THUNDER IN THE AIR

Brian Masters

THUNDER IN THE AIR

Great Actors in Great Roles

OBERON BOOKS
LONDON

First published in 2000 by Oberon Books Ltd.
(incorporating Absolute Classics)
521 Caledonian Road, London N7 9RH
Tel: 020 7607 3637 / Fax: 020 7607 3629
E-mail: oberon.books@btinternet.com

Extracts from Simon Callow, *Being an Actor* (1984) reprinted by permission of Methuen Publishing Ltd. Extracts from Bryan Forbes, *That Despicable Race* (1980) reprinted by kind permission of Penguin Books Ltd. Extract from Emlyn Williams, *Emlyn* (1973) reprinted by permission of the Maggie Noach Literary Agency.

British Library Cataloguing-in-Publication-Data

A catalogue record for this book is available from the British Library

ISBN: 1 84002 169 1

Cover illustration: Andrzej Klimowski; picture of Henry Irving by Millais, © theartarchive; photograph of Judi Dench, © Donald Cooper/Photostage

Cover design: Andrzej Klimowski and Richard Doust

Author photograph: © Juan Melian-Macias

Printed in Great Britain by Antony Rowe Ltd, Reading

1 3 5 7 9 10 8 6 4 2

Photographic Acknowledgements

For permission to reproduce the photographs in this book, the Publishers would like to thank: Donald Cooper/Photostage; Shakespeare's Globe; The Garrick Club (theartarchive); Musei Civici, Comune di Vicenza; Dominic Photography; The Mander and Mitchenson Theatre Collection; John Haynes; Mark Douet/Arena Images; The Shakespeare Birthplace Trust; Ivan Kyncl. Every effort has been made to obtain permission to use all the pictures in this book

Contents

To Michael and Judi

Illustrations

Being the fruit of nearly fifty years theatre-going and countless conversations on the nature of acting, it would be a daunting endeavour for me to acknowledge all the help I have been given throughout that time. I should like, however, to make especial mention of friends whose knowledge is so deep that I could not have dared attempt this work without them. In an order in which they should all be first, they are Henry McGee, Richard Bebb, Sir Donald Sinden, Michael Williams and Simon Callow.

1

Passing Traffic

Few boasts are more irritating than that of the enthusiast who insists that if you were not lucky enough to see John Gielgud in this or Laurence Olivier in that then you can have no idea what great acting is like. Your tormentor can savour in memory something that is forever denied you, since it is the nature of theatrical art to be alive and pulsing for a couple of hours, then vanish, evaporate into the night leaving scars on the mind and energy in the blood, but no tangible trace. Unlike the painter, sculptor or writer, the actor's art is necessarily ephemeral, and when it is artificially captured on film or tape-recorder it is only a distant, dim echo of the real thing. The experience actor and audience share is unique. As one actor ruefully put it, "Acting is the most mortal of the arts. Like perishable foods, it should be taken fresh or not at all." [1]

What makes this truth all the more infuriating is the knowledge that, for 400 years, the London theatre has consistently produced the finest actors in the world. They have all gone, leaving us little more than the rhapsodic accounts of people who saw and celebrated them. At the high point of Romantic excess, Coleridge nearly gave himself a seizure imagining Shakespeare himself on stage as Adam in *As You Like It*. "Think of having had Shakespeare in one's arms!" he wrote. "It is worth having died two hundred years ago to have heard Shakespeare deliver a single line. He must have been a great actor." [2] (He wasn't, as it happens, but legend blooms best in the dark.) There are scores of great performances, of specific actors in specific roles who for a moment brought thunder to the stage and who seem to be, quite naturally, irrecoverable. They are what Ronald Harwood called "the passing traffic of the stage" [3], a veritable phalanx of great men and women who retreat into the gloom of the wings never to be seen again. It will be part of the purpose of this book, no doubt presumptuous and foolhardy, to attempt to recover them, to glimpse what they may have been like in performance and record the magic they created. One must try to temper Garrick's pessimism, when he wrote, echoing Macbeth:

> But he who struts his hour upon the stage
> Can scarce extend his fame for half an age;
> Nor pen nor pencil can the actor save,
> The art and artist share one common grave. [4]

They should not be allowed to fall into oblivion merely because their voices are stilled. Justice requires, if it is at all possible, that they be heard again.

The stepping stones of theatre history are the moments of great actors in great parts. Some of their names may not even be familiar to the general reader, although he will hear of them again and again in the course of these pages and, I trust, know them well by the end – their style, their fame, their impact. We have to begin with Richard Burbage, Shakespeare's colleague and leading actor (the very one whom Coleridge ecstatically imagined carrying the Bard in his arms), if only because he was the original Hamlet, the original Othello, the original Macbeth and the original Lear, and has therefore created more famous roles than any other person in history. Indeed, it is an overwhelming reflection that Burbage's work, bringing to life for the first time the characters Shakespeare drew, while being presumably little more than a sequence of parts for him, has become the canonical basis of tragic drama for us.

We know precious little of Richard Burbage the actor, but it would be wrong to say we know nothing at all. He was also no mean painter, and it has been suggested that Burbage painted the portrait of Shakespeare known as the Chandos portrait, which is the most sympathetic and convincing likeness of the poet. There can be no proof, but it fits nicely that the first person to buy this portrait was the next great actor in our history, Thomas Betterton, who first played Hamlet in 1661, only 45 years after Shakespeare's death when there were still old actors about who had seen Burbage. Betterton dominated the stage for nearly half a century, dying in 1710.

Not long afterwards, an actor named Charles Macklin changed history by playing Shylock in *The Merchant of Venice* as a serious part; until then it had always been played for laughs, in burlesque fashion, a terrible travesty of Shakespeare's moving creation. Another revolutionary interpretation in the same year (1741) was given by a small, lively young man from Lichfield who was working in London in a wine-shop, and who decided to go on stage. In his first ever role as *Richard III*, he so astonished the audience that this has become probably the most famous first night in history. His name was David Garrick, and he continued working for another 34 years. He was the first "star" of the theatre, with over 400 different portraits or engravings of him circulating in his lifetime. Macklin was still performing long after Garrick's death, and himself lived to be nearly 100 years old.

Macklin saw the great actor of the next generation, John Philip Kemble, and his sister Sarah, known to the world as Mrs Siddons. Theirs was the first theatrical dynasty, for another acting Kemble, Charles, had a daughter Fanny, also an actress, whose career flourished in the early years of Victoria's reign. Her aunt, Sarah Siddons, is supposed to have never been surpassed in the role of Lady Macbeth, with which she is still identified today. The Kembles' supremacy was shattered by the arrival of a meteoric, untameable, tempestuous figure in the shape of Edmund Kean, whose debut in 1814 once more shocked the public into amazement and admiration in a way that was not to occur again for half a century. William Macready gave solid performances in the middle years of the century, but he never had the almost frightening impact of Kean, nor of the entirely different Henry Irving when he conquered London in the 1870s, and rose to become the first actor to receive a knighthood from his monarch. Irving died in 1905, amid scenes of lamentation not bestowed upon a dead actor since Garrick.

The twentieth century has given us Olivier, Gielgud, Ashcroft, Wolfit, Dench, and many others to whom I shall wish to return in due course, for I hope to show that the line of inheritance from Richard Burbage, though jagged and sometimes seismic in its leaps and jumps, is essentially unbroken, and may even allow us to see the great Kean, the impossibly versatile Garrick, the statuesque Kemble and the unbearably touching Sarah Siddons in some of their successors – our contemporaries. Hazlitt welcomed the fact that actors left no record of their art "except that of vague rumour", and that "the genius of a great actor perishes with him, leaving the world no copy." He said this might be mortifying for actors, but it was a great blessing to audiences, for it left an opening to originality. [5] Well, there is a limit to the amount of originality that can be invented with each generation, and I rather fancy that the same styles and essences of the actor's craft crop up fairly regularly. It was on those rare occasions when a great actor emerged, or more usually descended, as it were, unheralded, without warning, from the heavens, that audiences saw those essences illumined and made large. They are still there for us to see today.

When I was invited to contribute to a television programme about the career of Margot Fonteyn, I was surprised to discover that neither the producer, nor the editor, nor the cameramen, had ever seen her dance, and that though there are films of some of her performances, they had no idea of the effect she had upon an audience, the sheer joy of watching her and of accepting her gift to us. How could they? You would have had to be there at Covent Garden to experience a Fonteyn performance. She had only stopped dancing 20 years before, but that was enough to wipe her image clean, to make her invisible, or ungraspable in the real sense, to a young generation. Which is why the producers wanted to make the film; they wanted to *know*. And it is why I have chosen to attempt this book. It is *not* inevitable that all should be lost, and that if you never saw Olivier or Gielgud you can have no idea of their stagecraft. They can all be restored to us, by method and imagination, plus a little love.

Let us start by considering what all these disparate people had in common before we look at the differences in style and manner which distinguished them.

It may appear too obvious to merit observation, but is sometimes overlooked by the theorists. All the great actors have had extraordinary *personalities*, they have been much larger than the average whether on stage or off it, and consequently with a superabundance of energy, fire, vision and enthusiasm which must find expression. They are inevitably egocentric, for their very purpose in appearing before the public is to invite the public to look at them and forget the rest of life, but this egocentricity is not selfish in the usual meaning, save with some magnificently absurd exceptions who shall deserve a section to themselves. It is rather a recognition that they have something important, even urgent, to communicate, that nobody else can communicate it but them, and that their very life depends upon it. They would be bereft and insubstantial without it, like the empty hanging skin in Michelangelo's *Last Judgement*, and their hunger to perform must be satisfied at the cost of peace, serenity, rest and happiness, all those lesser blessings non-actors strive for. They are therefore driven creatures, and their effect upon an audience is to dominate it, to conquer and subdue it with the force of their extravagant personalities, make it malleable and in thrall to them. David Garrick wrote to an up-and-coming young actor of his day, William Powell (who sadly died young and disappeared from the history books), "A true genius will convert an audience to his manner, rather than be converted by them to what is false and unnatural." [6] An American critic observed of Henry Irving, "Take away Mr Irving's personality, and he is merely an awkward player." [7] The critic no doubt imagined he was being rude, but he had seen the essence of the great actor and failed to recognise it.

When a great performance happens, it is significant, and extraordinary to behold, how the audience willingly, even eagerly, surrenders to this domination by the actor. There is hunger on their part, too, and they welcomed Garrick, Kean, Irving and Olivier as sources of nourishment. There occurs a kind of seduction and submission across the footlights, and the resulting connection is utterly hypnotic in its power. When Irving performed in *The Bells*, a terrible Victorian melodrama which he converted into high art by the sheer force of his commitment, women in the audience shuddered. Georgian ladies became hysterical when faced with Sarah Siddons' pulverising wickedness as Lady Macbeth, and those present at Laurence Olivier's 1944 *Richard III* at the Old Vic say they were literally frightened *into* their seats by the opening speech and the actor's overpowering depiction of unmitigated evil (the film version has none of this); that is, they drew back and pressed themselves against the seats, not drawing breath until the speech (twice as long as usual owing to Olivier's crafty addition of a passage from *Henry VI*) was over and the actor had left the stage.

I can myself recall something of this hypnosis when Robert Stephens created the seemingly unplayable part of the Inca king Atahualpa in Peter Shaffer's *The Royal Hunt of the Sun*, also at the Old Vic. By altering his voice, his gait, his very shape, he seemed unearthly and overpoweringly regal. (I was reminded of the actor who, when asked if Irving had been a tall man, replied, "He was when he *wanted* to be.") It was important that the role should assume this god-like dimension, for it was necessary to the story that Atahualpa cause the cocky Spanish conqueror to hesitate in his rash destruction. But Stephens not only subdued the Spaniard, he subdued us also. We were loose-jawed with astonishment at the noble, exotic, sexually vivid creature we saw on stage. Similarly, the great American actress Uta Hagen left me drenched with fear, literally shaking, after her performance as Martha in Albee's *Who's Afraid of Virginia Woolf?* a role she created. Hagen took the audience and squeezed it.

The domination may also be inadvertent, unexpected or accidental. I have already mentioned one dancer, and if I introduce another it is because she is a great actress who happened to dance, just as Maria Callas was a great actress who happened to sing. Natalia Makarova stood in for another dancer at a private performance given by the Marquess of Londonderry (husband of the ballerina, Doreen Wells) at his seat, Wynyard Hall in County Durham. She had no time to rehearse, and only saw the stage a couple of hours before she was due to dance. Electricians and carpenters were still hammering and drilling, as the stage was built only for this occasion, but she decided she would "mark" her place on the boards. Wearing practice leg-warmers and a T-shirt, she proceeded to go through the movements of the Dying Swan to Saint-Saëns' music, and in the process transformed herself to a creature of nature, gasping and wilting towards a pathetic yet dignified death. Within seconds the hammering and drilling stopped. The workmen, watched in awe. She dominated them without knowing it.

So, if the great actors share this power to hypnotise or bewitch, they do so in a variety of ways. Categories are always invidious, for they invite the awkward or tantalising exception, but they will serve as a launching pad at least. Two divisions in particular are possible from the outset, the division between actors who perform in verse, the magisterial, iambic pentameters of the great tragic roles, and those who perform in prose, mainly the great comedians. And secondly, the division in style (within the tragic roles) between the classical and the mercurial, the impressively noble and the recklessly dangerous, the Apollonian and the Dionysian.

The distinction between Apollo and Dionysus is fundamental to an understanding of the actor's art, and it will underlie much of what is said in the course of this book. It is important, therefore, to clarify it from the very beginning and keep it in mind throughout. It will illuminate and reveal truths of interpretation which might otherwise appear arbitrary, cloudy or bizarre. In a sense, Apollo and Dionysus are antitheses in Greek mythology, and hence in human life; in another sense, they demand a fusion which the actor can achieve. That is his burden.

Apollo had care of the fruits of the earth, of animals and, by extension, of man himself, especially at that bursting, fruitful time of passage from youth into manhood. He was also the god of prophecy, and since prophetic signs were usually manifested in song, he came to represent music, and finally the arts as a whole. Apollo is always depicted as the epitome of physical beauty and moral purity, of the perfection of which mankind is capable (the finest statue of him is the Apollo Belvedere in the Vatican). He represents the best that human endeavour may achieve through order, control, discipline, restraint, the mastery over oneself and over the plastic world. Bach, Mozart, Nash, Palladio, Michelangelo, David Hockney are typically Apollonian figures, their work at once severely structured, balanced and calm, yet blazingly beautiful in its architecture and in the harmony it describes. Apollo finds revelation through restraint, truth in simplicity, beauty in the self-confident conquest of difficulty.

Dionysus was the god of vegetation and of wine in particular. He is known in Ancient Rome as Bacchus. His festivals were characterised by orgies and excessive licence, extending to the eating of raw flesh from a just-sacrificed animal, and he represented what human character may do when released from inhibition – unbridled, unrestrained, spontaneous and free. He was the god of licence, of the full expression of desires and instincts normally buried. Hence he was the bringer of madness, he was dangerous, anarchic, wild, instinctive, iconoclastic, revolutionary. He became the god of masquerade and of magical illusion, for his followers imagined the world to be other than what they had hitherto seen and experienced. The participants at a Dionysian rite were in state of hypnosis, possessed by their god and behaving like him rather than as themselves. They underwent a profound alteration of personality, entirely losing self-awareness for the period of the festival, and surrendering themselves to the experience. Blake, Picasso, Francis Bacon, Liszt and Stravinsky speak with the energies of Dionysus and can often be alarming as they do so. They make one feel the power of trance and hypnosis, that splendid but anxious sensation of being possessed.

It should be possible to see already the two strands of theatrical tradition identified by this definition – the one pure, seductive, satisfying; the other electric, intoxicating, unnerving. There have been Apollonian actors, ravishing us with their unearthly perfection of sound and subtle penetration of character; and Dionysian actors who have shattered and shocked us with unleashed, unpredictable passion. You would need to have all the Apollonian virtues to tackle Wilde's precious and precise masterpiece *The Importance of Being Earnest*, a play so economical and controlled that it can only be performed in the classical, restrained manner in order (paradoxically) to release its exuberant effects. A Dionysian approach would utterly smash its rococo beauty, a fact so obvious that no production has ever attempted one (it is, anyway, a naturalistic prose comedy, hardly suitable material for thunder). On the other hand, you need Dionysus to help you deal with King Lear, Othello or Macbeth, or you will merely skip across the words. For Hamlet, you need both Dionysus *and* Apollo, which is why the perfect Hamlet is so rarely accomplished on stage.

Let us select a handful of those exponents of the classical style through the centuries and see how they were considered by their contemporaries. The further back we go, of course, the more difficult this becomes. James Quin (1693-1766) was the acknowledged leading actor of his day before the explosive arrival of David Garrick in 1741. Richard Cumberland (1732-1811), incidentally the model for Sir Fretful Plagiary in Sheridan's *The Critic*, has left us a clear vignette of Quin's style. "With a deep, full tone," he wrote, "accompanied by a sawing kind of gesture, which had more of the senate than of the stage in it, he rolled out his heroics with an air of dignified indifference." [8] He rarely moved, but stood majestically centre-stage and spoke (as was the custom then) directly to the audience. He was there to be admired and to give tacit lessons in diction and deportment. This is not to diminish him, for he was indeed admired (in particular by Horace Walpole, who preferred him to Garrick), and both diction and deportment were expected of a great actor, who should set an example in manners. Cumberland also said that Quin "seemed to disdain the plaudits that were bestowed upon him," [9] which was again an acceptable gentlemanly attitude to adopt in the early Georgian theatre. But the important point is that no spark of danger touched a Quin performance. People said that he was always Quin, no matter what part he was playing, and they were very glad of that, too. An Apollonian actor is reassuring above all else.

But there were mutterings against this style of laboured gesticulation even during Quin's ascendancy. "I cannot believe any man the more," said Dr Johnson, "because he rolled his eyes, or puffed his cheeks, or spread abroad his arms, or stamped the ground, or thumped his breast, or turned his eyes sometimes to the ceiling and sometimes to the floor." [10] We shall have an opportunity to see just how Quin delivered a speech when we turn to the matter of technique. But for the moment, it is fascinating to recall that Quin and Garrick appeared on the stage together more than once, and that Garrick occasionally found himself outranked, withdrawing from the production rather than compete hopelessly. It is Quin's rueful remark which is more famously remembered, however, after first witnessing Garrick's astonishingly free and inventive style. "If this young fellow is right," he said, "then we have all been wrong."

John Philip Kemble (1757-1823) made his debut as Hamlet in his twenties, and gave his farewell as Coriolanus when he was 60. Throughout, he was noble, clear, impressive and striking, and there were many who thought the maverick qualities of Edmund Kean, who burst upon the scene only three years before Kemble's retirement and thereby mirrored the earlier overlapping of Quin and Garrick, would never match Kemble's faultless delivery and tone. Some critics found a chilling correctitude in his manner, however, and spoke of his being "cold, classical and correct", or worse, of having swallowed a curtain-rod. On his retirement, Hazlitt said that his manner "had always something dry, hard, and pedantic in it", and described him as "a stately hieroglyphic of humanity", but he did nonetheless allow that Kemble had been "the most excellent actor of his time" despite all this. [11] Leigh Hunt, writing much earlier when Kemble was at the height of his fame and Kean as yet unheard of, was somewhat harsher, referring to "an indiscriminate importance of manner" and chiding Kemble for attaching "a kind of loftiness to every sensation that he indulges" and for "a laborious and almost universal preciseness". As might be expected, he was best in soliloquies, which he delivered without indulging in "those complacent stares at the audience which occupy inferior actors". While thinking to chastise, Leigh Hunt unwittingly summarised the virtues of the classical, Apollonian, controlled style of acting which Kemble epitomised: "He does not present one the idea of a man who grasps with the force of genius, but of one who overcomes by the toil of attention. He never rises and sinks as in the enthusiasm of the moment; his ascension though grand is careful, and when he sinks it is with preparation and dignity." [12] Precisely.

Like Quin, Kemble was much admired for his clarity of diction, owing to which he was engaged to teach elocution to the Prince of Wales. It is recorded that he was so frustrated by the Prince's affected way of saying "much obleeged", that he implored with exasperation, "Sir, may I beseech Your Royal Highness to open your royal jaws and say 'oblige'?" [13] A silly story, perhaps, but it serves to illustrate how much attention was paid to the way in which classical actors said things, rather than to the substance of what they said. Kemble was not invited to lecture the Prince of Wales on the nature of human frailty or the emotional triggers to despair. It was significant that he deplored the way in which Garrick darted about the stage, and thought Garrick and Mrs Pritchard, as the Macbeths, had about as much dignity as the butler and the pastry-cook. King George III agreed; Garrick, he said, was "too much of a fidget".

William Charles Macready (1793-1873) was an intellectual and scholar as well as actor. It was he who rescued *King Lear* from a terribly mutilated version which had been played consistently for 150 years before him. Betterton had been the last to play Shakespeare's original text between 1663 and 1671 (when there were still old men alive who had known Shakespeare), but thereafter this was replaced by a version rewritten by the Poet Laureate Nahum Tate, which entirely wiped out one character – the Fool – and allowed Cordelia to live happily-ever-after with Edgar while Lear got his kingdom back. It is difficult to credit now, but this version was acted by Quin, Booth, Garrick, Henderson, Kemble and Kean. In bringing back the original, Macready "banished that disgrace from the stage forever" [14], and scored a great personal success. His performances were always of the highest standard, rich and rewarding, faithful and true, and audiences felt they had been brought closer to Shakespeare through the conduit of Macready's interpretations. He consistently gave the impression that he understood every word of what he was saying (unlike some maverick actors, both then and now), which gave both him authority and his audience confidence. In this he was like John Gielgud in our own century, of whom Donald Sinden has written, "he speaks Shakespeare's lines as if he had written them himself; we understand them because he understands them; if we do not, it is our fault, not his." [15]

Judi Dench is another artist who understands the roles she plays where other actresses merely impersonate them. She allows the architecture of the lines to reveal their meaning, and transmits that meaning to us with such conviction that we feel we are hearing the part for the first time, or that the words have just spontaneously occurred to her, and that there could be no others. In this way she gave the first truly intelligible Cleopatra of the twentieth century, and a few years later, the first portrayal of Désirée (after about 20 other actresses) in Sondheim's *A Little Night Music* which unlocked the sense of the part.

To return to Macready. He did not restrict himself to Shakespeare, but created over 50 parts in new plays, whereas Kean hardly ever tackled anything new. One might readily expect the contrary, but there it is. On the other hand, his cautious and respectful approach denied him the peaks of heroic stature that a more spitfire, intrepid actor like Kean could achieve. G H Lewes, admiring his range and flexibility, nevertheless noticed that "he was irritable where he should have been passionate, querulous where he should have been terrible." [16] Others were more damning. B R Haydon said Macready was like a machine one had to wind up before the curtain, then he could be relied upon to make exactly the same moves and utter exactly the same sounds as he had done at every previous performance. Kemble had been of similar stamp, he said, while Kean and Mrs Siddons would never have given the same performance twice. What Haydon did not recognise was that Kean could *not* have repeated a performance, because his genius did not spring from classical conceits and infrangible structures, but from the anarchic demon of inspiration, from Dionysian chaos. There is a story related of Laurence Olivier's controversial *Othello* at the National Theatre (when it was still located at the Old Vic). One evening some weeks into the run he gave such a profound and shattering performance that the rest of the cast burst into applause at the end of it. He, however, was hugely depressed and shut himself in his dressing room, refusing to see anyone. An actor knocked on his door and asked what was the matter. "Don't you know you were brilliant?" "Of course I know," said Olivier, "but I don't know *why!*"

Such a mysterious process would have been foreign to Macready, for control and mastery over one's instrument – the body and its voice – are the essence of classical acting. It would also have been foreign to Johnston Forbes-Robertson, a giant in his profession at the end of the nineteenth century, just after Irving and long before Gielgud, but now forgotten by all but other actors. Famous for his Hamlet, of which there exists even a rather jerky film made in the 1920s, giving no hint of its greatness, Forbes-Robertson held himself under such a dignified rein that his performances induced reverential hush. He was beautiful, impressive, reticent. "Artistic self-restraint is a very good thing," wrote William Archer, "but in this case it verges on timidity." [17] That was for a Hamlet in 1897 opposite the exquisite Mrs Patrick Campbell as Ophelia, of whom more later. The following year he played Macbeth and was greeted with this verdict by the anonymous reviewer of *The*

Athenaeum: "Our actors…are most courteous and well-bred and loth, apparently, to do anything that might not decently be done in a modern drawing room. Pleased as we are, however, we have ceased to be thrilled. To our pursuit of the beautiful we are sacrificing the terrible and the grotesque. His performance is beautiful and noble. Are we unreasonable that we want to be appalled?" [18]

And there you have it! Apollo does not seek to thrill or appal you, but to uplift and enlighten you. Dionysus delights in the shocking and needs to strike you with awe. It is, moreover, galling that audiences tend to want both experiences, and will only undergo that alteration in personality, that loss of self-awareness, if they are given both. If they have to choose, then they tend to prefer (and to remember) those occasions when they have been struck mute with wonder, when it is the Dionysian forces that have overwhelmed them. Such an experience they will receive only from the few unusual actors – at once obsessed and possessed – who seem almost prepared to risk self-destruction in their grim lunges after truth.

No one better exemplifies this kind of actor than Edmund Kean (1787-1833), a man so cluttered with faults and weaknesses that it was difficult to warm to him. He was often abusive and offensive, missed performances, made embarrassing scenes in the auditorium, and cut short his career and his life with alcohol, dying at 46. In fact, he was drunk throughout most of the period of his highest fame, sometimes even on stage. Excess marked his character and his art, and when he honed it, used it to serve his purpose, he was nothing short of a genius. Though small and far from imposing in "life" (before his triumph he was refused entry to the theatre by a protective Stage Doorman), on stage he assumed, heaven knows from where, a gargantuan power.

Kean had no idea who his father was and was abandoned by his mother. He was brought up by his aunt, who was an actress of note but not historically significant, and appeared on stage as a child. He spent all his formative years playing in undistinguished plays, living from day to day, virtually homeless and often starving. Noticed during a tour of Ireland, he was brought to London, completely unknown, where he waited during yet more months of inactivity for his chance. Eventually, he made his debut as Shylock at Drury Lane on 26 January, 1814 to a house which was almost empty (for he had been afforded no advance publicity) but which recognised genius as if they had been assaulted by it. Another actor sitting in the Green Room that night said that he wondered how so few people could make so much noise. Also in the audience was a great man of literature, William Hazlitt. What the one achieved, the other recorded, thus making this one of the great first nights of theatrical history. Edmund Kean was unknown no longer.

Two weeks later, on 12 February, he gave his first performance of *Richard III*, and a month after that his first *Hamlet*. The theatre was crammed every time he appeared, and he seemed to exhaust himself for each audience. He immediately became an idol, to such an extent that when it was reported that playing Richard III had made him ill and caused him to spit blood, the public rushed to his support and bombarded the theatre with demands he not be bullied into playing too often; they would not be satisfied until Kean had himself written to the newspapers to assure them he was restored to health. [19] All of this was true, of course. No publicity agent or public relations juggler had invented an exhaustion to draw attention to the actor; he so hurled himself into the part he was playing, stretching and squeezing his strength of mind and body, pushing his emotional endurance beyond the limits, that he was a husk by the end of it. He frequently appeared wild, loose, on the brink of madness, the sheer demonic energy of his performances causing the audience to tremble. A hero for the Romantic Age and the Romantic Temper, Kean could not have arrived at a better time. Meanwhile, the fans of John Philip Kemble deplored his lack of dignity and his habit of leaning against the scenery to rest.

Not that he minded; his salary was doubled and he was given a share in the theatre, whose fortunes he had single-handedly revived. A well-repeated story which demonstrates that genius does not preclude social ambition, has Kean saying to his wife, "Mary, you shall ride in your carriage, and Charlie shall go to Eton!" And they did!

How Kean achieved his remarkable effects on stage is a matter of technique, commitment and intensity, which must await a detailed comparison with other actors and their styles in the next chapter. For the moment, just listen to some of the reactions he provoked. "By Jove, he is a soul," said Byron. "Life, nature, truth without exaggeration or diminution." Leigh Hunt set him against Kemble's elevation of tone, all external, and said that Kemble showed the flower but had no idea about the roots or dirt or stalks and sinews which produced it: "Kean knows the real thing." Hazlitt said of his *Othello* that it was "the finest piece of acting in the world…a masterpiece of natural passion."

"Kean is all effort, all violence, all extreme passion," he later wrote. "He is possessed with a fury, a demon that leaves him no repose, no time for thought or room for imagination." Or again, "Mr Kean's acting is like an anarchy of the passions, in which upstart humour or frenzy of the moment is struggling to get violent possession of some bit or corner of his fiery soul and pygmy body." [20] A contemporary said of his portrayal of Sir Giles Overreach in Massinger's *A New Way to Pay Old Debts* (which had also been a favourite part of Garrick's) that it was "without doubt, the most terrific exhibition of human passion that has been witnessed on the stage." [21]

"Mr Kean's Othello is the masterpiece of the living stage," gasped *The Examiner.* [22] "You might fancy you saw the water quivering in his eyes," wrote Leigh Hunt (something similar would be said of John Gielgud over a century later). And G H Lewes spoke of his "rush of mighty power" which could leave no audience unmoved. It was not that he was perfect (as Gielgud would be) – far from it. Kean was splenetic and explosive, raving, storming one minute, inaudible, croaking the next. The most famous compliment paid to his art came from Coleridge, who said that watching him was "like reading Shakespeare by flashes of lightning". But Coleridge meant the compliment to be spiked, for when the lightning strikes, you see something startling and true, but when it doesn't, you are left in the dark. Kean lacked the ability to follow a dramatic line through thoughtfully to the end as Kemble had done. Lewes was quite aware of this, but concluded that the flaw shrank next to the genius. "All defects were overlooked or disregarded," he said, "because it was impossible to watch Kean as Othello, Shylock, Richard III, or Sir Giles Overreach without being strangely shaken by the terror, and the pathos, and the passion of a stormy spirit uttering itself in tones of irresistible power... I would again risk broken ribs for the chance of a good place in the pit to see anything like it." [23]

Universal enthusiasm such as this commands belief. But it is in a bad review, paradoxically, that we attain a better view of Kean's immersion in his art (or sheer cheek, if you prefer), and can see him with today's eyes. It was after a performance in Guernsey, where he was not well liked because he had been due to play Charles I in a forgotten heroic tragedy of that name, but cancelled the performance, sending word that the king had been beheaded on the way to the theatre; then he had sat in drunken bliss in the audience, heckling the understudy. It can hardly be denied that Guernsey had good cause to be angry. When Kean returned to give a performance of *Hamlet* in March, 1813 therefore, he did not have the islanders on his side. Remember that this was only ten months before his startling and historic conquest of London.

"It is one of the most terrible representations to which Shakespeare has ever been subjected," wrote the anonymous Guernseyite. "Without grace or dignity he comes forward; he shows unconsciousness that anyone is before him, and is often so forgetful of the respect due to an audience, that he turns his back on them in some of those scenes in which contemplation is to be indulged, as if for the purpose of shewing his abstraction from all ordinary subjects… [His] voice seems to proceed from a charnel-house." [24]

At which one is bound to cheer. It reminds me of Maria Callas in *Tosca* at Covent Garden in 1964, where she was so forgetful of the audience, so enveloped in the character, that she would hunch her shoulders in a most ungainly and un-*prima donna*-like way. She *lived* the part of Tosca, just as Kean had lived the part of Hamlet. The audience on both occasions were privileged eavesdroppers. And Callas' life offstage was hardly decorous.

If you prefer an example from the "straight" theatre, then you have Victor Henry, the great promise of the 1960s, now sadly overlooked, who played Jimmy Porter in Osborne's *Look Back in Anger* and Rimbaud in Christopher Hampton's *Total Eclipse*, both canonical plays in the history of twentieth century theatre. He was a nightmare. He picked fights with huge hulking strangers (he was, like Kean, a little man), insulted everyone, tormented himself, tortured himself, wounded himself, had a filthy imagination and a torrid tongue to match, was paralytically drunk and would sometimes appear on stage stumbling over the furniture and the words. Yet, as his friend and contemporary Simon Callow has written, "suddenly he'd do something so extraordinarily pure and intense that your heart would stop beating. He was the most absolute actor I've ever seen." [25]

So, Edmund Kean as an amalgam of Maria Callas and Victor Henry might be bizarre, but if it allows you to see him, then it will do. There are other actors working today who have something of his alarm and prickle, but nobody who has it all.

Kean was obviously not made to dine diffidently in society, and his social sins made it impossible for him to be invited to do so. His successor as dazzling maverick of the stage (with the cautious, puritan classicist Macready in between) could not have been more different. Henry Irving (1838-1905) not only conquered society, he subjugated it, rising to the very pinnacle as the first actor ever to be knighted, and so abjectly respected that people hushed when he entered a room. He made acting his mistress, and all else was time filled in. His seat at the Garrick Club was always the one with arms at the head of the table; nobody else dared use it, and even today people are reluctant to sit there lest his ghost softly chide. His profile was so famous that children used to parade beside the railway line to catch a glimpse of it as his train passed. It is probably no exaggeration to say that, next to Queen Victoria, he shared with Gordon of Khartoum the distinction of being the most revered English person alive. The Queen herself shared that veneration. When she conferred the knighthood on him in 1895 she said, "We are very, very pleased." She normally said nothing at all.

Despite this, there are some similarities with Kean's career, if none with Kean's temperament. Irving, too, was dismissed by a provincial journalist who advised him after a performance "to take the first steamer back to his comfortable home and to abandon all hope of becoming an actor." [26] After a performance on tour as Hamlet, he saw an old lady in tears and invited her to his dressing-room afterwards. He told her how moved he was to see her so upset. "Indeed I was," she said. "I've a young son myself play-acting somewhere in the north, and it broke me up to think that he might be no better at it than you." [27] Like Kean, Irving had disabilities, not in height but in speech and gait. He had stuttered as a child, retained abnormal speech rhythms, and walked like a praying mantis.

During his long apprenticeship, Henry Irving played 428 separate parts before attacking London in 1871. It was another remarkable debut, and another date in theatrical history. 25 November, 1871 was the first performance of Leopold Lewis' *The Bells*, a psychological melodrama about a respectable man haunted by the knowledge of a murder he had committed 15 years before. The secret of the acting lay in the contrast between Irving's untroubled demeanour in company, and his tortured soul when alone, with the latter gradually infecting the former and the audience watching in horrified sympathy as the man's spirit collapsed. Irving's performance was of such intensity, and so carefully wrought in development, detail, hesitation and nuance, that when the curtain came down the audience sat in shocked silence, as though they had been present at a confession. A woman in the stalls fainted. Irving's legend was born.

The response of his wife was quite different from that of Mrs Kean. "Are you going to make a fool of yourself for the rest of our life?" she asked on the way home. He stopped the carriage, got out, and never spoke to her again.

The story of women fainting, by the way, is no mere theatrical anecdote embellished by repetition. The great comic actress of the next generation, Athene Seyler, who died as recently as 1993, saw Irving in *The Bells* when she was a young girl. "When he came to his death scene," she said, "I actually fainted in my seat." [28]

Irving's magic was not the quicksilver, dangerous kind that Kean had worked, but it was just as hypnotic, just as potent and urgent. He seemed somehow to command total attention, to expect the audience to concentrate with him and go through a tunnel from which they might or might not emerge secure. He sucked their energies by focusing his own with such intensity as to draw them to him, then discarded their caterpillar carcass when once they had shared his exotic experience. He disdained applause, but tolerated it. That was not the purpose of the exercise. Magic was the purpose, magic and domination.

For more than 20 years, Irving managed and played at the Lyceum near the Strand playing only melodramas and Shakespeare, scorning the new-fangled notions of Ibsen and Shaw, and becoming a British institution with his leading lady, an extraordinary actress in her own right, Ellen Terry, at his side. John Gielgud said that Irving did a disservice to Shakespeare by "putting his acting between the lines" rather than through them [29], and certainly Shaw agreed, asserting that Irving played "in flat contradiction of the lines, and positively acted Shakespeare off the stage." [30] But none of that seemed to matter. He mesmerised a generation, and when he died in 1905 flags were flown at half-mast all over the country, and London cabbies tied black handkerchiefs to their riding-crops.

Ellen Terry was appearing at the Gaiety, Manchester, in a play called *Alice Sit-by-the-Fire,* in the closing scene of which she had to say, "I had a beautiful husband once, black as the raven was his hair…" She faltered, choked, was overcome and broke down utterly. The curtain descended, and the audience filed out in silence, feeling they had intruded upon a private sorrow. [31]

No other actor has earned such general respect from among the rest of his profession – except John Gielgud. Gielgud was also the only one to have surpassed Irving in honours, although Olivier was elevated to the peerage. [32] Gielgud had both the Order of Merit and the Companion of Honour, marks of deep resonance.

On the other hand, it was upon Olivier rather than Gielgud that the mantle of Betterton, Garrick, Kean and Irving fell, for he it was who dared to flourish himself as the instrument of his art, while Gielgud appeared always to subordinate himself to the work and the words. I have already had cause to refer to Olivier's opening as Richard III in 1944 and the devastating effect it had upon all who witnessed it. As with Garrick, Kean and Irving before him, Olivier's sudden ascendancy was unexpected. He was not unknown, but he had just returned from being a film star in Hollywood, and there was much prejudice against him. It was not felt that he would measure up to the demands of a great classical role; Gielgud had already established himself with Richard II and Hamlet and his pre-eminence was already thought to be unassailable. The doubters had not reckoned with Olivier's rogue ability to astonish, nor his demonic energy, what Kenneth Tynan called "his unparalleled animal powers". Nor, apparently, had he. The night before, he still was not sure how to attack the part, and told his friend John Mills in the dressing room that he was very worried, that it was going to be dreadful, that he simply did not know what he was going to do.

What he did do is history, and to quote Kenneth Tynan again, "Olivier's Richard eats into the memory like acid into metal." [33] He made it virtually impossible for any other actor to tackle the part, and until Antony Sher, with blind panache, swept the memory clean in 1983 with his demented spider interpretation, when one imagined Richard III, one saw Olivier's appalling leer through those icy eyes. I hope later to examine his technique in this part and in others, but for the moment it is instructive to reflect that the two powers of ordered beauty and disquieting chaos were felt in the same era through the special talents of John Gielgud and Laurence Olivier, the one exquisite, fine-wrought, brooding and introspective, with "silent inner lightnings"; the other large, shattering, exploring unknown territories pungent with threat. Tynan said that the contrast between them was like that which Dr Johnson pointed out between Milton's ability to carve a colossus out of granite, and his inability to carve heads on cherry stones. "One thinks of Olivier in terms of other species, of panthers and lions: one thinks of Gielgud in terms of other arts, of ballet and portrait painting." [34] Never has the distinction been better expressed, and rarely have Dionysus and Apollo been better depicted.

Olivier consolidated his position as Kean's heir in 1945 with an overpowering performance as *Oedipus Rex*. The high point in the drama came when Oedipus was finally made to realise that he had unknowingly slept with his mother and killed his father, and the audience watched, horrified, as the knowledge sank in. Richard Bebb describes the moment thus: "There was a long pause while the whole house held its breath. He stood perfectly still, threw his head back, and emitted from a distended throat two of the most blood-curdling screams that can ever have been heard in any theatre. They had the brightness of a high trumpet, and pierced every one of us like the sharpest of swords." [35] Tynan was also there. He knew what was coming, and waited for the rack to move into the final notch, "but I never hoped for so vast an anguish." The scream, brilliantly caught in Irena Sedlecka's statuette, "must still be resounding in some high recess of the New Theatre's dome," he wrote. "Some stick of wood must still, I feel, be throbbing from it. The two cries were torn from beyond tears or shame or guilt: they came from the stomach, with all the ecstatic grief and fright of a newborn baby's wail." [36] Olivier himself said he imagined the pain of a wolf whose tongue was stuck to ice.

The point is that Olivier had made the earth move. One knew that, from then on, acting would have to be different, just as James Quin knew it would be as soon as he first saw David Garrick, just as a whole army of young hopefuls knew it would be after Marlon Brando's electrifying début in Tennessee Williams' *A Streetcar Named Desire*, in which he was so new and vivid and surprising that you did not know, could not tell, when he was going to open his mouth to speak, or whether he would finish a sentence once he had started it. It is this element of surprise which I am trying to emphasise as crucial to the nature and personality of the great actor.

You can positively feel the surprise, the excitement, in Richard Cumberland's report of Garrick's playing of Lothario in *The Fair Penitent* by Nicholas Rowe (who was, incidentally, Shakespeare's first biographer, and whose principal researcher for this was the actor Thomas Betterton). I have already quoted his account of Quin's manner and style – the rotundity of phrase, the nobility of figure – but his account of Garrick comes immediately after; they were appearing, remember, on the same stage at the same time: "But when I first beheld little Garrick, young and light and alive in every muscle and in every feature, heavens, what a transition! It seemed as if a whole century had been stepped over in the transition of a single scene; old things were done away, and a new order at once brought forward, bright and luminous..."

Garrick was said to have brought a refreshingly "natural" style of acting to the stage, which was why the whole of London, tired of the formal declamatory style, flocked to see him. But then, before him, Betterton was famed for his naturalism, and after him Kean, Irving, Olivier, Alec Guinness, have all been heralded as bringing a new naturalism to the art. This is clearly impossible to sustain, as a moment's thought will show that if it were true then a journey back into theatrical history would lead us into darker and darker abysses of progressively "unnatural" acting until we reached a stark, rigid figure opening his mouth like a goldfish. There is no such actor. The farthest we can go back is to Burbage, Shakespeare's colleague and leading actor. We have no detailed account of his style or presence, but we do at least know that it was *convincing*, as this elegy, written on his death in 1619 only three years after Shakespeare himself, eloquently suggests:

> How to ye person he did suit his face,
> Suit with his speech, while not a word did fall
> Without just weight to balance it withal.
> > ...tragic parts you see
> Die all with him.
> Oft have I seen him leape into a grave
> Suiting ye person (which he seemed to have)
> Of a sad lover, with so true an eye
> That then I would have sworn he meant to die. [37]

This is potent testimony that Burbage acted in a style true to nature, a style upon which everybody has been meant to be improving ever since.

The point is, surely, that being "natural" is being true, giving the audience an experience that they accept as being rooted in reality. The actor has to *impose* that acceptance, and there are many ways of so doing. This man who saw Richard Burbage *believed* in his anguish when he was in character (probably as Hamlet), to such an extent that he felt for him. Irving's audiences believed in the torment of Irving's soul, Kean's in the destructive passions which besieged him, Kemble's, Macready's and Gielgud's in the heartrending doubts and fumblings which lay heavy on their minds, Olivier's in the earth from which he sprang – full-blown – and those who applauded Charles Mathews in the nineteenth century and Alec Guinness in the twentieth believed in the accuracy and subtlety of the characterisations they offered. All were "natural" insofar as they persuaded the audience they were.

Naturalism is also affected by the nature of the audience and the size of the theatre. The Elizabethan theatre was intimate and at times rowdy. Both then and during the Restoration period the audience were encouraged to treat themselves as part of the experience, not spectators gawping at it from afar. The apron-thrust stage of the Restoration, with doors forward on either side, often meant the actors making their entrances would be closer to the audience, at that point, than they were to other actors on stage; hence the proliferation in comedy of the "aside", a remark directly made to the audience around them. In the early eighteenth century boxes were on the stage itself, and the nobility often sprawled over it getting in the way of actors, until Garrick banished the practice in mid-century. With the rebuilding of Drury Lane and Covent Garden in the early years of the nineteenth century and the creation of vast auditoria seating 3,000 people, the actors were so far away from their audience that Mrs Siddons complained she had to bellow and make herself hoarse. Clearly, the declamatory style became necessary in such a house, or the actor would not be heard at all. But that did not preclude "naturalism"; it influenced the technique by which naturalism might be attained. The aim to convince has never been abandoned.

There is also a different kind of "naturalness" required for high tragedy than there must be for light comedy, the former being generally written in verse, with its own emphases, internal music and rhythms, which the actor must adhere to at the same time as mapping a route whereby he can discover natural expression and truthful characterisation within them. This is a tall order, for the actor must have a sense of pace, of poetry, of the architecture of language, before he can even think of acting a role. Most of this chapter has been concerned with acting the tragic parts, to which I shall return in due course. Comedy is usually in prose, and so much closer to the rhythms and tones of everyday speech that it presents a much easier task and requires a quite different technique. (Not that playing comedy is *easier*, only that it is easier to *speak*.) The different vocal controls and shapes needed for comedy and tragedy, not to mention the different insights into human experience and character, explain why so few actors manage to triumph in both genres. Kean, Macready and Irving were only successful in grand tragic roles. Olivier acted in many comedies, but was never really convincing in any of them; you could see the wires being pulled, watch the steps being taken to build a comic picture, so that he was always a technician displaying his tricks. Charles Mathews, who *only* played comedy, built the character from the inside out, so that you were never aware there was any technique involved at all; Mathews played so many different roles in one evening, you could never be sure whether any or all of them were him or some other actor taking the role, because you could never recognise him. Alec Guinness had the same chameleon talent, changing his face from within. Olivier in comedy was always Olivier dressed up and doing funny things.

It should come as no surprise, therefore, that the Apollonian actor, sure on his feet and strongly in control of his art, is apt to straddle better the chasm between the comic and tragic styles; John Gielgud was a brilliant comedian. The daring, self-demanding risk-taker, through whom the torrents of human confusion and despair pass, is scarcely likely to submit to the rigorous, meticulous jewel-building required of comedy. He would crush it and trample it in his sonorous tread.

In fact, only one actor throughout our history has managed to be both a terrifying tragedian and a comic actor of genius, and that is David Garrick, 250 years ago. Though he has been mentioned much in this chapter, wherein tragedy has dominated, he played far more comic roles in his career than he did tragic ones, and it is as Abel Drugger in Ben Jonson's *The Alchemist* that he achieved his highest distinction. It remained his and his alone until Alec Guinness shone in the same role in 1947, making it in turn one of *his* two most famous roles (the other being the Fool in *King Lear*), far exceeding his more famous film portrayals. Garrick was also the only actor who could come off stage having played Lear and immediately tell a funny story in the Green Room.

A similar division obtains among actresses. Sarah Siddons played only tragedy, Nell Gwyn and Mrs Jordan only comedy. Maggie Smith is a comic actress of genius who lacks the red corpuscle when she adopts the tragic vein, and (to flick abroad for a moment) Marie Bell, Edwige Feuillère and Nuria Espert were actresses only when suffering the agonies of human despair. In the last generation, Edith Evans straddled the divide with distinction on either side, and Judy Dench does so today.

In the end, acting must use the best of Apollonian restraint and Dionysian licence and fuse the two, as they are fused in life. Both influences work upon us, and both must therefore inform the actor's art. The actor who has only good sense and good judgement is cold, said the French philosopher Diderot, while the actor who has only excitement and sensitivity is mad. (Perhaps Kean was mad, and Kemble was often frigid.) This is why the very best acting sometimes goes entirely unnoticed, because it may lack that grand expansiveness of acting which attracts attention, and yet still be amazingly true. "Pianists always pour scorn on the idea that Rachmaninov is harder to play than Mozart because it looks like it," says Simon Callow. "Similarly, real virtuosity in acting is passed over in favour of mere flashiness." [38]

No wonder Garrick's contemporaries marvelled at his abilities. "I pity those who have not seen him," wrote Hannah More. "Posterity will never be able to form the slightest idea of his perfections." [39]

Well, was she right? Can we form not the *slightest* idea? I have already suggested that you can see some of Garrick and much of Charles Mathews in the art of Alec Guinness, and that you can rediscover more of Garrick and some of Kean in Laurence Olivier. I feel sure we see something of Thomas Betterton in John Gielgud's work. Irving is probably unmatchable, at least in manner, but his hypnotic effects have on occasion found parallels in the work of Michael Gambon, Anthony Hopkins and David Suchet. I often think of Edmund Kean's strength of attack when I watch Antony Sher. Of the younger actors who have known work only in television no such inheritance is possible, for their level is necessarily shallower. That cannot be helped – the camera emasculates great acting, or makes it look ridiculous, unless years of experience predate it; Olivier's masterful TV performance in his old age in John Mortimer's *A Voyage Round My Father* comes to mind.

Actors on the whole distrust this idea, while all the time seeking to discover how their predecessors acquitted themselves, and with what stroke of emphasis, "business" or melodic line. They are proud to recognise that they are part of a profession with a long tradition of excellence and magic, but they resist any implication that their art may itself be inherited. This is because their greatest fear (and it is hardly news to say that all actors are a cocktail of apprehensions and dreads of one kind or another) is of being thought a mere copy of something that went before. To this end they will sometimes go to extremes to avoid impersonation, and only ape the style of others in order to make affectionate mock of it. The only time I have seen an actor consciously try to recreate a former actor's style with respect rather than mischief was when Richard Pasco played a scene from *The Bells* as Irving would have done, at the Fortune Theatre one Sunday evening in 1995. This was a special occasion, to celebrate the centenary of Irving's knighthood, and I suspect that if the public had been admitted Pasco would have approached his task in a different spirit; he would not have risked being seen as an imitator.

In a lecture given at Harvard University, Massachusetts, in 1885, Irving himself deflected the notion of inheritance. "You cannot possibly be taught any tradition of character, for that has no permanence," he said. "You may learn down which trap the ghost of Hamlet's father vanished; but the soul of interpretation is lost, and it is this soul which the actor has to recreate for himself." At another time, he said, "Traditions, though excellent for those who invented them, are often singularly bad for those who try to carry them on." [40]

But traditions are not entirely without weight. They may be frustratingly little documentary evidence to support them, but it does not take long to find their backbone with a little warm deduction. We know that when Thomas Betterton began his career, he was in William Davenant's company. Davenant had known Shakespeare, and did not go out of his way to deny rumours that he was Shakespeare's love-child as well as his godson. Be that as it may, there was a clear line from Richard Burbage, who created the role of Hamlet for William Shakespeare, to an actor in the company called Joseph Taylor, who subsequently learnt it from him, and from him through Davenant, who taught it to Betterton, "every particle of it". We also know that Betterton gave lessons, and compiled notes on the art of acting, so it is hardly guesswork to suppose that he taught Hamlet. There is an eye-witness account of him in performance, according to which when Hamlet saw the Ghost in Act I, Betterton turned white as a sheet, the audience shuddered and "partook of the astonishment and horror with which they saw this excellent actor affected." [41] Quin may even have been there – he was a teenager when Betterton retired. Within 30 years Garrick had arrived on the stage, and the line from him is straightforward: Kemble saw him, his sister Sarah Siddons played with him; Macready acted with Mrs Siddons and taught Samuel Phelps; Phelps acted with and gave advice to Johnston Forbes-Robertson, whom some today can still remember (he died in 1937).

1. Shakespeare's Globe, London.

2. James Quin, by Hogarth, in stylised pose.

3. David Garrick, by Zoffany.

above: 4. Garrick and Mrs Pritchard in *Macbeth*, caught by Zoffany at one of the performance's "points".
below: 5. Peg Woffington, by Mercier, an actress celebrated for her beauty.

6. Charles Macklin, aged 92 and still performing, by Opie.

7. Palladio's Teatro Olimpico in Vicenza,
a complete surviving example of an eighteenth century stage

8. Mrs Siddons as *Lady Macbeth*, by Marlowe.

9. John Philip Kemble in *Cato*, by Thomas Lawrence (The Apollonian Actor).

There are other strands from Shakespeare, too, but gossamer-thin. When Aubrey was compiling his *Brief Lives* he interviewed an old actor called Beeston, then living in Shoreditch, who had acted with Shakespeare. Shakespeare also appeared as an actor in his friend Ben Jonson's *Every Man in His Humour* (1598) and *Sejanus his Fall* (1603); alas, though his name is in the cast list, no record tells us what parts he played, and the plays were out of the repertoire for so long that no tradition could skip one or more generations; otherwise, we might even have known, through inherited example, how Shakespeare acted! All we hear is that he wasn't a very good Ghost.

Charles Mathews (1776-1835) gave several one-man shows in the latter part of his career. One of them was designed to illustrate his massive collection of theatrical portraits (now the backbone of the Garrick Club's collection), during which he impersonated the styles of the various actors depicted, bringing the portraits to life, as it were, through his art as well as the painter's. Thus he developed "a theory of mimicry as a means of theatrical immortalisation" [42], his way of fighting against oblivion, and climbing the connections all the way back to the Bard.

Incidentally, and irrelevantly, theatrical stories pass down as surely as do echoes of theatrical style, and one of the earliest concerns Burbage and Shakespeare. Burbage had been playing Richard III and was so captivating that a young woman in the audience, falling under his spell, sent word inviting him to call on her that night, and announce himself as Richard III. Shakespeare overheard her message, took note of the address, and went to see her himself. Either she was not choosy, or he pretended to be Burbage, but they were both enjoying themselves when word came that Richard III was at the door. Shakespeare sent a message back saying that William the Conqueror came first.

This story is told in much the same way today, 400 years later, and there are no grounds to suspect it be apocryphal. It first appears in the diary of John Manningham, when a student at the Middle Temple, as a tale told him by a fellow student, Edward Curle. The date is 13 March, 1601, when both Burbage and Shakespeare were not only still alive but still working in the theatre. There could be no obvious reason for Curle to make it up or embellish it, or for Manningham to disbelieve him (as sometimes happens with stories which gain currency long after the death of the people in them), because it was clearly common gossip going about town *at that very time.* [43] Nor was Manningham writing for publication; his diary was not discovered in the British Museum until some two centuries later. My excuse for mentioning this is to show that enduring traditions often come from secure sources. By the same token, stories about how so-and-so used to play a particular part, in what style, with what inflection, accompanied by what piece of "business", should not be discredited merely because they are exotic. Contrary to popular belief, theatrical stories are on the whole faithful; exaggeration would undermine rather than improve them. When Irving was preparing *Hamlet* for a performance early in his career in 1864, when he was still unknown, he went to Birmingham to see Chippendale, who had played Polonius to Kean's Hamlet.

Mrs Patrick Campbell was the first person in England to portray Ibsen's *Hedda Gabler*. Long after her retirement, she gave her rehearsal copy of the text, with her own emendations and stage instructions in the margin, to John Gielgud, who gave it to Peggy Ashcroft when she played Hedda half a century later. She in turn passed the text on to a modern Hedda, Janet Suzman, in 1977. It is now in the Ellen Terry Museum near Winchelsea, Kent.

Mrs Abington created the part of Lady Teazle in Sheridan's *The School for Scandal* in 1777. Sitting on the stage as Sheridan rehearsed the play was a young woman, who heard the playwright give notes to Mrs Abington; one she especially recalled was how to deliver the line, "How *dare* you abuse my relations?", not pettishly, as the actress had done, but like a volcano. That young woman lived to 90, and her son, the playwright Charles Reade, passed on Sheridan's hints to his own protégée, Ellen Terry, whose nephew, John Gielgud, directed the play in 1962. [44] Who is to say Sheridan's instructions were not still being heard, as in an echo, 200 years after they were given?

There is the additional, tangential phenomenon of actors playing Shakespeare himself, as if in some way by becoming the Bard they might creep closer to the secret of his intentions, might even take "notes" (as they call directors' instructions) by osmosis directly from him. Thomas Betterton appeared as Shakespeare in the Prologue to Dryden's version of *Troilus and Cressida* in 1679. John Philip Kemble took the role in an entire play about Shakespeare by C A Somerset called *Shakespeare's Early Days*, in 1829; it was a huge success. Granville-Barker was Shakespeare in Bernard Shaw's *The Dark Lady of the Sonnets* in 1910. And there have been others.

Just as stories are inherited, so may styles be passed down. The easy, apparently effortless comic style of Kenneth More and Rex Harrison was learnt from Ronald Squire, before him from Charles Hawtrey, back to J L Toole and the great Liston of the early nineteenth century. Donald Sinden is the inheritor of the broader, bolder style an earlier generation saw in Seymour Hicks. Sinden likes to step out of the proscenium arch and address the audience directly, in a conspiratorial manner, sharing the theatrical experience, not just bestowing it; in this he harks straight back to the Restoration period and the subsequent comic tradition of the nineteenth century. He was most at home as Sir Harcourt Courtley in the 1972 production of *London Assurance*, a comic creation of genius in which he purposefully spoke direct to the audience as if the other actors might not have been there except as props for him to act with; he was consciously inheriting the style of a previous century, and played the part with the same panache as the original, William Farren, might have played it.

Another style, quite different, is that introduced by Gerald du Maurier at the beginning of the twentieth century, in which the actor seemed to be talking to himself and not even know the audience was there; they were eavesdropping, listening in. This style passed to Noël Coward and dozens of players in "situation comedy" who contrive to look as if they are not acting at all. It requires special skills, and nobody was a greater master of them than Richard Beckinsale, sadly dead at the age of 31. They are oceans away from the grand styles of Kean, Kemble and Irving, and a case could be made for their being in direct line from the deceptively, seductively easy style of Garrick himself, but what they have in common with these giants is the actor's central aim, the discovery and representation of truth.

The actor's material is himself – his voice, body, presence – and his tool is his technique. Donald Sinden once demonstrated to me how, when he was engaged to appear for the first time in Vanbrugh's *The Relapse* (1696), he was anxious about the technique required to deal with an "aside" – that confidential whisper to the audience which the other characters are not meant to hear; an "aside" is a character thinking, and the audience is privy to that thought. He went to an old actor called Baliol Holloway, who had overlapped with Irving's period, who proceeded to give him a two-and-a-half-hour demonstration on how to do it: 1. Fix one person in the audience with your eye; 2. make sure it is a different person in a different part of the house each time; 3. turn your head as far round as you can away from the actor you are talking to on stage, to emphasise your complicity with the audience, *away from* and *despite* him. Baliol Holloway had been given those tips by another actor from another age, whose lesson went back to the mists of time and probably (why not?) to the original cast. The audience who watched Donald Sinden in 1967 were perhaps also watching, without knowing it, something of Colley Cibber (1671-1757). That is what I mean by the actor's hidden inheritance. It is transmitted above all by technique, and that is what we must look at next.

1 William Redfield, *Letters from an Actor* (1967)

2 Samuel Taylor Coleridge, *Shakespearean Criticism*, ed. T M Raysor (1930), Vol II. One of the earliest researchers at Stratford-upon-Avon in the seventeenth century questioned an old man who may have been related to Shakespeare but, at any rate, had certainly known him, whose dim recollection could only summon the image of the Bard being carried in one of his plays. On this slender evidence, Coleridge built the picture of Burbage carrying Shakespeare in *As You Like It*.

3 Ronald Harwood, *All the World's a Stage* (1984), p 187

4 David Garrick and George Colman, *The Clandestine Marriage* (1766), Prologue

5 William Hazlitt, *The Examiner*, 15 January, 1817

6 David Garrick, *Letters*, 12 December, 1764

7 J A Hammerton, *The Actor's Art* (1897), p 134

8 T Cole and H K Chinoy, *Actors on Acting* (1949), p 94

9 John Timbs, *The Romance of London*, (1985) Vol II, p 224

10 James Boswell, *Boswell's Life of Johnson*, (1949) Vol I, p 211

11 *The Times*, 15 June, 1817

12 Leigh Hunt, *Critical Essays on the Performers of the London Theatres* (1807)

13 Brian Masters, *Georgiana, Duchess of Devonshire* (1981), p 65

14 John Forster, *The Examiner*, 4 February, 1838

15 Donald Sinden, *A Touch of the Memoirs* (1982), p 61

16 G H Lewes, *On Actors and the Art of Acting* (1875)

17 William Archer, *Masks or Faces: A Study in the Psychology of Acting* (1888), p 189

18 *The World,* 15 September, 1897

19 Cole and Chinoy, *op. cit.,* p 297

20 W A Darlington, *The Actor and His Audience* (1949), p 104

21 Cole and Chinoy, *op. cit.,* pp 297-299

22 *The Examiner,* 4 October, 1818

23 Lewes, *op. cit.*

24 James Agate, *Ego 6,* (1935-48), pp 150-151

25 Simon Callow, *Being An Actor* (1984), p 12

26 Edward Gordon Craig, *Henry Irving* (1930), in Darlington, *op. cit.,* p 122

27 Ned Sherrin, *Theatrical Anecdotes* (1991), p 126

28 Athene Seyler and Stephen Haggard, *The Craft of Comedy* (1943), p 172

29 Lewis Funke and John Booth, *Actors Talk About Acting* (1961), p 7

30 *The Saturday Review,* 26 September, 1896

31 James Agate, *Ego 1,* (1935-48), p 146

32 So too were Brian Rix and Richard Attenborough, but for reasons unconnected with acting.

33 Kenneth Tynan, *A View of the English Stage* (1975), pp 15, 39

34 *ibid.,* pp 20, 22

35 Catalogue to series of statues by Irena Sedlecka, 1994

36 Tynan, *op. cit.,* p 27

37 Cole and Chinoy, *op. cit.,* p 90

38 Callow, *op cit.,* p 97

39 Hammerton, *op. cit.,* p 100

40 *ibid.,* pp 70, 136

41 *Dictionary of National Biography,* Vol II, p 435

42 Desmond Shawe-Taylor, *Dramatic Art: Theatrical Paintings from the Garrick Club* (1997), p 42

43 Harleian MSS, 5353, in the British Museum Library, in S Schoenbaum, *Shakespeare's Lives* (1970), p 38

44 Ellen Terry, *The Story of My Life* (1908), p 49

2

Learning the Lines

The "rogue and peasant slave" soliloquy in *Hamlet* comes shortly after the prince has watched an actor, known in the text as First Player, deliver an impassioned narrative speech with such technical skill that he assumes a grief more convincing than the actual grief which Hamlet himself feels:

> Is it not monstrous that this player here,
> But in a fiction, in a dream of passion,
> Could force his soul so to his own conceit
> That from her working all his visage wann'd,
> Tears in his eyes, distraction in's aspect,
> A broken voice, and his whole function suiting
> With forms to his conceit? And all for nothing!
> For Hecuba!
> What's Hecuba to him or he to Hecuba
> That he should weep for her? What would he do
> Had he the motive and the cue for passion
> That I have? [1]

There is the wonder of it all, that an actor can *pretend* so persuasively. Hamlet implies that he cannot see how it's done, but since he has earlier asked the actor to dredge his memory for the words, only a few of which Hamlet himself can recall, he suggests that the very act of memorising triggers the transformation. Is it the emotional weight of the words which create a feigned emotional condition? Or is it simply the mechanical process of memorising which permits the actor to slot into place, like changing gear, a robotic, obedient personage-not-himself? Does it all boil down to clever technique?

Well, yes and no. The debate is as old as the theatre itself and there have been, in all ages, proponents of the idea that technique must only serve, that it must never be allowed to smother the reality that the actor is trying to unleash. Even a superb technician such as Gielgud could say that technique is "very dull and empty if there is no spark behind it, like cold virtuoso playing of an instrument" [2], and Mrs Bancroft, a prominent actress of the 1880s, made a similar point when she spoke of "a bell with a wooden tongue; it makes a sound, but there it ends." [3] The eighteenth century was in many ways the high point of dramatic technique, but argument on the matter was still vigorous, and a verse by Robert Lloyd positively deplored the reliance upon technique alone:

> Acting, dear Thornton, its perfection draws
> From no observation of mechanic laws:
> No settled maxims of a favourite stage,
> No rules delivered down from age to age,
> Let players nicely mark them as they will,
> Can ne'er entail hereditary skill…
> …The strongly felt passion bolts into his face:
> The mind untouched, what it is but grimace?
> To this one standard make your just appeal,
> Here lies the golden secret: LEARN TO FEEL.
> Or fool, or monarch, happy or distrest,
> No actor pleases that is not *possessed.* [4]

This was written at a time when Voice, Deportment and Eye were lauded as the marks of an Actor and a Gentleman, resulting in some particularly stuffed performances, so one may readily understand why Lloyd was so frantic for a bit of Dionysian freedom. It was precisely because Edmund Kean appeared "possessed" that the public rushed to watch him, but it would be wrong to imagine that he was not also a secret technician, plotting his every effect; he wrote to Garrick's widow to complain that everyone assumed he did it all without work, merely because that was the way he made it look.

A sworn enemy of technical imprisonment in the late Victorian and Edwardian era was Herbert Beerbohm Tree, an exuberant character and showman who put on great spectacles at Her Majesty's Theatre (in the same spirit and in the same place as Andrew Lloyd-Webber a few generations later) and was sometimes mocked for professional shallowness. "I hate technique," he said, "It does destroy the inspiration so dreadfully!" The original Professor Higgins in Shaw's *Pygmalion* (1914), he attempted to indulge his inspiration in rehearsal by giving the character a Scots accent and a limp, and making him take snuff, until

Shaw told him simply to say the lines as they had been written, as any actor with proper technique would know how. Tree was even reluctant to learn the lines properly, preferring to leave at least something to chance; "when a performance is fixed, it ceases to live," he claimed. He went so far as to alter Shaw's ending, some time into the run, to enable him to fall in love with Eliza before the curtain falls, and was mystified when the playwright did not seem pleased. "My ending makes money, you ought to be grateful," he said, to which Shaw imperiously replied, "Your ending makes nonsense, you ought to be shot." [5]

It must be admitted that Shaw had never been an admirer of Tree's flamboyant, idiosyncratic acting style, and once reviewed his performance as Falstaff with the withering remark that he might as well try to play Juliet.

On the other hand, there was an adaptation of Dickens' *Oliver Twist* in which Beerbohm Tree devised devastating effect. Bill Sikes had just murdered Nancy offstage, and there was anxious tension in the audience. Tree, playing Fagin, walked on slowly and alone, carrying a candle, which was virtually the only light on his face. When he reached the centre of the stage, he stood there for several seconds, then suddenly, and in absolute silence, blew the candle out and enveloped everything in dark hush. The sense of finality and pity was so shocking that the audience gasped, and I must say one's heart can miss a beat merely in the telling of the story a century later. Tree would put that incident down to theatrical intuition or "imagination". But in order to be effective the idea had to rely on the actor's considerable technical experience in timing, in building tension, in suggesting mood, finally in commanding an audience and making them feel what he wanted them to feel. Tree was no amateur.

Technique also depends upon preparation, which must include as a starting point knowing one's lines. This was not always so simple as it might appear. Samuel Pepys complains several times of being disappointed at the theatre because none of the actors knew their lines. This was scarcely surprising when a play was given only two or three performances before being replaced by another, and actors had to learn two or three parts every week. Thomas Betterton was required to master over 120 major roles, a task which would make any modern actor weep. Short cuts including casting the same actor for the same type in each play (e.g. the villain was always expected to be played by the actor who specialised in villainous parts, and the Heavy Man, the

Low Comedian, the Walking Gentleman and the Singing Lady were the originals of what we now call "type-casting"), which allowed him, if he "dried" (forgot his words), to substitute a speech from another play without anyone noticing; limiting the plastic and visible aspects of acting to a few recognised gestures; and making it up as you went along. Ad-libbing was rife, and casts used frequently to make each other "corpse" during a performance (i.e. stifle involuntary and unprofessional hilarity) by the extravagance of their mid-race inventions. There were even anecdotes during Pepys' time of actors rehearsing their latest tragedy in the street, and being arrested and tied up as madmen. [6]

The provincial repertory system which developed in the nineteenth century and was still thriving until 20 or so years ago, made similar demands on actors, requiring them to play at least one part while learning two or three others – J L Toole learnt 18 parts a week in repertory at Edinburgh – with similar results. They were creative on their feet, they stayed within type, they "corpsed", but at least there is no record of their being arrested and locked up.

There were occasions when the leading man was ill, with no understudy to take his place, so the play was put on with the principal part entirely left out. Kemble and Cooke once played a scene from Act III by mistake in the middle of Act II, but put the matter right later on, by playing the Act II scene in the middle of Act III. Nobody seemed to mind. On the Georgian stage, performances tended often to have this haphazard character. An actress, having dried just after the beginning of a soliloquy, told the audience, "It is a long speech, we will pass it over." [7] A pair of actresses who dried during a performance of *The Beaux' Stratagem* starting filling in by quoting from other plays, the one from *Venice Preserv'd*, the other from *Cato. Romeo and Juliet* was sometimes abbreviated to the garden scene, the grave scene and the funeral procession, with passers-by roped in for the latter, clad in sheets. At a performance of *Hamlet*, noting the audience were getting restless, the actress playing Gertrude proposed to them "that the Lord Hamlet would favour the court with a hornpipe." [8]

Until Macready's time, the leading actors would learn only their cues, and would not all appear together until the actual performance, at which point they might very well meet one another for the first time. The practice continued into modern times, and I am told by those who have experienced it that there is little more terrifying than being thrown on stage under such conditions.

Not only that, but actors would jealously guard the secret of their interpretation from the rest of the cast, revealing nothing until the actual performance (some still do, and Charles Laughton was notorious for it). This is why Macklin's celebrated *Merchant of Venice* took everybody by surprise in 1741. "He did not let any person, not even the players, see how he intended to act the part, he merely repeated the lines…and did not, by so much as one single look, tone, gesture, or attitude, disclose his manner of personating this cruel Israelite." [9] When Macready played with Mrs Siddons in 1811, he had only one rehearsal.

Little wonder it was he who instituted full rehearsal, with the whole cast doing the whole text without an audience. "No one should ever hazard an unrehearsed effect," he said. [10] To an actor who breezily promised he would be "all right on the night", Macready said, "Sir, if you cannot do it in the morning, you cannot do it at night." Like all actors (although not all are strictly honest about it) he had his own favourite ways of preparing for a part. He could very easily give in to expansiveness, and to curb this tendency he used to recite the most explosive passages from *Macbeth, Othello*, or *King Lear* while lying on the floor, standing still against a wall, or with his arms tied to his side. He would pretend to be whispering when uttering blasted rages, so as to protect himself from exaggeration. He had three large mirrors in his room and would spend hours scrutinising his facial muscles as he rehearsed a speech, alert for over-emphasis or grimace, trying to pare expression down to the eyes alone. At the seaside he would address the waves, to give himself confidence. "The easier an actor makes his art appear," he wrote, "the greater must have been the pains it cost him." [11]

There is a story that Voltaire (who, it is now generally forgotten, wrote masses of plays) tied the arms of an actress to her side to eliminate excessive or unnecessary gesture. She complied for a time during rehearsal, but finally burst her bonds and flung her arms up, then was contrite and apologetic about the lapse. Voltaire said no, the gesture was absolutely right at that moment, because it could no longer be repressed.

On the other hand, Macready could not go on to the stage cold, but had to work himself up if the text demanded it. He prepared himself for Shylock's notoriously difficult rage and grief at his Act III entrance by standing in the wings cursing to himself, or rattling a ladder against a wall as if it had caused him offence. If he was still not satisfied, he would return to the theatre on Sunday when it was "dark" (i.e. empty) and tackle his speeches, his moves, his entrances and exits, all alone.

One night when he was playing *Macbeth*, he was disconcerted to find that his servant, who normally stood in the wings with a bowl of cochineal ready for him to smear over his hands to represent blood, was not in his appointed place. Macready had only seconds to think what to do. Standing nearby was a commercial traveller who had been permitted by the stage manager, as a special treat, to watch the Great Actor from this privileged spot. Macready punched the poor man violently on the nose and proceeded to wipe the resulting stream of blood over his hands. At the end of the performance he apologised to the startled stranger, and slipped him a £5 note. [12]

Edmund Kean, who seemed to be the very epitome of the impulsive, inspirational actor, did and said things about his meticulous preparation which anticipated Macready almost word for word. He, too, constantly practised before a mirror to perfect that "spontaneity" with which he would impress his public. He rehearsed repeatedly in front of his wife at home. He visited a lunatic asylum to study gait and behaviour before he attempted Lear. He scorned those actors who, to portray a drunkard, lurched all over the stage. "The great secret of delineating intoxication," he said, "is the endeavour to stand straight when it is impossible to do so." (He should know!) If appearing in a theatre with which he was unfamiliar, Kean would count the steps from the wings to the spot where a particular line or speech would be given, and patiently re-rehearse every detail. "There is no such thing as impulsive acting," he said in his letter to Mrs Garrick. "All is premeditated and studied beforehand." [13] (Part of his preparation occasionally involved sleeping with a whore in his dressing room before curtain-up, but he never explained how this helped.)

As with Macready and Kean, so with Irving. Trusting to the inspiration of the moment, he said, was like "trusting to a shipwreck for your first lesson in swimming." To a successful young actor, perhaps rather too pleased with himself, Irving gave sober advice: "I will give you a year to learn that speech so that you will make your audience imagine for the moment that you have not got it by heart." How many times has one heard of an actor so convincing that he seems only to have thought of the words a second or two before, that you could watch him thinking. It has been said of Gielgud and Judi Dench, just as it was said of Kean and of Garrick. It is all a matter of technique.

If Irving thought it would take a year to master it, Betterton suggested it could take a lifetime. [14]

Charles Macklin asserted that he could take almost anybody from the street and, by the application of technical rules, change their speech and interpretation of character to that of an actor. This is obviously going too far, but Macklin was echoing the spirit of the age in which he lived, when it was believed by some philosophers (John Locke in particular) that man was a *tabula rasa* or blank page upon which experience and instruction would write their lessons. Horace Walpole, unimpressed by Mrs Siddons' acting, said there was nothing in what she did that a little instruction could not supply. [15] This was what they wanted to believe, that there was nothing *beyond* technique, that man was, in other words, as perfectible as the actor.

Nobody went further along this line, and I suspect with a great deal of mischief thrown in, than David Garrick, who would perform the dagger soliloquy from *Macbeth* at the drop of a hat and return to his dinner undamaged, and who claimed he could make love to a lamp-post with the same emotional depth as Romeo made love to Juliet. It was all an illusion, a pretence – in other words, an art. As his friend Dr Johnson rudely remarked of the acting profession, "Punch has no feelings!" Pushed to its extreme, this notion gave rise to a treatise by Denis Diderot and one of the most spectacular rows in theatre history, Diderot's thesis being that the best actors were those who felt nothing at all.

Manifestly, Macklin was wrong, and Mrs Bancroft right; technique alone cannot produce an actor, though it may well produce the semblance of one – the form without the fire. Shaw was fond of pointing out those actors and actresses who, in his august opinion, might benefit from some help, among them Miss Hope Booth, "a young lady who cannot sing, dance, act or speak, but whose appearance suggests that she might profitably spend three or four years in learning these arts, which are useful on the stage." [16] Shaw was dismissive of actors in general, considering them to be vehicles for his own genius, and sought to use them only to create the musical, aural equivalent of the orchestral interplay of words and character which he had created. To this end, he was insistent upon the deployment and refinement of technique through the period of rehearsal, but even more adamant that once the rehearsal period was over, the finished performances should no longer be tampered with. Beerbohm Tree's continual embellishments from one week to the next infuriated him.

But actors now believe that technique is a living, moving, generating pulse which enables them to participate in the creation of theatre, to collaborate; it is not fixed and frozen as it too often was in the seventeenth century. Technique evolves during rehearsal and polishes afterwards, and actors have many different, personal routes towards this synthesis. When Ralph Richardson and Peggy Ashcroft were rehearsing *The Heiress* in 1949, Richardson built up his character day by day, adding a little new touch that had not been there before, whether the raising of a hand or the movement of a knee. Ashcroft, on the other hand, worked in the opposite direction, toning down her original instincts and simplifying more and more each day, until only the essentials, barely visible, remained. [17] Simon Callow makes the very useful analogy with culinary art. "For me a rehearsal room is a kitchen," he writes, "where you combine ingredients as they come to hand, testing, tasting. Finally, you apply flame, and the thing grows; exactly how, one never knows." And because one never knows how this mysterious fusion of talent and technique takes place, most actors are very reluctant indeed to talk about it, as if examination might dispel it altogether. Still in his kitchen, Callow says, "To write about it might anyway be quite rash: like taking a loaf out of the oven to see how it actually rises." [18]

Technique also feeds on experience. The actor is condemned to pry, to watch everyone closely and see how they "tick", how they respond to surprise, disaster, grief, wealth, and never to forget anything he observes. Character is his medium, and every new manifestation of character must be pounced upon and snatched away for his own personal archive. During rehearsal and performance, he is then engaged upon what Simon Callow calls "a plumbing job", as he digs out these accretions of observation, these interior notes and jottings, and uses them to give verisimilitude to the character he is portraying.

It has always been so, notwithstanding fashionable changes in technique through the ages. David Garrick enjoyed significant success as King Lear. It was said that the madness he assumed for this demanding cathedral of a part was utterly convincing, not extravagant or "actorish" in any way, but real and frightening. The success was put down to Garrick's extraordinary technique, but he told his biographer, Arthur Murphy, that it was based on observation. He had known an upright and decent man who lived in Leman Street, Goodman's Fields, and had a two-year-old daughter. One day he was cradling this daughter at a first-floor window, dangling her in his arms, when all of a sudden he lost grip and dropped her into the street below, where she fell upon solid flagstones and was immediately killed. He stayed at the window screaming in agonies of grief, disbelieving, helplessly wishing the clock back five minutes, and when the neighbours delivered the dead baby to him, he filled the street with lamentation. From that day, the man lost his senses, never to recover them. He spent the rest of his life cradling the child in his imagination, standing at the window, then dropping it and collapsing in despair. The drama was repeated almost daily, and Garrick used frequently to visit him. He said that what most affected him were the man's pensive moods, when he would sit and stare distractedly, then look slowly around the room as if pleading for help from each corner. This he used in his portrayal of Lear, and even, perhaps to his discredit, at dinner parties, "doing" the poor man to perfection. [19]

Actors are, similarly, prone to feed their technique with repeated self-analysis, or at least self-observation (for, unless they are modern "Method" actors from New York pre-occupied with motivation, they are concerned with the truth of behaviour more than psychological explanations for it). "It is the private curse of all good actors that they develop abnormal powers of self-observation," wrote Richard Bebb. [20] Gielgud is on record as having concentrated on his own response when he first saw somebody dead (his mother) in order to give Hamlet's most famous soliloquy its resonance – he was thinking how she had looked in death, and found himself reliving the reflections of that moment. [21] When Kean was knocked over in a fencing match, he implored those present to make him do it again, exactly the same way: "How did I fall?" The great Irish actor Micheal MacLiammoir was yet more ruthless. On holiday with a friend in Morocco, he received news one day that the friend had been involved in an accident and was feared dead. MacLiammoir burst into tears and rushed downstairs to the hotel lobby, and as he did so, he caught sight of himself in a mirror on the wall. He stopped briefly. "Oh, so *that's* what one looks like when the person dearest to one in the whole world has just died," he thought. [22] The note was coolly taken and lodged in the memory bank.

Yet another reason for keeping one's technique in good repair is to freshen a performance which might risk becoming stale after a few months (a problem which did not arise until the twentieth century invented the "long run"); actors dread the moment when they find they are doing exactly what they did the night before, on automatic pilot, and thought is replaced by "a sound pattern accompanied by the making of appropriate faces." [23] Gielgud's answer was to ignore the audience, to pretend in effect that they were not there, in order to achieve that relaxation without which all technique is so much irksome baggage. "Relaxation is the secret of good acting," he once said. "Young actors when they are nervous tighten up as soon as they start. This tension sometimes is effective, but it is terribly exhausting and only briefly effective." [24] On the other hand, given that the best way of delivering a soliloquy is by addressing it to the audience and imagining a dialogue with them, which helps you shape the different thoughts within the soliloquy as responses to their unspoken questions, it would be difficult to carry relaxation to the point of continuing without them. Gielgud himself recognised that mysterious, unfathomable fact, that you will hear from every actor, that no two audiences are the same. Few nowadays would talk of "good" or "bad" audiences, but all get the feeling of a house within seconds of curtain-up, and must adjust their performance to that particular house on that particular night. It would be impossible to achieve this fine-tuning without a mastery of technique which has to be taken for granted, like a bag of tools always in the boot. Gielgud said it is "a continual adjustment, like putting screws in a wireless."

Ultimately, technique must be at the service of truth, and of that domination of an audience which we identified in the last chapter as the mark of a great actor. More than 300 years ago, Thomas Betterton said that no amount of applause was equal to an attentive silence, and though it might on occasion be awkward to persuade an actor that he is appreciated when the audience is stubbornly still, the moments when one feels that it would be easy to make them clap, and the actor chooses instead to control them, to fill them with respect and awe, are unforgettable. The first night of Peter Shaffer's *Equus* in 1973 was one such. We had not known what on earth to expect from this eclectic and inventive playwright, and the fact that the title was Latin for horse helped as little as he knew it would. The play rolled over us like a tidal wave of emotion and discovery, of shock and wonderment at the revelation of a boy's unique derangement in blinding horses to prevent their seeing his sin, as well as providing some stunning stage effects (four actors actually playing horses in ritualised, balletic, fully convincing poses). By the end we were trembling, and Alec McCowen came to deliver the final speech direct to the audience from downstage. He chose to take us in his grasp and keep us quiet, make us think what he and the playwright wanted us to think as we left the theatre. It was a brilliant display of technique, no less so for being invisible. He left the stage. The curtain came down (not literally, for there wasn't one at the Old Vic then). The stage darkened. Nobody applauded. There must have been up to 12 seconds of absolute silence before we emerged from being McCowen's creatures. Similarly, in a revival of Ionesco's *The Chairs* in 1997, Geraldine McEwan took one and a half seconds to switch the audience's mood from sniggering delight to solemn, embarrassed hush, solely by her authourity.

Another display of almost foolhardy audience control was Donald Sinden's famous double-take in *London Assurance*. Sir Harcourt Courtley has arrived with all his urban sophistication and style to stay at a house in the country. The last person he expects to find there is his son, so when he is introduced to him, he greets him in a perfunctory manner, as befits a great man-about-town, and does not recognise him. But the audience does, and waits for the fact to penetrate beneath Sir Harcourt's fulsome wig. It seems to take forever. Sinden played on the audience's expectations with such practised skill that he was able to keep them waiting for the penny to drop, and let them share in the illusion that he really *hadn't* recognised his son, so confidently that he actually strode off the stage into the wings, to all appearances putting an end to the scene. By this time the audience could scarcely contain itself, and when a few seconds later Sinden came storming onto the stage again, pointing his finger and looking outraged, we knew he had finally realised and the house exploded. Other actors were astonished that he dared test the "double-take" so far, but he knew he had the audience in his control, and it was for him to tell them when they could erupt.

This is wholly a matter of technique. Sinden picked it up from a Laurel and Hardy film in which Hardy sees Laurel's photograph in the newspaper years after he was supposed to have perished in the trenches. The audience recognise the picture, Hardy does not. Until, minutes later, the camera is following him down a corridor when he suddenly stops as if tugged from behind, and we know from the heaving of his shoulders that enlightenment has struck.

Technical devices can sometimes escape control, at which dangerous point they become predictable mannerisms. An example is the device passed down in theatrical lore as "The Macready Pause". The great classical actor liked to avoid elision at all costs, and to this end would interpolate a pause in the middle of a sentence, where it was hardly justified, to keep the audience on its toes; or insert a pause between two words, keeping them artificially apart. It sounded like this:

> Be innocent-a of knowledge, dearest-a chuck,
> Till thou applaud-a the deed.

Fanny Kemble somewhat maliciously proposed that Macready did this because he was so bad at speaking blank verse, he had to chop it up into prose. Be that as it may, chop it up he did, and moreover the device had become so commonplace to him that he no longer noticed he was doing it. [25] You may occasionally hear actors do something similar today. Garrick kept his audience alert by emphasising unexpected syllables or stopping in mid-thought, as in "I will speak *daggers* to her, but use *none*"; "making the green...one red"; "I think it was to see...my mother's wedding." These are dangerous technical detours, for they can make an actor stub his toe on the technique, when he should be clearing a way for the sense.

Garrick defended himself for the pause before "my mother's wedding" (during Hamlet's greeting to his old university friends Rosencrantz and Guildenstern) in a letter he wrote in response to criticism. "As I certainly *suspend* my voice, by which your ear must know that the sense is suspended too; for Hamlet's grief causes the break, and with a sigh, he finishes the sentence – 'my mother's wedding'." [26]

Much the most distracting habit to audiences nowadays is the technical insistence upon theatrical gesture, although there was a time when you were considered no actor unless you had mastered it. Shakespeare's advice to the Players is as fresh and vivid and useful today as it was then:

> Speak the speech, I pray you, as I pronounced it to you, trippingly on the tongue; but if you mouth it, as many of our players do, I had as lief the town-crier spoke my lines. Nor do not saw the air too much with your hand, thus; but use all gently: for in the very torrent, tempest, and – as I may say – whirlwind of passion, you must acquire and beget a temperance, that may give it smoothness. O! it offends me to the soul to hear a robustious periwig-pated fellow tear a passion to tatters, to very rags, to split the ears of the groundlings, who for the most part are capable of nothing but inexplicable dumb-shows and noise [27]

The first audience of this play would know, of course, that their dramatist and his instrument, the actor Richard Burbage, were offering a criticism on technique which had got out of hand and which they may well have seen on that very same stage. No doubt it raised a laugh, too, especially if some of the offending actors were present.

Hamlet's most visible advice, which would have been instantly recognised, is not to "saw the air". We have an eye-witness account of a much respected actor doing precisely that a generation or two later. James Quin had considerable success in a play called *Zanga*, in one speech of which he appears to have gone over the top. He is telling a story, in which a letter is read. He then says:

> He took it up;
> But scarce was it unfolded to his sight
> When he, as if an arrow pierced his eye,
> Started, and trembling dropped it to the ground.

And here's how he acted it. On "He took it up", he picked up a piece of paper and held it in front of him. On "unfolded to his sight", he opened it. On "as if an arrow pierced his eye", he raised his right hand up far above his head and brought it down, his finger jabbing his own eye. On "started", he recoiled with great violence, as if somebody had punched him in the chest. On "trembling", he shook like a man in a fit from head to toe, and then, of course, dropped the terrible letter to the ground. [28] Try as I might, I cannot think of any actor alive today (outside schoolboy performances) who would deliver a speech with quite this grandiloquence of gesture. Frankie Howerd, perhaps, but then he would not have expected to be taken seriously as Quin did. James Quin was demonstrating his mastery of technique.

His immediate predecessor, Thomas Betterton, died before he could witness Quin's style in action, but we may surmise that he would have found it difficult to approve. His own apparently dispensed with any gesture but the unavoidable. He rarely lifted his arms higher than his stomach. He would customarily lodge his left hand on his breast, tucked between coat and waistcoat, and with his right hand he would quietly support the content of his speech. [29] Physical exertion was kept to a minimum. Having short, fat arms and a corpulent figure, this is perhaps just as well, yet the more one hears of Betterton, the more one is prone to acknowledge him as one of the great masters of the English stage, and attention must be paid to how he did it, how he appeared to an audience. Contemporaries all agree that a gesture from him was so rare that when one did occur it was conspicuous, and that all his energies went into the words and the facial expression (remember, once more, that in his day the spectators were very close). Everything was in the face and in the eyes. His art lay in economy rather than in extravagance. "Betterton kept his passion under, and showed most (as fume smokes most) when stifled." [30]

One finds similar tributes paid to both Garrick and Kean for their eloquence of facial expression, but in their case it was combined with much physical athleticism. Hazlitt wrote of Kean's face that it was "the running comment on his acting, which reconciles the audience to it. Without that index to his mind, you are not prepared for the vehemence and suddenness of his gestures...it is in the working of his face that you see the writing and coiling up of the passions before they make their serpent-spring; the lightning of his eye precedes the hoarse burst of thunder from his voice." [31]

The reference to Kean's eye needs to be elaborated. His eyelids were so short that one could see the white of the eyeball above the pupil, and since the eyes were large, black, brilliant and penetrating, as he well knew, their glance could be haunting. One spectator confessed that after a performance of *Othello*, he "saw those eyes all night." [32] One may clearly see what he meant in portraits of Kean on stage.

As for Garrick, he was the recipient of the finest compliment ever paid an actor, when a young painter called Shireff named him as the one actor he best understood. What made this so significant a remark was that Mr Shireff had been deaf and dumb since birth. Garrick's biographer Arthur Murphy met Shireff in 1798 and enquired, with rudimentary sign language, how he could judge of an actor's performance if he could not hear what was being said. His reply, expressed without articulation but with ample demonstration, was astonishing. The meaning he finally conveyed was that Garrick's face was a language in itself. Shireff only had to look carefully and he understood the entire play, and to prove it, he reproduced the story of Richard III entirely in sequences of facial expression, remembered from David Garrick. [33] One recalls James Agate's celebration of Edith Evans' face in 1924 – "a city in illumination". [34]

Garrick was not being entirely innovative in using his face as a tool of technique – he was following established rules which all actors were expected to observe, but he was better at it, more agile in expression, than the rest. A treatise on acting written by a dramatic coach by the name of Aaron Hill (1685-1750) and published in 1746, five years after Garrick's debut, listed the ten dramatic passions which needed to be expressed clearly and carefully differentiated. They were Joy, Grief, Fear, Anger, Pity, Scorn, Hatred, Jealousy, Wonder and Love. This was one of the many "mechanistic" schools of acting technique which have arisen from time to time. Hill's idea was to match muscular control of facial expression with the inner passions they were designed to express, so he first defined the ten passions, and then demonstrated to the actor how to conform his physiognomy to make the corresponding manifestation on his face. He instructed his actors to practice the expressions in front of the mirror until they got them right, after which they would only have to think about the emotion, imagine it, and the proper expression would automatically register on their faces. Variations from the rules were to be discouraged, or people in the audience would be misled and confused.

A similar "scientific" approach towards technique had been recommended by no less a man than Betterton, who averred that "extreme propensity to winking in some eyes proceeds from a soul very subject to fear, arguing a weakness of spirit and a feeble disposition of the eyelids. A bold, staring eye, that fixes on a man, proceeds either from a blockish stupidity, as in rustics; impudence, as in malicious persons; prudence, as in those in authority; or incontinence, as in lewd women." [35] Which certainly renders a bold stare more interesting.

Aaron Hill's theories were inspired by a scientific enquiry made some 50 years before, and published with illustrations in Le Brun's *Méthode pour apprendre à dessiner les Passions* (1702), wherein it was possible to see drawings of faces in horror, grief, surprise, joy and so on, and learn to copy them. Horror would be delineated by bulging eyes, a severe frown between the eyebrows, mouth down-turned at the corners and slightly open. Detailed examination of paintings showing Garrick in performance reveal just how closely he echoed these precepts; they were considered essential to theatre technique, because they were accurate and recognisable, a "descriptive inventory of the soul". [36]

Complimentary to this theory was the notion that "types" of people reflected the characteristics of the animal they most physically resembled, so that those who looked like sheep behaved like sheep and others who resembled eagles, with cold gaze and fathomless intention, would have the regal dignity of the eagle. John Philip Kemble, of course, was always depicted thus. This theory gained further currency in the next century and tended towards serious type-casting of actors who could not escape their physical features; it harked back, in some respects, to the stock characters of the Commedia dell'Arte, whose origins were mediaeval, and persisted into the present day with the predictable and comforting casting of the *Carry On* films. You can still spot Aaron Hill's ten facial expressions in these films.

Also in Garrick's day, rules were applied to the position of the body for the accurate expression of the emotions. Hill said that you must stand correctly for the required passion, as the body dictated the mood of the voice; words of joy, for example, could not convince and would not sound joyful if the body were in a flopping, languid position. Another theorist advised that, in order to portray terror, the left leg should be placed somewhat behind the right. One may readily surmise that Garrick ignored all this and went his own way, but in the paintings of actual performance, where a special "moment" in the play has been caught, even Garrick may be seen adopting the appropriate position.

There was a very good reason for this. The painter's job was to fix for posterity that scene in the play which had been most effective and which the audience most remembered; and to aid the painter (or perhaps craftily to anticipate him), the actor would establish a "point" in the play wherein he adopted a particular position or invented an especial piece of "business" to highlight the argument of the moment. This would then be translated on to canvas. The actors might even pause slightly at that point, once the audience had come to expect it and look forward to it, and many of the paintings in the Garrick Club, particularly those by Zoffany (whom Garrick personally commissioned), celebrate these bravura displays of technique within the weird silence of the frame; they now seem almost fossilised, but retaining that vestige of life which makes them itch to escape the restrictions of the canvas.

But you do not have to seek out a Zoffany painting to see a "point" made during an eighteenth century performance. You can go to a pantomime at any provincial theatre this Christmas. There you will find the entire cast freezing at certain moments in the plot to let you take it in, and the Good Fairy will undoubtedly pose for you as she passes her wand from the right hand to the left, as protection against the villain.

One hundred years after Aaron Hill, theorists of the mechanistic school were still laying down the law. A book on gesture for actors published in 1822 recognised 69 distinct postures as essential standards to learn. Defiance had to start in the boots, travel to the top of the head and back down again to the feet. [37] Obviously, one should wring the hands to show despair, drop to the knees to show supplication, and strut about to show arrogance (in *Nicholas Nickleby* Dickens describes a "stage-walk" as consisting of a stride and a stop alternately). A popular actor called Pope had learnt all this well enough, and it drove Leigh Hunt to distraction. "He has but two gestures," he wrote, "which follow each other in monotonous alteration, like the jerks of a toy-shop harlequin; one is a mere extension of the arms, and is used on all occasions of candour, of acknowledgement, of remonstrance, and of explanation; the other, for occasions of vehemence or of grandeur, is an elevation of the arms, like the gesture of Raphael's *St Paul Preaching at Athens*...if Mr Pope, however, is confined to two expressions in his gesture, he has but two expressions in his look: a flat indifference, which is used on all sober occasions, and an angry frown, which is used on all impassioned ones." [38] Which suggests how insidious artificial rules for dramatic technique may become; they give rise to what we call (and no actor does) the "ham" actor, a type we shall come to later. "A man, when he tells his friends he hopes to go to heaven, does not point towards the sky to demonstrate his meaning. Why, then, should it be done on the stage?" [39]

Leigh Hunt was exasperated by Young and Kemble as well. "We see how little is to be done, in any varying character, with only one or two tragic looks and feelings," was his lofty judgement on Charles Mayne Young. The trouble was, he thought, that actors were too ready to subordinate truth to technique. "They open their mouths with astonishment, bite their lips with vexation, raise them with smiles, drop them with tears, and do all that any common actor can do, or perhaps a little more; but they never chase the expression about with fugitive variety; passion sets them or shakes them, but it does not scatter them...they have not the power to *re-create*; they can only copy." [40]

Technique is the actor's tool; it should never be his teacher. And when it has been absorbed and adapted by the individual actor to his or her own tastes and talents, it should become invisible. It was, indeed, one of Olivier's main difficulties in comedy that you could (nearly always) see the technique being applied. Shaw's extensive notes to Mrs Patrick Campbell just before the press night of *Pygmalion* indicate how technical expertise must always be present as a subterranean source from which to draw sustenance, but his desire to manage her performance by technique alone and rob it of its natural effervescence must surely have had unwieldy results. He told her to speak the line to Professor Higgins, "I'll let you see whether I'm dependent on you", as if she were telling her own child, "I'll let you see whether you will obey me or not." The line "I could kick myself" was delivered, he told her, as if she meant, "anitz your turn Srerbert [i.e. Tree]." He instructed her on exactly how wide the mouth should be on a certain smile. "You're not, like me, a great general," he wrote. "You leave everything to chance, whereas Napoleon and Caesar left nothing to chance except the last inch that is in the hands of destiny." [41] One must sympathise with those many actors today who feel more and more redundant and frustrated as directors grow ever more Shavian in their manner. One of Michael Pennington's favourite directors, alas unappointed, was the 11-year-old boy who advised him over a pizza to make the Ghost's voice wobbly and high in *Hamlet*, while Claudius' should be deep and nasal. "Do quick jerks for Claudius, and play the Ghost on tiptoe." [42]

Two examples of technical flair at the service of actors who know what they are doing, stretch across three centuries. One is now so famous that it threatens to paralyse any actress who is cast for it, namely Edith Evans' handling of the bag scene in *The Importance of Being Earnest*. Her magisterial, incredulous, affronted pronunciation of "A handbag!", injecting a whole octave and six syllables into one word, is justly admired. What has been forgotten is her pacing of the entire scene leading up to this word, with gradually growing crescendo leading to a climax which she would deliver as she intended – a perfect example of technical perfection so absolute that it even improved upon the text; well, the very least one may say is that Edith Evans, in that scene, was not merely Wilde's interpreter, but his complicit partner. (Incidentally, the only actress I have seen conquer the scene since her was Barbara Leigh-Hunt, who welcomed the mountain, climbed it with guts and energy, challenged us to feel for her as she approached that dreadful summit, and then merely mouthed the famous word in astonishment.) Asked what she would do if she wasn't sure how to say a line, Edith Evans replied, "I think dirty."

The second example is Edward Kynaston (1640-1706), an historically interesting actor since he started as a boy, and was the last boy-actor to play the female leads of Juliet, Ophelia, Beatrice and Desdemona in the Shakespearean canon, acting opposite Betterton himself until Charles II's edict allowed women to appear on stage for the first time, and Betterton's wife took over. [43] Pepys recorded that he "made the loveliest lady that I ever saw in my life", when he was 20 years old. [44] But Kynaston survived this early start, stayed in the profession, and grew into one of the most respected actors of his day. Colley Cibber praised his ability to speak a line as if he had just thought of it, like Judi Dench and John Gielgud. Kynaston's mastery of technique showed on the line to Hotspur, "Send us your prisoners, or you'll hear of it!" While lesser actors might have looked daggers, frowned, stormed and braced their sinews, Kynaston paused after "prisoners", then whispered the last five words so low that audience had to strain to hear them, attaining an effect far more pregnant with menace than shouting would have done. [45]

Perhaps the most challenging test of technique is the reflective wordless moment, when the actor has to hold an audience by his concentration alone. Richard Bebb has recalled Paul Scofield in *Hotel in Amsterdam,* as the play opened, gazing through an imaginary window out into the audience and fixing every one of them "with those amazing eyes", and keeping them still and attentive. He compares this with Noël Coward in the closing moments of *Song at Twilight,* looking out to the audience and simply remembering. [46] For myself, the best example was offered by the ballerina Lynn Seymour in Kenneth Macmillan's version of *Romeo and Juliet* (1964). Juliet is secretly married to Romeo, the murderer of her brother Tybalt. Her family, who do not know of the marriage, have betrothed her to Paris, and she must accept him or be banished. It is a moment of sheer panic, Prokofiev's music surges and soars, using strings and brass to express the turmoil of her anguish. A more obvious choreographer would have made a spectacular solo dance for her, plunging no doubt into despair at the end, and a lesser actress would have demanded it. But Juliet sat throughout the two or three minutes of that stupendous music, still and upright on the foot of her bed, thinking. She did not have to move for us to know what she was going through, and when she finally made up her mind to consult Friar Laurence, her thrilling flight around the whole stage, cloak aloft behind her, expressed the relief we felt on her behalf.

In Ayckbourn's *The Norman Conquests* (1974) the central scene was a dinner party for six. Michael Gambon, as Tom the Vet, was the last to be seated, and found himself allocated the one odd chair, lower than all the rest, brought in from the children's room. His subsequent wordless, ungainly embarrassment, gorilla arms lifted above his head to reach knife and fork, roused the audience to such a pitch of laughter that the actors were unable to continue the scene for some minutes. It was not merely the visual joke which succeeded, but Gambon's subtle drawing attention to it, while acting the part of someone who is trying *not* to be noticed. This is technique of a telescopic kind.

Here are accounts of two superlative actors showing how technical colour can enlarge a role. The first is Edmund Kean, whose abrupt transitions from the grandiloquent to the colloquial, from the fleet to the reflective, left his audiences breathless. They had been used to the beautiful and predictable Kemble, and did not know what this startling man was going to do next. "His style was impulsive," wrote an actor of the next generation, who had seen him as a child. "Fitful, flashing, abounding in quick transitions; scarcely giving you time to think, but ravishing your wonder, and carrying you along with its impetuous rush and change of expression." [47] Kean's audiences were hungry for surprise.

The Examiner wrote of such a variety and expressiveness in all his gestures that one might say "his body thought". Hazlitt described him vividly in the death scene of Richard III: "He fought like one drunk with wounds; and the attitude in which he stands with his hands stretched out, after his sword is taken from him, had a preternatural and terrific grandeur, as if his will could not be disarmed, and the very phantoms of his despair had power to kill." [48] *The Morning Post* was almost lost for words: "one of the finest pieces of acting we have ever beheld, or perhaps that the stage has ever known." It is just possible to picture Kean in this scene, strong and determined yet beaten, imploring, placatory, and still proud, ultimately pathetic. In front of the tent, before the battle when he was disarmed, he had drawn circles in the ground with the point of his sword, testing fate, brooding on his own destiny, forcing the audience to contemplate his thoughts with him.

Other actors have taken up this piece of technique, not necessarily by imitation, but by shared inspiration. (Michael Pennington has revealed, for instance, that he and other actors, independently of one another, have felt the need to wear something belonging to the Players when Hamlet begins the speech, "Tis now the very witching time of night", and is about to display his resolve at last. Pennington put on a cloak, Stephen Dillane put on the Player King's crown, Ralph Fiennes put on a Player's mask. They all, says Pennington, felt that at the moment when Hamlet had proof of his uncle's wickedness, he retreated into a world of gesture and pretence the better to avoid action.) [49] The Richard that most reminds me of Kean in this scene is Ian Holm, in the Royal Shakespeare Company's trilogy *The Wars of the Roses* in 1963. The three plays were occasionally performed in the morning, afternoon and evening of the same day, enabling the audience to follow the chronicle with some concentration. When Richard fought for his future, the stage was black, dim light piercing through enough for the action to be visible, smoke swirling, irons clanking, and Richard alone in the centre, desperate, furious, knowing the truth but not resigned to it, and finally swirling along with and into the dark, dank mist like a creature demented, a bear wounded and driven mad by pain. I can never forget the loud shattering clang of sword upon breastplate, which must have been heard outside, nor the demonic wrath of Ian Holm's despair. The ghost of Kean walked the stage that night.

And here is Hazlitt's account of Kean's technique in *Macbeth* after the murder of Duncan: "The hesitation, the bewildered look, the coming to himself when he sees his hands bloody; the manner in which his voice clung to his throat and choked his utterance; his agony and tears, the force of nature overcome by passion – beggared description." [50] He had such control of his body that, when Othello dies, Kean managed to fall as a dead weight, with no bounce or rebound as living muscles would manifest, and no self-protective reflex; it was the "dull weight of clay seeking its kindred earth". [51]

Forward almost exactly a century to Olivier's Richard III, already referred to more than once. The critic W A Darlington has left a detailed account of that first entrance which had such a frightening impact upon the audience. Darlington expected the king to come limping on and straight into "Now is the winter of our discontent" as many others had done. But no. Olivier "came in at the back, and made his progress downstage a thing of so many artfully contrived but deeply significant pauses and hesitations, of so much play of expression, that it seemed as if the time that elapsed before he spoke could be reckoned by minutes rather than seconds... Before the first line was delivered the actor had told us so much about the man he was impersonating that he had me (and, I could feel, the rest of the audience) sitting forward, tensely attentive, and quite certain that I was about to see the best Richard of my experience. And after the first speech I could, if it had been necessary, have written a notice." [52]

Twenty years later, Olivier's Othello showed what may happen when technique smothers interpretation. It was a famous first night, much anticipated, and opened with another stunning effect. Olivier walked on carrying a single rose, his gait unmistakeably that of a West Indian, his entire body blacked up, his eyes rolling, and when he spoke, his voice down an entire register. It was a thrilling demonstration to behold. But as the play proceeded, I felt uneasy that I was being asked to watch a demonstration of technique *alone*, and that the character of Othello had been forgotten. Olivier was not thinking as he acted, he was mimicking. The reviews were nevertheless ecstatic, and at a special benefit matinée, at which admission could only be obtained upon production of an Equity card, Olivier's fellow actors packed the auditorium and rushed down the aisles at the end to applaud an astonishing event.

An eighteenth century German tourist called Lichtenberg left an account of Garrick's technique so precisely drawn that we may still see it now. He is describing one of Garrick's famous "starts", which he used in virtually every play, the abrupt step backwards in alarm, the startled look in face and body, which terminated in a held attitude. He was good at this, both because he had natural light grace, and because he had trained himself to attain the balance of a ballet dancer. [53] This is the moment when Hamlet meets the Ghost: "Hamlet has folded his arms under his cloak and pulled down his hat over his eyes; it is a cold night, and just on 12; the theatre is darkened, and the whole audience of some thousands are quiet, and their faces as motionless as if they were painted on the walls of the theatre… Suddenly, as Hamlet moves towards the back of the stage slightly on the left, and turns his back to the audience, Horatio starts, and, saying, 'Look, my lord, it comes', points to the right, where the Ghost has already appeared and stands motionless before anybody is aware of him. At these words Garrick turns sharply, and at the same time staggering back two or three steps, his knees giving way under him; his hat falls to the ground, and both his arms, the left most noticeably, are stretched out almost to their full length, his hands as high as his head, the right arm bent more with its hand lower, and the fingers apart; his mouth is open: thus he stands rooted to the spot, with legs apart, but no loss of dignity, supported by his friends who are better acquainted with the apparition, and who are afraid lest he should collapse. His whole demeanour is so expressive of terror that it made my flesh creep even before he began to speak." [54]

Another member of the audience wrote, "No actor ever *saw* a ghost like Garrick. For my part, I must confess he has made me believe my old friend Bransby (who is tolerably substantial) to be incorporeal." [55] And Dr Johnson said that if he had looked like that on seeing a ghost, he would have frightened the ghost.

That is how technique may supplement, enrich and illuminate the text. Cynics are ready to point out that it is the actor's only real contribution, a view echoed by theatrical gossips for amusement, and by other actors out of embarrassment or self-protection. Because they do not know themselves wherein *really* lies their secret, they prefer to disguise the subject under the blanket of "mere" technique. Edmund Kean appeared together with his son Charles in *The Fall of Tarquin* in October, 1828. There is a great judgement scene in which Kean had to fall upon his son's neck at the words, "Pity thy wretched father!" The audience was overcome and burst into rapturous applause. At which point Kean whispered to his son, according to Charles' own account, "We are doing the trick, Charlie!"

Frankly, I don't believe him.

Obviously, the actor's finest technical tool is his voice. It comes as a surprise, therefore, that many of the greatest actors have had very poor voices. Mrs Barry and Mrs Oldfield, two of the most illustrious figures of the seventeenth century, both started very badly and were initially sacked because they had appalling speaking voices. Some may say Maggie Smith's nasal rasp is not attractive, and not suited to many parts, that Albert Finney's voice is too soft, Kenneth Branagh's too shrill and Daniel Day-Lewis' too introspective, as if resentful of being heard. When we look at the giants of the past, the catalogue of their vocal shortcomings is amazing.

John Philip Kemble, the noblest of the classicists, "is proof how much may be done by an expressive countenance and manner with the worst voice in the world", according to Leigh Hunt. [56] Returning to the subject on another occasion, Hunt wrote, "His voice is hollow and monotonous from the malformation, as it is said, of his organs of utterance." Having allowed that Kemble spoke distinctly and exactly, even with confidence, he said, "the art with which he supplies the natural weakness of his voice by an energy and significancy of utterance is truly admirable." [57]

Henry Irving's voice was a talking point throughout his career and remains so today. Shaw said it was "made resonant in his nose [and] became a whinny when he tried to rant." [58] "His voice was so poor that it would have prevented him from obtaining any success at all," he proclaimed, "had he not had a large and cavernous nose. By throwing his voice forward into it, he gave it an impressive resonance, which sometimes produced a strikingly beautiful effect, in spite of its nasal tone." [59] Drama students have ever since been trying to imitate it, avoid it, make fun of it, but none has been able to make of it the majestic instrument that Irving secured for himself. (It is said that Olivier's sinister nasal whine as Richard III was inspired by poor imitations of Irving, yet another example of the serpentine inheritance of the stage.)

Edmund Kean is an even more surprising example. When he raised his voice, it was harsh and discordant. He tended to gabble between the big speeches, which were the high points he used to support his intuitive understanding of the part, giving them all his vocal strength and treating the rest as so much irrelevance. One famous vocal trick has passed down to us by virtue of its brilliant description by G H Lewes. As Sir Edward Mortimer in *The Iron Chest*, Kean had an exit line of two words – "Wilford, remember." The first word was enunciated quite normally, then came a pause and "his face underwent a rapid series of expressions, fluently melting into each other, and all tending to one climax of threat. And then the deep tones of 'Remember' came like muttered thunder." [60]

Charles Macklin taught his students voice control by making them walk on opposite sides of his garden, with himself in the middle, and greet one another across the space. One obtuse student caught the full Macklin treatment when the old man thrust forward his face and poked him in the chest with the words, "Look at me! First, sir, you should have a *silvery voice*. And secondly, sir, a *pleasing face*!" [61] Macklin, of course, had neither.

Garrick's voice was not exceptional, but, again, he used it with great skill. "He spoke blank verse very ill; rhyme despicably," went one lament, "and every player, man and woman, now on the stage, has caught the infection." [62] The same writer, by the way, deplored Garrick's "awkward hobble", by which we must construe a natural way of using stage space, as opposed to the stiff stance of the declaimers; although, perversely, he still said the actor was the greatest performer he ever saw. Garrick's friend Dr Johnson notoriously pointed out that there was not one of his scene shifters who could not have spoken the "To be or not to be" soliloquy better than he. [63]

He was capable, too, of losing the voice altogether or swallowing words if the emotion of the speech demanded, the last word of a sentence disappearing beneath his tears. An example was Hamlet's soliloquy after the encounter with the Ghost. The words "So excellent a king" were mangled, inaudible. You could tell only from the movement of the mouth, which then quivered and shut tight "to restrain the all too distinct expression of grief on the lips", what the actor was trying to say. [64] This is very modern acting indeed, the sort of emotional nakedness we are accustomed to witnessing in Juliet Stevenson, Emma Thompson or Daniel Day-Lewis, but it must have been shocking to behold in 1741, after the operatic and perfectly pronounced declamations of James Quin. Here was the voice at the service of the art; it is technique just the same, but wrung from the depths, not seen hopping elegantly along the surface.

"In tragedy," wrote a contemporary, "the voice should pierce; and there are voices suited to it. Of all others', Mr Garrick's, which in its full perfection, and on a proper occasion, pierces and strikes the heart, as the sound of a trumpet." [65] There is a story that, at the beginning of his career, when he had poor breath control (he had not, remember, been trained as an actor, but was a wine-merchant by trade), Garrick would let rip with his voice and so wear it out that he became hoarse as the performance progressed. A friend in the audience threw him an orange, which he gratefully sucked on stage. [66]

This is not to say that Garrick shouted, but that he projected, which is quite a different thing and should be less exhausting. In this regard, Irving paid handsome tribute to one of the nineteenth century's finest comedians when he said, "I never knew an actor who brought the art of elocution to greater perfection than the late Charles Mathews, whose utterance on the stage appeared so natural than one was surprised to find when near that he was really speaking in a very loud key." [67]

In every age there have been bad actors who confuse projection with shouting, and we may see them deplored all the way from Shakespeare himself ("I would as lief the town-crier speak my lines"), through Betterton to Kenneth Tynan. In the pre-Garrick period there was "little or no applause to be gained in tragedy, but at the expense of the lungs" [68], and in the nineteenth century Leigh Hunt reserved particular scorn for Mr Pope, "who has the finest lungs of any man on the stage", and defined a fine actor, sarcastically, as one who makes a great noise. [69]

So what was it that Garrick, Kemble, Kean and Irving had (despite the handicap of imperfect voice) which actors like Pope manifestly lacked? The answer lies in an innate sense of music.

This becomes plain when one reflects that the large plays of the canon, especially Shakespeare's and particularly those written in blank verse, were never intended to be conveyed in "naturalistic" speech, of the kind one would use at the greengrocer's or in conversation at club or pub, so that when Garrick and others are lauded for being "natural", it is not meant that they are vulgar, common, or ordinary in their speech. What is meant is that they contrive to convey natural emotion through the internal music of the lines, and not let the lines artificially imprison the emotion in a straitjacket of form. All the best actors are singers in speech. Gielgud said, "It's like swimming, you know. If you surrender to the water you keep up, but if you fight it you drown." [70] Simon Callow found a similar image, "like surfing", when he began to "taste" the verse: "Unlike most modern writing, the words, the metre and the rhythm contain their own energy. Once you've liberated it, it carries you forward effortlessly." [71]

With this music in mind, we can look at Edmund Kean afresh. The actor George Vandenhoff said that Kean used his voice like a musical instrument, interpreting a musical score. There were tones and semitones, *fortes* and *pianos*, *crescendos* and *diminuendos*, all orchestrated by a master of pace, so that when Kean appeared to relax his vocal colour, it was in preparation for a burst of amplitude to come. "What beautiful, what thrilling music it was!" exclaimed Vandenhoff. "The music of a broken heart – the cry of a despairing soul." [72] Another contemporary proclaimed that an actor "requires as fine an ear as a musician" [73], and another that an actor must keep his voice in tune, so that when he feels the passions he will send out the appropriate tone without having to struggle for it.

Colley Cibber likewise makes the musical analogy. When Thomas Betterton spoke, the audience no more needed explanations from him or anyone because the music of the voice carried meaning implicitly with it, in much the same way as it was possible to enjoy an Italian opera without glancing simultaneously at the score. "Does not this prove that there is very near as much enchantment in the well-governed voice of an actor as in the sweet pipe of an eunuch?" Cibber returns to the theme later in his chapter on Betterton, written in 1740, that is 30 years after his death: "The voice of a singer is not more strictly tied to time and tune than that of an actor in theatrical elocution. The least syllable too long or too slightly dwelt upon in a period depreciates it to nothing; which very syllable, if rightly touched, shall…give life and spirit to the whole. I never heard a line in tragedy come from Betterton, wherein my judgement, my ear and my imagination were not fully satisfied; which since his time I cannot equally say of any one actor whatsoever." [74] In the following year came Garrick.

Of Charles Kemble's voice it was said that one could not imagine there could be "so much charm in words as mere sounds", and that his technique enabled him to give a "perfect, most musical delivery of the meditative passages". [75] A popular actress like Mrs Patrick Campbell was well aware of how to seduce an audience with the controlled use of her beautiful voice, which was said to have the deep, warm rich tone of a cello. The French actor Coquelin (the original *Cyrano de Bergerac*) told her that she made an ugly language sound beautiful, and when she was old and miserable in New York, too proud or perverse to accept help from friends, she told James Agate mournfully, "my voice at least has not gone, and Brenda can always make me another face." [76]

Macready took lessons when young from an actress of an earlier era, the immensely popular Mrs Jordan (incidentally mistress to the future William IV and mother of his many children), of whom he said, "Her voice was one of the most melodious I ever heard, which she could vary by certain bass tones, that would have disturbed the gravity of a hermit." [77]

She used it also to turn laughter into an instrument of enchantment, with better effect than anyone since. Leigh Hunt describes it perfectly. "The laughter of Mrs Jordan," he says, "in all its branches, from the giggle to the full burst, is social and genuine; it dips, as it were, and tickles the dialogue; it breaks in and about her words, like sparkles of bubbling water; and when the whole stream comes out, nothing can be fuller of heart and soul." [78]

Then there is Ellen Terry, Irving's leading lady for 20 years and the favourite actress of even those who never went to the theatre! She spoke blank verse "with a perfection of music" and "a clarity and meaning which made it seem her own natural language." The point is, the clarity followed *from* the musicality – the one was the result of the other. She herself made light of this quality, informing an interviewer that she had been taught to have "a chest thrown out and a head thrown back" and the rest would follow. Mrs Kean had also taught her to keep all five vowels distinct, as one would five musical notes, and not "mix them all up together as if you were making a pudding." [79] But the beauty of her voice was not an accident. It was "magical: slightly veiled, seeming to enfold herself and those to whom she spoke in a glow of happiness." [80]

One does not have to seek far to discover who in our day might be said to have the Terry voice. Judi Dench can melt the most cynical just by speaking, and when she turns that velvet, comforting voice into the instrument of her art on stage, using its many colours and textures to heighten a word or phrase and bring out its hidden resonance – more than its meaning, its *unsuspected* meaning – then she becomes the medium through which truth is told. She, too, makes light of it, having once caused a notice to be placed outside the theatre where she was appearing, to warn that "Miss Dench does not have a cold – she always sounds like that." But there can be no doubt that it is the intuitive musicianship in managing the voice that makes it more than merely speak.

Where some of the critics of the day found Johnston Forbes-Robertson to be temperate, unexciting, others were exalted by the conviction carried in the lusciousness of his voice. One may perhaps judge the effect by assessing the extraordinary language it evoked in his admirers: "For sheer beauty Forbes-Robertson's delivery of Buckingham's farewell speech remains something of a sacred memory. The impression, night after night, left on the audience whose eyes were riveted on the actor as they drank in the intonations of his matchless voice, was that one of the noble army of martyrs had already crossed the dark river and was speaking from an unseen world." [81] It was as if words were inadequate to fix the experience, in the same way as they would be if one were trying to describe a tidal wave from Wagner. Conscious hyperbole takes over, because the musical moment is ungraspable, but Richard Bebb has come close to it using just such an analogy. He says that quite a lot of the best effects in the theatre are operatic, and as Flagstad rides the orchestra in *Götterdämmerung*, so the actor must ride the emotions and orchestration of the voice.

Forbes-Robertson treated his voice with great respect and understood what a vital element it was in dramatic technique. When a young actress sought his advice in the 1920s, and gave a private audition for him, he concentrated his remarks on her voice. He told her to sit at a piano every day, decide on a note in the middle of her voice, strike it on the piano, then speak some line of verse to it, firmly, vocalising it without singing it. After that, she should do exactly the same with the next higher note on the keyboard, and so on to the octave, always repeating the same line. She should use a different line of verse each day, but not miss a day of the exercise. This, he said, would improve her tone and inflection.

That Forbes-Robertson himself kept the musical instrument of his voice in order cannot be doubted. It was said that not only could he make the brass candelabra in his drawing room go "ping" when he spoke at a certain pitch, but in the cavernous Drury Lane Theatre, he could be heard clearly at the back of the top gallery, when apparently speaking in a whisper.

This is the province of the Apollonian, classical actor, the disciplined and reverential servant of his art; it is not the province of the maverick and the magical. What is interesting is that it has been a constant throughout the history of the acting profession, despite the upheavals of the Garricks and the Keans, and that this recognition of the musical duty owed by the actor both to his text and his audience is at the root of technique. In 1788 we read, "The first necessary step is to acquire the true tones of your voice, which must be by moderately articulating in various keys, and this must be your employ for some time, suppose an hour or two each day…divide your notes in the same manner as if you were learning to sing – one, two, three etc., till you arrive at our highest note, and then accustom yourself to speak in every one of these tones (for singing is no more than speaking in an elegant mode)." And in 1772: "In the repeating of poetry, besides the continuity and exquisite delicacy of cadence, every word must have its proper tone, every syllable its due proportion of breath; for by the smallest inaccuracy in any of these four things, all the fine effect of the verse is lost." [82]

The finest voice of our time has been that of John Gielgud, described by Tynan as having had an east wind blown through it. The odd thing is that using the voice as a musical instrument does not, as a non-actor might suspect, isolate it from sense, render it affected and remote and non-human; it is not at all like chanting. On the contrary, musical discipline reveals meaning and releases truth of character, God knows how. The mystery is intact. As Lee Strasberg said, "When Gielgud speaks the verse, I can hear Shakespeare thinking."

I also believe a quite different actor, Robert Stephens, achieved a sustained musical performance with his portrayal of the Inca king

Atahualpa in Shaffer's *The Royal Hunt of the Sun.* On the face of it, it might appear that this was a performance of Kean-like fireworks, all dash and bravura. The make-up, the costume, the way in which Stephens made us revere him and understand how he could be worshipped as a god, the way he changed his very shape, all was spectacular and utterly new. But it was the amazing voice which carried the king into the auditorium, its careful modulations, unearthly pitch, strict definition of strange vowel sounds, its unchallengeable majesty. This was technique of a very high order. Stephens left nothing to chance and there were no flashes of impulse. It is only when you have technique at your command that you can finally forget it and so immerse yourself in character that you yourself disappear. Like a ballet dancer who must perfect her *arabesques* and *attitudes* before she can even dream of becoming Giselle, so the actor must arrive at the stage where he takes technique for granted, before he can leap into the unknown. Technique is the springboard, not the purpose.

What happens when technique is assured and the actor flies, we shall look at in the next chapter. Not even he can know in advance. Which is no doubt why he does it in the first place.

1 *Hamlet,* Act II, Sc. 2

2 Lewis Funke and John Booth, *Actors Talk About Acting* (1961), p 8

3 J A Hammerton, *The Actor's Art* (1897), p 26

4 *ibid.,* p 21

5 Richard Huggett, *The Truth About "Pygmalion"* (1969), pp 80, 159, 162

6 *The Diary of Samuel Pepys,* ed. Latham and Matthews, Vol II, p8; Vol III, p 39; Vol V, p 224; Vol X, p 4416

7 V C Clinton-Baddeley, *All Right on the Night* (1954), pp 28, 35

8 William Appleton, *Charles Macklin; an actor's life* (1960), p 15

9 James Kirkman, *Memoirs of the Life of Charles Macklin* (1799)

10 Hammerton, *op. cit.,* p 26

11 William Charles Macready, *Macready's Reminiscences and selections from his diaries and letters* (1875), *passim*

12 *The Everyman Book of Theatrical Anecdotes*, ed. Donald Sinden (1987), p 87

13 Hammerton, *op. cit.*, p 103

14 Charles Gildon, *Life of Thomas Betterton* (1710); Hammerton, *op. cit.*, p 137

15 T Cole and H K Chinoy, *Actors on Acting* (1949), p 121; Horace Walpole, *Letters*, ed. Cunningham (1906), 3 November, 1782

16 Michael Holroyd, *Bernard Shaw* (1988), Vol I, p 343

17 Sinden, *op. cit.*, p 126

18 Simon Callow, *Being an Actor* (1984), pp 105, 169

19 Arthur Murphy, *The Life of David Garrick* (1801), in W A Darlington, *The Actor and His Audience* (1949), *op. cit.*, p 69

20 Richard Bebb, *Tragedians of the City*, talk broadcast on BBC, 12 April 1972, and published in the *Journal of Recorded Sound*

21 Funke & Booth, *op. cit.*, p 9

22 Callow, *op. cit.*, p 173

23 Michael Pennington, *Hamlet: A User's Guide* (1996), p 192

24 George Arthur, *From Phelps to Gielgud* (1936), in Bertram Joseph, *The Tragic Actor* (1959)

25 Hammerton, *op. cit.*, pp 38, 115

26 *Private Correspondence of David Garrick*, ed. James Boaden (1831), Vol I, p 133

27 *Hamlet*, Act III, Sc 2

28 Hammerton, *op. cit.*, p 46

29 Anthony Aston, *Brief Supplement to Colley Cibber* (1748)

30 *Dictionary of National Biography*

31 William Hazlitt, *Table-Talk* (1821-2), p 378

32 Arthur Sprague, *Shakespearian Plays and Players* (1954), p 85

33 Murphy, in Darlington, *op. cit.*, p 63

34 James Agate, *Red Letter Nights* (1944), p 34

35 Cole and Chinoy, *op. cit.*, p 101

36 Desmond Shawe-Taylor, *Dramatic Art: Theatrical Paintings from the Garrick Club* (1997), p 13

37 Joseph Donohue, *Theatre in the Age of Kean* (1975), p 68

38 Leigh Hunt, *The Essays of Leigh Hunt*, ed. Arthur Symons (1903), p 291

39 J L Styan, *The English Stage* (1996), p 316

40 Leigh Hunt, *Dramatic Criticism 1808-1831* (1949), p 24

41 Huggett, *op. cit.*, pp 116-118

42 Pennington, *op. cit.*, p 145

43 It is not recorded exactly who was the first actress on the English stage, although it is known what part she played. On 8 December, 1660 a woman appeared for the first time as Desdemona in Thomas Killigrew's production of *Othello*. (*The Diary of Samuel Pepys, op.cit.*, Vol I, p 5, footnote)

44 *ibid.*, 18 August, 1660

45 Cole and Chinoy, *op. cit.*, p 107

46 Bebb, *op. cit.*

47 George Vandenhoff, *Leaves from an Actor's Notebook* (1860), pp 22-23

48 Hazlitt, *op. cit.*

49 Pennington, *op. cit.*, p 92, ft.

50 Westland Marston, *Our Recent Actors* (1888)

51 Sprague, *op. cit.*, p 85

52 Darlington, *op. cit.*, p 175

53 Bertram Joseph, *The Tragic Actor* (1959), p 112

54 *Lichtenberg's Visits to England*, trans. Mare and Quarrell (1938)

55 *St James's Chronicle* (1772), in Joseph, *op. cit.*, p 128

56 Leigh Hunt, *Essays and Sketches op. cit.*, p 293

57 Leigh Hunt, *Critical Essays on the Performers of the London Theatres*, (1807)

58 Holroyd, *op. cit.*, p 351

59 Bebb, *op. cit.*

60 G H Lewes, *On Actors and the Art of Acting* (1875)

61 Colley Cibber, *An Apology for the Life of Mr Colley Cibber* (1826)

62 Thomas Morris, *Miscellanies in Prose and Verse* (1791)

63 James Boswell, *Boswell's Life of Johnson*, Vol II, p 483

64 Mare and Quarrell, *op. cit.*

65 John Hill, *The Actor* (1755), in Joseph, *op. cit.*, p 119

66 Hammerton, *op. cit.*, p 31

67 Hammerton, *op. cit.*, p 137

68 John Wilkes, *General View of the Stage* (1759), in Joseph, *op. cit.*, p 46

69 Leigh Hunt, *Critical Essays on the Performers of the London Theatres* (1807), p 284

70 Funke and Booth, *op. cit.*, p 7

71 Callow, *op. cit.*, p 85

72 Vandenhoff, in Donohue, *op. cit.*, p 60

73 John Wilkes, in Joseph, *op. cit.*, p 97

74 Cibber, *op. cit.*

75 Joseph, *op. cit.*, p 312

76 James Agate, *Ego 5*, (1935-48), p 111

77 Claire Tomalin, *Mrs Jordan's Profession* (1994), p 214

78 Leigh Hunt, *Dramatic Criticism 1808-1831* (1949), p 88

79 Hammerton, *op. cit.*, p 174

80 Holroyd, *op. cit.*, p 346

81 George Arthur, *From Phelps to Gielgud* (1936), in Joseph, *op. cit.*, p 392

82 Joseph, *op. cit.*, pp 92, 389-392

3

Total Surrender

Most of us can recall a time when we first, as infants, played a game which involved the wearing of a mask. It might have been on Guy Fawkes' Night, or in the United States especially at Hallowe'en, or it might simply have been the merry outcome of a birthday present. Whatever it was, we should not find it difficult to remember also the unfamiliar feeling of freedom which the mask bestowed. It took some time to get used to it, maybe a few minutes or even longer. Although we could not see ourselves, we knew we must look different, for our friends' reactions and responses to an ordinary movement or word were quite bizarre. We wondered if they knew that we also *felt* different, that we were subtly changed by the disguise in a way which even we could not comprehend. We felt we could say things we had not said before, and they would not be misunderstood, or do uncommon things without being reprimanded for it. Why? Because the unspoken assumption was that we had *become* somebody else, through the magic of donning a face which was not our own. It was a weird feeling. And as we got used to it, we abandoned ourselves more readily to the new vocabulary and the new kind of behaviour. We grew to relish them.

Throughout the history of drama, the wearing of a mask has been a crucial element of the art, and not only metaphorically. The ancient Greeks wore actual physical masks, as did the Romans, and as have done for centuries the Japanese actors of the Noh plays. In fact, the Noh mask is an object of veneration in Japan. The acting troups of the Commedia dell'Arte wore masks as guides to the characters they were portraying, and the traditional rites of Bali, New Guinea, the Basque country and North American Indians always involve the disappearance of the individual behind a transforming mask. One could go on. The habit is so widespread across the world, through a multitude of societies and over thousands of years, that it is safe to call it universal.

Actors rediscover that tingle of daring excitement at throwing off their skins to assume the character, the past, the beauties and sins of another, and the mask in drama was the symbol of their abandonment of self. It represented their total surrender, for a specified and finite time, to the character it suggested. The actor shed his personality and took on the personality of the mask. Of course, in modern theatre the mask is worn only metaphorically, and we rely upon the actor to change the contours of his face into that of the character he portrays; the wonder of it is that so many do, today as miraculously as in Garrick's time. But on the few occasions when *actual* masks are worn in the modern theatre, the effect is eerie and awesome. This was done in Peter Hall's production of Aeschylus' *Oresteia* in 1981, when the actors of the chorus were suddenly cloaked in anonymity behind plaintive white masks. It was also done in a play I have already mentioned twice, *The Royal Hunt of the Sun*, when the elders of the Inca kingdom, not believing it possible that their immortal god Atahualpa would not rise after being slain by the impudent foreigner, turned their exquisite, eloquent masked faces slowly towards the audience, and without a word, drew choked gasps from us at the pity of their trustful ignorance. We sat in absolute silence, not daring to disturb their concentration.

The silence is another significant factor. In a way which is imperfectly understood, the theatre divorces us from quotidian life and plunges us closer to spiritual forces which we have all but smothered, closer to fine truths and unfathomed revelations which we secretly yearn to experience. The mask aids this mysterious process, suggests a religious ritual of sorts. And because this is not properly understood, we ask our actors to go through exhausting magical transformations night after night in an attempt to make it understood. The mask is their burden, and we are their congregation. "Je suis un prêtre", says "Kean" in Jean-Paul Sartre's 1953 adaptation of the earlier Dumas play about the actor, "*tous les soirs je célèbre la messe et toutes les semaines je reçois des offrandes, voilà tout.*" ("I am a priest: every evening I say mass, and every week I receive alms, it's as simple as that"). [1] But instead of showing us God, they show us Dionysus. It is in this sense that actors are in touch with the primitive and child-like in us all, and that, by their exertions, they enable us to re-engage with this elementary potential by proxy. To do that, technique will avail them only so far.

Whereas technique will assist the actor in creating the illusion of transformation, it is after technique that genius comes into play and he may go that little inch further to tumble over into true self-forgetfulness, which is what the audience expects of him. For they are involved with the actor in a process of joint loss of self-awareness, a shared adventure whereby the actor releases himself in order to release them. With technique, he can only show them how it is done. Simon Callow says that the actor feels "a hunger from the audience, a feeling that they were getting something they'd done without for too long." He talks of a "magnetic pull", to which he has to respond by wilful (and, it should be added, courageous) abandonment to the part. "Unless it's your own lust, longing or craving, the audience will be only intellectually aroused: the thing will have been referred to, but not experienced." [2] This is what Tom meant in Fielding's *Tom Jones* when he described Garrick's portrayal of Hamlet in the presence of his father's ghost: "if that little man there upon the stage is not frightened, I never saw any man frightened in my life." And on one occasion when Garrick was playing King Lear, his crown of straw fell off, threatening a potentially disastrous alteration of mood. Yet not one person laughed, because not one person noticed; they had gone so far in the process of self-forgetfulness that they thought of him as a king and not as an actor to whom an awkward accident had befallen. [3]

There is something indefinably sensual about the way in which the actor approaches this part of his task – the leap through technique into the beyond. Michael Pennington talks about a "sweet optimism", and "an intense personal heat". Gielgud said he knew the moment when he could "smell" a part. Simon Callow "tastes" it; Herbert Beerbohm Tree "felt" it – all expressions of candid wading into the senses. They suggest the actor "forgets" himself, leaves his "self" in the dressing room, by virtue of a frank sensual communion with the person he has to impersonate. Dionysus again! This is why, of course, politicians, who like our pleasures to be ordained and regimented, have always distrusted the theatre, been timid of its mysterious power to disorient and place us in touch with a power of which they know nothing. Polonius represents them all when he responds fearfully to the Players' performance in *Hamlet.* Pennington puts it like this: "Men like him hate the theatre: it can be awfully unsettling. The Players are specialists and tricksters, as well as shamans, priests, the hub of the matter: they have brought in an air more fantastic and artificial than life but yet truer to life, and a lot healthier than the air of Elsinore." [4] I fancy this is why Arts Councils are sometimes reluctant to support theatrical endeavour as long as they are controlled by politicians. The theatre represents for them an Alternative Church, unmanageable and more exciting that the one they offer in their legislations. "In the theatre," said Gielgud, "I can pour out emotion to beat the band."

It is fascinating to discover how little actors have changed across the centuries in their conviction that this final plunge of almost blind immersion takes them elsewhere, onwards to a different existence. "The actor's art," wrote Macready, "is to fathom the depth of character, to trace its latent motive, to feel its finest quiverings of emotion, to comprehend the thoughts that are hidden under words, and thus possess one's soul of the actual mind of the individual man." [5] What is demanded here is nothing less than the "turning into" somebody else, which is so obviously crazy that one hesitates to say it out loud, and yet that is precisely what audiences have felt in the presence of great acting, and evidence for it crops up time and again. The theatre is, after all, magic.

There was an occasion when Helen Faucit was playing Hermione to Macready's Leontes and, at the scene in which Leontes discovers Hermione to be alive when he had thought her dead, his rapture was so overwhelming that she momentarily felt frightened in the presence of it.

One of the famed partnerships on stage was David Garrick and Mrs Pritchard, particularly in *Macbeth*. Dr Johnson tells us that Mrs Pritchard offstage was a pretty ordinary woman, rather boring and plain, without conversation. She was not what one would nowadays term a "star", full of glamour and wit. Yet as Lady Macbeth she was a revelation. The fictional role possessed her so much that she fell into fits behind the scenes, unable to shake it off, and onstage she was so wracked with sobs that she could unwittingly deflect attention from other actors. (Garrick once called it "tiresome blubbering".) In the scenes she shared with Garrick, however, she was totally with him in conspiracy, revealing by shifty looks and snatched whispers what the text hinted. In the banquet scene she took pains not to reveal to the individual guests what she thought of Macbeth and his fright, but stole furious glances at him when they were not looking. These were Lady Macbeth's reactions, not simply those of an actress.

One of the great parts we see so little of now is Sir Giles Overreach, a monster of greed and wickedness in Massinger's *A New Way to Pay Old Debts* (1621). It was played by Garrick, Kean, Irving, and, almost to the present day, Wolfit, and one can see why, for it is flamboyantly written, with many an excuse for extravagance. It is also demanding, and one is bound to wonder yet again why actors feel drawn to roles which are guaranteed to prostrate them. Here are a few lines from the final scene, in which Overreach is driven into paroxysms of wrath by the turn of events which has spoilt his perfidy. You need some imagination to hear the words in all their cancerous splendour:

> LADY ALLWORTH: How he foams at the mouth with rage!
> OVERREACH: Oh, that I had thee in my gripe, I would tear thee
> Joint after joint...
> ...But that I will live, rogue, to torture thee
> And make thee wish, and kneel in vain, to die,
> These swords that keep thee from me should fix here,
> Although they made my body but one wound,
> But I would reach thee...
> ...though Hercules call it odds,
> I'll stand against both as I am, hemmed in thus!
> Since, like a Libyan lion in the toil,
> My fury cannot reach the coward hunters,
> And only spends itself, I'll quit the place:
> Alone I can do nothing; but I have servants
> And friends to second me; and if I make not
> This house a heap of ashes...or leave
> One throat uncut – if it be possible,
> Hell, add to my afflictions!

Two pages later, Wellborn comments that "his looks are ghastly" and the parson Willdo says,

> Some little time have I spent, under your favours
> In physical [i.e. medical] studies, and if my judgement
> err not,
> He's mad beyond recovery: but observe him,
> And look to yourselves.

Whereupon Sir Giles Overreach launches into his final speech and ends a raving madman:

> Why, is not the whole world
> Included in myself? to what use then
> Are friends and servants? Say there were a squadron
> Of pikes, lined through with shot, when I am mounted

Upon my injuries, shall I fear to charge them?
No: I'll through the battalia, and that routed
(*Flourishing his sword.*)
I'll fall to execution – Ha! I am feeble:
Some undone widow sits upon mine arm,
And takes away the use of 't; and my sword,
Glued to my scabbard with wronged orphans' tears,
Will not be drawn. Ha! what are these? sure, hangmen,
That come to bind my hands, and then to drag me
Before the judgement-seat: now they are new shapes,
And do appear like Furies, with steel whips
To scourge my ulcerous soul. Shall I then fall
Ingloriously, and yield? no; spite of Fate,
I will be forced to hell like to myself.
Though you were legions of accursed spirits,
Thus would I fly among you.

It is best read aloud. At this point Sir Giles rushes to the front of the stage and hurls himself to the ground, is disarmed and tied up, foaming at the mouth, cursing and ranting, biting the earth, before being carted off to the madhouse. [6]

When Edmund Kean took this role, it was felt no such depths of depravity had ever before been seen upon the stage. His screams reverberated around the dumbstruck theatre, the tortured cries of a real madman, and several women in the audience became hysterical. So did some men; Lord Byron was seized with a convulsive fit. The people in the pit (the crammed backless benches on the ground floor) rose to their feet en masse, at which the entire audience followed their example, standing, stamping, waving hats and handkerchiefs and cheering with unparalleled enthusiasm; "thunders on thunders of applause swept over the theatre."

Kean had not just shown them lunacy; he had taken them into the soul of a lunatic.

It goes without saying that Kean had also the technical command to arrive at the effects he intended, but that this was not apparent to the spectators. The same was true of Olivier in *Oedipus*, whose primordial scream on realising his incest I have already mentioned. When, shortly afterwards, following the dreadful speech by the Chorus telling how Oedipus has stuck pins in his eyeballs not once, but several times, Olivier appeared with blood streaming down his face from dark hollows, you could hear the sound of seats banging as people left the theatre; the St John's Ambulance Brigade were on duty every night, 15-strong, just in case.

One who was famous for "losing" herself, and, like an unbridled horse, left to rampage within her assumed character without the useful guidance of a proper technique, was Fanny Kemble. As Belvidera in *Venice Preserv'd* she had also to go mad under the pressure of acute despair. Miss Kemble said that she could not do this "in cold blood" and so would not prepare her effects in advance, because this would have been feigned, not true. Once on stage, Belvidera took over and she went berserk, becoming deranged to such a degree that she could not stop even after she went offstage; she shrieked down the stairs, in the corridors, and rushed out into the street, still shrieking. She told this story herself and said that she had to be "captured" and brought back to her dressing room. [7] Lest we suspect the lady exaggerated, her father corroborated the phenomenon on a separate occasion, as the diarist Greville reports: "She was so affected in Mrs Beverley that he had to carry her into her dressing room, where she screamed for five minutes; the last scream (when she throws herself on his body) was involuntary, not in the part, and she had not intended it, but could not resist the impulse." [8]

I cite the example only as an illustration of that loss of self-awareness that the drama may induce. Another was Miss Kemble's contemporary Helena Faucit (later Lady Martin), who recalled one of her performances as Juliet: "When the time came to drink the potion, there was none; for the phial had been crushed in my hand, the fragments of glass were eating their way into the tender palm, and the blood was trickling down in a little stream over my pretty dress. This had been for some time apparent to the audience, but the Juliet knew nothing of it, and felt nothing, until the red stream arrested her attention." [9] It should be pointed out that this never happened again, since she afterwards used a wooden phial of poison, and that the story relates to when the actress was only 13 years old.

Mary Anderson was a late Victorian actress of note, and incidentally the last to play both Hermione and Perdita in *The Winter's Tale* (a difficult feat, as they appear together in the last scene) until Judi Dench in 1973. Anderson tells how one night she was in her dressing room at the interval when her dresser began to prepare her costume for the tomb scene. "Don't do that," she said, "I have to play the potion scene yet."

In fact, she had already done it, but it took some time to convince her. Her colleagues on stage said it was one of the finest performances she had given. So committed to it was she, that she must have performed in some sort of trance.

Miss Kemble, Miss Anderson and Miss Faucit may appear to us now to have overdone matters slightly, but that is because we were not present and cannot conceive the effect of such immersion in character. There are dozens of witnesses through the ages to actors, from Betterton onwards, having actually grown pale when their character was in a situation to induce fear. Betterton was a ruddy-faced, healthy man, yet as an actor his face could turn as white as his shirt. How could this be, if he was *only* acting, that is, if he was applying the technique of his craft in order to dissemble? No amount of technique can arrest the blood supply in one's veins; that can only happen when the body so determines, and the body's chemicals would only so determine when the body was threatened by emotional trauma. Therefore, Betterton was no longer Betterton; he was inhabited by the character he was portraying, and it was this character who was afraid.

Another example, Ellen Terry describing how Irving "lost" himself when he played Matthias in *The Bells*: "Every time he heard the sound of the bells, the throbbing of his heart must have nearly killed him. He used always to turn quite white – there was no trick about it. It was imagination acting physically upon the body." [10]

The actor as witch-doctor. It is a beguiling thought, spiralling into endless possibilities, absurdities, philosophies, and ultimately the white hole of mystery. If I have mentioned Simon Callow several times already, it is because few actors have pondered their fate *as actors* with the clarity he brings to the subject. This process of losing one's identity in that of the Other is something he describes in detail: "It is a sure sign that the character's blood is flowing through your veins and that you have discovered the iceberg of which his words are the tip when you can put him in any situation and speak as him. This fusing of lives – yours, his and the author's – is the vital anarchic energy without which the play, whatever its superficial energy, will be a dead thing... Once you've caught the bug, it will start to do the work for you: your conscious brain will sit back, while your motor system – yours and his – takes over. Until you've got hold of the character, you'll be in misery: you'll feel false and laboured; the words will cling to your palate like burrs; your body will drag like lead. You'll blush a lot."

Callow says it is not enough to understand the character, nor to impersonate him; the actor must locate him inside. "Then, indeed, you will feel almost irrelevant: a receptacle, a conduit, because the character will start to follow his own instincts and live his own life, just as he did when he first came flowing out of the author's pen. It's an incomparable feeling. Another person is coursing through your veins, is breathing through your lungs." [11] Notice how twice on the same page the actor refers to blood and veins, the language of surrender and possession. Of course he cannot mean it literally or he would be psychotic, and I have unfairly cut him off before he makes the admission that what is really happening is a rearrangement of himself. Dr Johnson once questioned John Philip Kemble as to whether he was one of those "enthusiasts" who believed himself transported into another character. When Kemble said he was not, Johnson replied, "The thing is impossible. And if Garrick really believed himself to be that monster Richard the Third, he deserved to be hanged every time he performed it."

Quite so, but notwithstanding Kemble's denial and his well-attested technical mastery, we have evidence that he *did* immerse himself in character to the point where he behaved like somebody else, exactly as Callow describes. For a change, the character was not somebody who had to be frightened to death or despatched to an asylum, but one who was a mild, pensive, melancholy and sweet-natured character whom sadness attacks, Penruddock in *The Wheel of Fortune.* Hazlitt praised it as one of the most perfect performances he had ever seen, adding significantly that Penruddock's recollection of disappointed hope "became a part of himself". Kemble's biographer James Boaden tells us that he did this through weeks of intense meditation. "I saw in his walk, and occasionally in his countenance, the image of that noble wreck of treachery and of love, which was shortly to command the tears of a whole people." In other words, Kemble would remain in character offstage, and Boaden further states that when he saw him socially, he would have a pretty good idea of what sort of part he was preparing by the way he stood, sat or looked. When he played The Stranger, "I certainly never knew any other take such severe hold upon his countenance and general manner. He relapsed from his usual kindness into gloomy abstraction; and admirably neat as he was in general, I saw for some days a carelessness about his person." [12] Once more, the language of possession.

Of peculiar interest is a talent of Kean's which was pointed out by G H Lewes. He called it the expression of "subsiding emotion", whereby the actor continues to suffer the residual effects of anger, jealousy, suspicion or whatever, in decreasing doses long after the textual justification for them has passed. "Although fond, far too fond, of abrupt transitions," wrote Lewes, "nevertheless his instinct taught him what few actors are taught – that a strong emotion, after discharging itself in one massive current, continues for a time expressing itself in feebler currents. The waves are not stilled when the storm has passed away. There remains the groundswell troubling the deeps. In watching Kean's quivering muscles and altered tones you felt the subsidence of passion. The voice might be calm, but there was a tremor in it; the face might be quiet, but there were vanishing traces of recent agitation." [13] How much one should attribute this to technical skill, and how much to psychological insight is a moot point. We have already observed in the last chapter that Kean was a far more careful technician than his audiences realised, and perhaps this was a very clever piece of manipulation on his part. On the other hand, while technique may tell you how to achieve a certain effect, but it cannot instruct you that such an effect is required. Kean's intuitive understanding of this very human quality would seem to indicate that he was reacting naturally "in character" and no longer as himself, that he had been "taken over". He may not even have been aware that he was doing it, and it needed a critic to point it out. An actor today who has inherited this very special ability for recording the aftershocks of emotion is David Suchet.

Ellen Terry regularly reduced her audiences to tears by the genuineness of her distress when in character. The Terry tears, inherited by her nephew John Gielgud, are famous; they would cascade down her cheeks, and her body would shake and tremble with sobs. This, too, may easily be ascribed to technique, but Terry did not always think so. "Though I may *seem* like myself to others," she wrote, "I never *feel* like myself when I am acting, but someone else." She went further, and sometimes deplored the continual loss of self which her profession demanded of her. She said she could not go on acting, being alive on stage and only half-alive off it, experiencing somebody else's character and, paradoxically, being cherished by an adoring public for that – for a reality she assumed, not the reality she was born with. "They love me, you know! Not for what I am, but for what they imagine I am." [14]

That is the eternal price the actor must pay for erecting a temple of illusion and submitting to possession within it. It has been said from time immemorial that actors are busy escaping from themselves, and that their art is self-protection; Shaw said it of Irving, Lamb said it of virtually everyone on stage. But if so, what an odd self-indulgence it must be wilfully to expose oneself to pain, and *somebody else's* pain at that, in order to evade one's own. The loss of selfhood is, I should have thought, a perilous matter, and the fact that actors have for so long and so consistently been prepared to undergo it must say something about the exigent pull of the theatre to those it entraps. It cannot be refused. An actor is almost condemned to be on stage. Even somebody like Richard Burbage, so far as we know sane and sensible, was apparently possessed by the part he was playing in a way which looks like voluntary surrender. He wholly transformed himself, we are told, "putting himself off with his clothes", and so absorbed the character, or was so absorbed by it, that he could not re-emerge until well after the performance. Betterton stayed in his assumed character for the rest of the day (performances then took place in the afternoon). I have myself seen something akin to this; actors call it "winding down", but their slowness and vacancy for a couple of hours looks more like recovery from illness.

Nobody epitomised this capacity for self-abandonment better than Sarah Siddons, in which regard, surprisingly, she was the opposite of her brother John Philip Kemble. Whereas he always appeared firmly in control of himself and did not cease to be the professional actor giving a considered performance, she was all clamour and collapse, instinctive, impulsive, and terrifyingly real. "On the stage I never felt the least indication that she had a private existence, or could be anything but the assumed character," wrote her biographer. "When Mrs Siddons quitted her dressing room, I believe she left there the last thought about herself." [15] Her identification with the part was total, and it totally dominated her. Even her face changed according to the part she had hurled herself into, and she manifested the same difficulty in emerging from trance as we have seen in others. Her daughter Sally said she was regularly ill when she came home after a performance, for her body and mind still played host to another, and until that other was expelled she would feel "drained". The day after a performance as Belvidera in *Venice Preserv'd* she said, "It was hardly acting last night. I felt every word as if I were the real person, and not the representative." [16]

Another of her favourite parts was Constance in *King John*. She told how she would always keep her dressing room door open throughout the play so that she could hear what was going on on stage. She would then, without affectation, be Constance in her reactions to what she heard long before she herself appeared; she would not have to be Sarah pretending. "The spirit of the whole drama took possession of my mind and frame, by my attention being incessantly riveted to the passing scenes." Note the use of the word "possession". Whenever Fanny Kelly played Constance's son, Arthur, "her collar was wet with Mrs Siddons' tears." [17] Experienced, one might expect hardened, actors like Macready, John Philip Kemble and Charles Young all confessed, separately, that they had been on stage with Sarah Siddons and had been so astonished and overcome by her acting that they had been momentarily stopped in their tracks, unable to carry on with the scene. They had not "dried"; they had been stunned.

Charles Young has left a personal account of what it felt like. He was playing Beverley to her Mrs Beverley in *The Gamester*, which has a climactic scene terminating with his death. Mrs Siddons threw such grief into the line which was his cue that his throat swelled and tightened, and he found himself literally, physically, unable to speak. He was given several prompts, but to no avail, for he had not forgotten his lines at all. His organs of speech were paralysed. She had ultimately to help him by whispering, "Mr Young, recollect yourself." Young the man had vanished; he was now Beverley, and Young would have to be found and "collected" once more.

A young actor playing a small part in *Henry VIII* had a scene with Mrs Siddons which may well have stunted his career. As Queen Katharine she had to turn upon him and utter dire warnings, which she did with a look so menacing that he came offstage sweating and trembling. "That woman plays as if the thing were in earnest," he stammered. "She looked on me so through and through with her black eyes, that I would not for the world meet her on the stage again." [18]

Sarah Siddons' portrayal of Lady Macbeth is an historical wonder, and her sleepwalking scene is still discussed 200 years after she gave it. Until her time, it had been customary to carry a candlestick through this scene, and Mrs Pritchard, playing it with Garrick, had been acknowledged the finest embodiment of the part. Siddons decided to break with tradition and free her hands for expression, so she dispensed with the candlestick and was much criticised for it by old-timers. Yet that is only the surface of her interpretation. More important was her depiction of walking while asleep. Other actresses had imagined (and perhaps some still do) that it should be slightly dotty, not knowing where you're going, being hesitant and weak, spreading our your arms, gliding rather than walking and behaving generally as if in a hypnotic state. Mrs Siddons realised intuitively that a sleepwalker would not know she was putting on a dumb-show and, not realising she was supposed not to see where she was going, would have no need to be hesitant. Though asleep, she could see as well as if she were awake, and thinking herself to be awake, would behave accordingly. Her Lady Macbeth washed her hands thoroughly from an imaginary jug, stooped to listen to what she thought she heard, went about her business with as much firmness of purpose as a woman fully conscious; yet her audience felt she wasn't, and were stupefied by what they saw. She whispered to herself on her exit, muttering secrets. Lord Harcourt frankly admitted she made him "shudder". [19] The moment was captured in oils by Zoffany.

Mrs Siddons was not a success the first time she appeared in London, at the age of 20, possibly because she had yet to conquer the problems of technique, but her intuitive imagination was already at work when she first read the part of Lady Macbeth, and it was clear that her destiny as an actress would be to soar. She said that the night she read the play was a night she could never forget. "I came to the assassination scene, when the horrors of the scene rose to a degree that made it impossible for me to get further. I snatched up my candle, and hurried out of the room in a paroxysm of terror. My dress was of silk, and the rustling of it, as I ascended the stairs to go to bed, seemed to my panic-stricken fancy like the movement of a spectre pursuing me. At last I reached my chamber, where I found my husband fast asleep. I clapped my candlestick down upon the table, without the power of putting the candle out, and I threw myself on my bed without daring to stay even to take off my clothes." [20] Never mind that the language now sounds to us somewhat overblown – the lady is obviously describing the sensual moment of "feeling" a text and being consumed by it, as she would do time and again at the height of her power, challenging her audience to dare tread with her.

The most astonishing instance of this was her performance as Aspassia in Rowe's *Tamerlane*, in the last act of which Aspassia's lover Monesis is strangled before her eyes, driving her to such a pitch of agony that she too falls dead. In the moments before her collapse, Siddons spoke with convulsive jerks and in all reality was horrified beyond endurance by what she had witnessed. When she did fall lifeless upon the stage, the audience sat for a few moments in stricken silence, then they rose in a clamour and insisted the curtain be lowered. The conviction throughout the theatre was that Sarah Siddons was truly dead, that she had exerted herself too far and cut the very breath to her lungs. A witness described the scene: "She fell back, violently clutching her drapery, and her dress all disordered – a swoon in earnest, which caused such a rush from the pit and boxes of part of the excited and sympathising audience. The agitation of the actress was almost perilous to her life." [21] The manager came out before the curtain and assured them that she was all right, and would be better for a rest. Thus placated, the audience nevertheless refused to allow the play to proceed towards its end, and the curtain remained lowered. Scenes like this were repeated over and over. The King went to see her five times in four weeks, and was seen to shed tears. Sheridan wept so loudly his body heaved. The entire audience appeared collapsed in grief, as at a mourning.

If Edmund Kean could boast to his son Charles that they had "done the trick", with how much more justification might Sarah Siddons have laid such claim 20 or 30 years earlier. But was it a "trick", or did she actually suffer? One is bound to wonder. The audience were not provincial dullards, prepared to believe anything. They were not fools. They were sophisticated and experienced. Most impressive of all, there were two fine actors amongst them, Joseph George Holman and William Macready (father of William Charles), and when Siddons collapsed in a heap, Holman went ashen-faced and, turning to the other, said, "Macready, do I look as pale as you?" [22]

Hazlitt noticed something idolatrous in the enthusiasm Sarah Siddons excited, but did not misprise her for that. "She was regarded less with admiration than with wonder," he wrote, "a being of superior order…it was something above nature. We can conceive of nothing grander… To have seen Mrs Siddons was an event in everyone's life." [23]

She had a presence on stage, also, which commanded attention by itself, in the way suggested in Chapter One: she hypnotised, dominated, subdued her audience. At her entrance as Margaret of Anjou in *Henry VI*, another actor on stage (playing Edward IV) called her a "giantess". Guards preceded her upon the stage, then parted to reveal her motionless, standing in the centre of an arch: "Her head was erect, and the fire of her brilliant eyes darted directly upon mine. Her wrists were bound with chains…nor had she, on her entrance, used any action beyond her *rapid walk* and *sudden stop*, within the extensive archway, which she really *seemed to fill.* This, with the flashing eye, and fine smile of appalling triumph which overspread her magnificent features, constituted all the effort." [24]

We are fortunate to have seen something like her, in that same role, in our own day. Peggy Ashcroft played Margaret of Anjou in the RSC's *Wars of the Roses,* which started with *Henry VI, Part One* and terminated with *Richard III.* Ashcroft was an 18-year-old at the beginning, and an 80-year-old by the end, with equal conviction throughout. She did not appear to use any overt technical devices, but rather did she assume authority by osmosis, and exude majesty as the chronicle progressed. At the close she was the very definition of incandescent wrath. She dominated the stage whenever she was on it, and she cowed us as well; no one would have wanted to face her. I fancy we may have felt an echo of the awesome power of Sarah Siddons on that occasion, as the veils of pretence were brushed aside and naked impulse revealed.

And there has also been a Lady Macbeth of primeval force in recent times. Judi Dench (1973) gave the impression that evil stuck to her like burrs, and her handwashing scene was a terrifying exhibition of the panic instilled by contamination. In the sleepwalking scene she was like a creature driven mad by the cage. In fact, Dench found her own revelation of such wickedness and its destructive power so deeply unsettling that she was ill for most of the run, a strangely stilled version of her normal exuberant self. Hers was yet another an instance of the dangers run by actors who practise their magic at their own expense. James Bridie once advised Flora Robson to "flick Lady Macbeth through your soul faster than thought." This has nothing to do with analysis or explanation, but everything to do with inner knowledge.

It does occasionally occur that the liquid veracity of an actor's portrayal may come less from absorption in the part through concentration and surrender than from accidental identity with the part, a collision of the actor's private and professional selves. One obvious example is that of Charles Kean and Ellen Tree playing *Romeo and Juliet* on the evening before their marriage in 1842, when their rendering of the balcony scene was by all accounts beyond compare. (Another actor less commendably positioned his girlfriend in the wings when he needed to express extraordinary desire for an unlovely Juliet.) Molière himself played the part of the hypochondriac Argan in his own play *Le Malade Imaginaire* (1673), in which he had to protest his clutter of illnesses and the threat of his imminent death in the face of incompetent quacks who encouraged him and made his condition worse. During the fourth performance Molière felt unwell but carried on. When the curtain fell he was spitting blood. He died a few hours later.

The most arresting example is the Hamlet of Ian Charleson at the National Theatre in 1989. It was universally recognised as a performance of unexampled intensity, not in the sense of being expansive or hot-blooded, but rather because the actor and the part seemed to fuse before our eyes; by the end of the first act they could no longer be severed, as Charleson appeared to *become* Hamlet in the most mysterious manner. It was as if he was in touch with Shakespeare himself, or, better still, that the Danish Prince was no more a semi-fictional character given a fascinating personality by the greatest of playwrights, but a young man plunged into deep distress by the most intractable of emotional problems. The cliché, I'm afraid, is unavoidable: you could hear a pin drop.

Nobody had expected Charleson to be that magnetic. He had taken over the part at short notice from Daniel Day-Lewis, who had left in mid-run following an attack of stagefright. Nor was it the first time Charleson had played Hamlet, and his interpretation had previously been acknowledged to be fine and thoughtful, but not so penetrating. He had played a number of other roles with distinction. He was rare in being admired by other actors, who predicted the peaks for him in time. (In fact, I recall that when he was at drama school and could not afford to pay for the third term, the other students thought so highly of him that they clubbed together and covered his fees.) He was secretly considered a Kean-in-the-making.

What most of that attentive audience could not know was that Ian Charleson had been diagnosed as being HIV-positive, which had progressed into AIDS and had severely weakened him. He had only weeks to live. The intensity which reached out to every seat in that theatre arose from the unhappy circumstance of "Poetry Come to Life", for one can only imagine a fraction of the movements of soul and mind which must have buffeted him (or perhaps comforted him?) when he spoke of his flesh thawing and resolving itself into a dew, or of suicide and the passage into death (perchance to dream, aye, there's the rub). It is difficult wholly to avoid extravagant language in a case like this. Charleson was not so much possessed by the character of Hamlet as possessed by the spirit of Shakespeare. No doubt that sounds too much. Nevertheless, anyone who reads the part, let alone anyone who has to act it, inevitably finds within it a personal truth – even many of them – moments when one stops abruptly in astonishment at the inner rumblings and reverberations which Shakespeare's words have set in motion. The reader pauses and looks ruminatively out of the window. What does the actor do? What can he do, but surrender himself to the moment? Ian Charleson must have felt that Shakespeare had been writing expressly for him.

It is as well that the audience did not know he was dying, for they are already eager to confuse drama with reality and forget they are watching an illusion. If they knew for certain that they were not, they might be assaulted or even traumatised by guilt. We saw earlier that audiences want to surrender to Dionysus and look to the actor to do it for them, by proxy and in pretence. Dull reality outside the theatre should then be a kind of reassurance, a return to sanity. One does not cast a murderer to play Macbeth (although both Charles Macklin and James Quin were incidental murderers, offstage and out of character!), and one must hope that the story of the provincial who drew his revolver and shot Iago for being so villainous is apocryphal. Stories of members of the audience who identify the actor with his part, however, abound. A wealthy widow left Kean a very handsome sum of money after seeing him play Othello, then revoked it when he played the nasty Luke in Philip Massinger's *City Madam*. Another lady had fallen desperately in love with David Garrick as Romeo. Garrick said he would give her a ticket to see him play Abel Drugger in *The Alchemist* and she would be cured on the spot.

The actor who surrenders to the part is engaged on a voyage of self-discovery, tasting some emotions perhaps for the first time and willing to expose himself publicly to the havoc they sow. A fine line must be drawn, because if the audience is to share that experience they must believe for the length of the performance that it is happening, and yet they must emerge from that belief afterwards, just as the actor slowly emerges from his possession. It is a shared exploration of truth, with the actor bearing the brunt, on our behalf, of all those unpleasant surprises which attend every explorer. Callow puts it best: "If acting wasn't about confronting oneself in the darkest alleys of one's life, what was it?" he asks. "Giving vent to the creatures in one's own black lagoon, in the presence and with the support of one's closest colleagues, might enable one to give them to the audience too." [25]

The trouble is, if you give too much vent, and that too frequently, there is an obvious risk of mental disturbance. A wonderful ballerina at the Maryinsky Theatre in St Petersburg (Leningrad then), who trained at the best school in the world – the Vaganova – was Olga Spessistseva. Having conquered all the technical hurdles very early, she grew into a superb artist, recognised as the best Giselle of her day, because she no longer thought about technique but concentrated on abandonment, on leaving herself and becoming Giselle (or Odette/Odile in *Swan Lake*). But she went too far, and spent her long retirement in an asylum in the United States, where she had an erratic grasp of reality and occasionally thought herself to be a swan or the very embodiment of Giselle (who in the ballet does in fact go mad at the end of Act I).

Then there is the mystery of Daniel Day-Lewis and his experience in Hamlet. I mentioned earlier that Ian Charleson took over his remaining performances after he walked out in the middle of one, suffering from stagefright. It was not so much an attack of nerves which assailed him as a fusion of identity. When Hamlet beheld the ghost of his dead father, Day-Lewis saw before him the ghost of his own father, the distinguished poet Cecil Day-Lewis. Some years passed before he explained what had happened, after a fashion. "Well, of course I was talking to my father, as I do every day," he said. "Wouldn't it have seemed stranger not to have been? It was simply that what he said to me on that night seemed particularly hard to bear." [26] One is not much wiser.

Technique must be the engine and the pistons, and emotional courage the fuel. Neither can work without the other; the great actors manage a synthesis of the two, and the measure of their success is that the audience cannot tell which is in the ascendant. Leigh Hunt wrote, "Too great a sensibility seems almost as hurtful to acting as too little. It would soon wear out the performer. There must be a quickness of conception, sufficient to seize the truth of the character, with a coolness of judgement to take all advantages; but as the actor is to represent as well as to conceive, and to be the character in his own person, he could not with impunity give way to his emotions in any degree equal to what the spectators suppose. At least, if he did, he would fall into fits, or run his head against the wall." [27]

Some years ago, I wrote an account of the experience of seeing Maria Callas in *Tosca*. It seems to me now a fairly accurate depiction of the kind of self-forgetfulness I am trying to celebrate in this chapter, and I would like to repeat part of it: "The audience felt they were witnessing an agonising personal drama, not a performance of professional skill... When Tosca sang of her jealousy, one wanted to get out of one's seat and calm her, explain things to her. And when she was reassured, one saw that she was ready to cleave her body to her lover's there and then, on stage, in front of us all, and give herself passionately. This was conviction of a rare order: Callas was nowhere to be seen – she was lost inside Tosca... Everything she did sprang from the dramatic imperative, and sprang naturally, intuitively. If she felt like it, she sang into her armpit – the movements, the gestures rose from within her and accorded with those of a woman in anguish." [28] The point, I now see, was that she *was* a woman in anguish.

Even better, when you have the luck to encounter two actors on stage at the same time, each of whom has achieved the balance and can take the measure of the other in total freedom, with mutual gifts of flight, then the magic is more than doubled. Callow has a good expression for the phenomenon: acting, he says, becomes jazz. I can think of a dozen examples: Anthony Quayle and Gwen Ffrangcon-Davies in *Long Day's Journey Into Night* (1958), Uta Hagen and Arthur Hill in *Who's Afraid of Virginia Woolf?* (1962), Judi Dench and Ian McKellen in *Macbeth* (1972), Judi Dench and Anthony Hopkins in *Antony and Cleopatra* (1987), Margot Fonteyn and Rudolf Nureyev in *Marguerite and Armand* (1966), Maria Callas and Tito Gobbi in *Tosca* (1964) and above all, perhaps, the two occasions when John Gielgud and Ralph Richardson acted together in non-classical plays, David Storey's *Home* (1970) and Harold Pinter's *No Man's Land* (1975).

The rapport on stage on both occasions was more than just professional, yet it relied upon nothing so thin as friendship. They were a team, two halves of the same being – the actor acting. To abandon oneself to a role in the way I have suggested here – to make that dizzy leap – requires a special kind of recklessness, and however many other people are on stage at the time, you are alone, with your heart in your mouth. Richardson and Gielgud gave the impression of having banished fear. They were so totally in character that we the audience felt like eavesdroppers, peering in on private colloquy between two highly individual men. They were a partnership of fancy, playing make-believe to perfection, to the extent that Gielgud and Richardson disappeared to be replaced by these two odd fellows in desultory conversation leading to little conclusion. Their use of space and pause, the charges of current between them (what is nowadays called "body language"), their forgetfulness of the audience, no doubt betrayed technical skills of a supreme order, but they were entirely invisible. With both of them one felt the impulse to say something was theirs and theirs alone, that it did not depend upon lines being written for them, but on the mood their characters felt descend upon them at any one moment. They were free, strange, ungovernable. They seemed magically independent of the play they were in, which was just as well, for neither play was particularly substantial. There is much truth in the notion that, the less good the play, the more creative the actor has to be to inject life into it. Gielgud himself said that Irving's greatest performances were those he improvised out of very clumsy old texts, which he rewrote during the intervals. One would not care to suggest that either Pinter's or Storey's texts were in need of the radical dismemberment due a Victorian melodrama – on the contrary, they were taut and spare and every word had a purpose – but they would not have been remembered were it not for the actors who made them flesh and spirit, just as *The Bells* is remembered today only for Irving's performance in it. To watch Richardson and Gielgud gently lob, their words interlocking and sparking unanticipated echos, was indeed "like jazz".

It is also evident when the match purposefully does not meet, as in the 1996 revival of *Who's Afraid of Virginia Woolf?* David Suchet and Diana Rigg eddied around one another, but there was no confluence. Suchet was entirely within the skin of George, a part which he had anyway wanted all his life to play; he smelt of stuffy American academia, he shambled and shuffled with weary frustration, his invective was intellectual and arid, his whole personality was congested by years of hostility, humiliation and vicious amusement, tempered by an understanding of Martha which went deeper than love. Diana Rigg was outside the skin of Martha. She shouted and raved and teased, because that was what the role demanded. She was all technique, which meant that she never stopped being an actress saying lines, saying them brilliantly as a pianist might dazzle his way through Liszt's B Minor Sonata but not intuit what it felt to compose it. She treated the part as a technical mountain to climb, and though she climbed with energy and a sure foot, when she reached the summit she never forgot that she was a mountaineer. Consequently, the intensity of these two fine players was at variance, one entirely forgetful of self, the other consciously and visibly hitting for effect, the one metamorphosed by the process of acting, the other palpably moulding herself on to it. It was an object lesson in the difference between technique and absorption. Rigg was terrifying in character because Suchet, in character, could not make her listen to him.

One could see the same actor in quite different circumstances two years earlier in David Mamet's *Oleanna*, in which he played opposite Lia Williams. Suchet was a university teacher to whom a shy and diffident, long-haired female student has gone for advice. She is worried that she does not seem to understand the course he is teaching, she does not know what he means half the time, and she thinks she must be unassailably stupid and ought to leave college. The meeting takes place in his study. He sympathises with her and tries to encourage her, telling her that he too, at her age, wondered whether he would ever get his mind round some things, but that it does come with experience, and she should persevere. He offers to help her catch up with the course by giving private lessons in his room once a week. Throughout the first act, he is helpful and kind, and when she bursts into tears he puts a considerate hand on her shoulder.

All is different after the interval. The student accuses him of élitism, of purposefully using words she does not understand in order to proclaim his ascendancy over her. She tells him that she and her "group" have therefore decided to ban his books and require him to teach from others they have selected. She questions his right to tenure and reports before a committee who duly revoke it. About to lose his job, he must also sell his house. His wife occasionally telephones during these increasingly fraught conversations with the student, and we hear him trying desperately to explain matters to her; at the same time he must placate the girl who, by now, is bent on destroying him. He is cornered and incredulous, blinking at the abyss before him; she is scornful and triumphant. He tries to reason with her, placing hands on her upper arms, but it is beyond hope. By this point the tension throughout the theatre was pressing upon one's chest, and one could feel the heartbeat quicken. Suchet and Williams were creating a different world and sucking us into it.

In the last scene we learn that the girl has reported him for attempted rape. He is about to be arrested, and telephones his wife to warn her before she learns the fact from the police. On the telephone he says "Don't worry, baby." The girl strides over to him and commands, "Don't call your wife 'baby'," whereupon the teacher's civilised restraint snaps and in an explosion which ought to have been expected but which nevertheless comes as a shocking surprise, he punches her in the face and knocks her to the ground. Nor does he stop there. Completely out of his mind, he kicks her in the stomach; she seeks refuge under a table; he kicks her in the head. Finally he comes to and realises what he has done, but the ripples of the horrific scene still play over his body, in exactly the same way as Edmund Kean was said to have displayed "subsiding emotion".

If I describe this play in rather too much detail for a paragraph, it is because you have to imagine the audience. They had been whipped up into such a state of shaking indignation that when Suchet attacked Williams there arose a great cheer from the stalls, and a number of people stood up and shouted their encouragement. I have never seen an audience reaction anything like it. The actors were so deeply into their assumed roles that we, idiotically one might think, drawn by their own forgetfulness of David Suchet and Lia Williams, *forgot* they were actors. It was an emotional forgetfulness, usually referred to as suspension of disbelief (because, of course, belief is an emotional not a rational exercise). Moreover, we too experienced that "subsiding emotion" as conversations about the events we had seen continued on the way up the stairs and into the street, leading in several visible instances to heated argument. Supper engagements were cancelled on the pavement, as men took the lecturer's side and women the student's, and one suspected other kinds of engagements might also have suffered. I ate alone, the heart still pounding.

This was a magnificent illustration of that fusion of technical ability with actual melting into character, art plus adventure, which only the greatest theatre achieves. I am told that it was so sly, so inclusive, that Suchet and Williams were victims of it, too; they went on arguing in character when they were not on stage, he defending the lecturer, she arguing for the student. If that is not being "possessed" by a character, to the extent that it contrives to replace your own, I don't know what is.

Not everyone would agree. There are those who continue to maintain that emotional commitment on this level is hazardous to good acting, or that I may be a fool to have given it credit for what is only in my imagination. The first objection is certainly valid, and I think that when acting becomes this intense, it is only a centimetre away from the ridiculous, or what is sometimes known as "ham" acting. And the second objection bears upon the first, because it raises the dispute as to whether the best actors should feel anything at all. Are ham actors those who feel too much? Has their headlong dive into the personality of another killed off whatever dramatic technique they may once have had? Or have they simply got the balance wrong, are they, in other words, disordered?

The question is an old one. "We no more think feeling a necessary ingredient in acting than we should deem it expedient for a painter, after he had finished a likeness upon the canvas, to represent the heart, liver, brains, and the internal formation, on the back of it." [29] This nineteenth century view is, in effect, a plea to guard the mystery, disguised as common sense; of course actors should not feel anything – that's why they're actors! In 1747 Sainte-Albine had published a book called *Le Comédien* in which he flatly claimed that only people in love could act the part of lovers, and only those with an elevated soul could play the hero. Three years later, François Riccoboni contradicted him roundly with the claim that only by repressing emotion could the actor keep the voice free for acting (by which he meant, in those days, speaking clearly), and with the publication of Denis Diderot's *Paradoxe sur le Comedien* in 1830 an almighty row broke out on both sides of the Channel, which went on spluttering for over a century. Diderot's startling thesis was that extreme sensitivity, or the ability to feel the emotion of a part, made for very bad actors, and that a sublime actor could only occur in a man who had absolutely no capacity to feel whatever. The "paradox" lay in the fact that a man or woman thus wooden, blocked and emotionally stunted should be the best equipped to find the intellectual core of the play. He wanted the theatre to serve like a sermon, a lecture, and he therefore demanded that actors stifle any emotion or character, both of which would interfere with their function as conduits for his didactic intention.

Sensitive men or women make bad actors, he says, for four main reasons: a) they tend to rely upon the inspiration of the moment, and not do their homework, b) they identify too closely with the character they are portraying, c) they are too deeply involved in the business of acting and forget who they are, d) they may well end up by playing themselves rather than the character. It is immediately obvious that d) contradicts both b) and c), and that b) and c) are the very qualities which the present chapter has been celebrating as the triumph of self-forgetfulness. Those on Diderot's side warned that excess of sensitivity led not to the art of acting but the absurdity of "ham" acting, drowning the stage in hysterics. Those against Diderot claimed that absence of sensitivity led to empty technique, "the school of the tragic cadence and the struck brow", which is itself "ham" acting.

I am not sure sure either is right, and I use the term "ham" with reluctance and apology. Actors detest it, for it makes overt fun of their vocation, and yet they know well enough that it exists and are not slow to deride it themselves. The over-emotional actor and the over-technical actor are both at fault, and both in danger of slipping over the edge into ham, because neither has emerged from himself in order to devote his energies to the part. The one is showing off his artistry, the other displaying his emotional baggage, both are being themselves. Self-indulgence is at the root of ham, it lacks originality and invention, it lacks genuineness and quivering spark, it is either copying, striking up other people's attitudes to show one can do it, or it is self-love, demonstrating the beauty of one's heart and soul and foisting them upon whichever character happens to be on that night. Ham never forgets itself.

Examples abound, but they must be examined with care, for we shall find even Garrick and Kean among them if we fail to hold to our definitions. As Ellen Terry very wisely remarked, "All great acting has a certain strain of extravagance which the imitators catch hold of and give us the eccentric body without the sublime soul." [30]

Haidée Wright, now forgotten, was a considerable actress in the early part of the twentieth century, who, in John Gielgud's words, "knew how to dominate the stage with absolute authority in what my father always described as The Grand Manner." In Somerset Maugham's *The Unknown* she had a line many actresses would beg for – "Who is going to forgive God?" – and she gave it her best. She had "a touch of the barnstormer" in her, and the throbbing tremolo of her incessantly quavering voice was much imitated. Gielgud admitted she was "blatantly stagey", but paid tribute to the passionate intensity which she could always evoke and to the "great spirit in her little body". "I never liked to hear anyone make fun of her," he added, and one knows that it was politeness, respect for his profession, and human decency which prevented him from calling her "ham". [31]

He was very fond of Mrs Patrick Campbell, which gives him the right to say "she boomed too much" without offence, and even to be humorous about her: "Neither Shakespeare nor the Bible served to exhibit her to real advantage." As Lady Macbeth she looked like "the Queen of Hearts about to have the gardeners executed", and towards the end of her career she mischievously clowned in the serious scenes and hammed up the light ones with grand gesture. [32] She had been a "star", a beauty, and an actress capable of making the audience hold its breath, but she was perhaps never too far from being a ham.

The trap is ever lurking, half-open, waiting for the actor to trip in, like a fly-eating plant which closes on its prey and will not heed its struggling. Once you have toppled into ham, you are more or less condemned to continue the performance in the same vein; you cannot just climb out of it again. And it can catch the very best. Flora Robson was a fine actress, distinguished in many superb performances from the 1920s to the 1960s by her truth and restraint. She gave the best account of Nurse in *Romeo and Juliet* that I ever saw. In Somerset Maugham's *For Services Rendered* (1932), however, she apparently went over the top. This is what James Agate had to say: "Miss Flora Robson contrives to give both the undercurrent of deep emotion and its ultimate flood, though I think her hysterics would gain in force if she would put a little less power into them. This is no time to argue the paradox of acting, but Miss Robson is a good enough artist to realise that because a character is at the end of its tether is no reason why the actress should be at the end of hers." [33]

If that might be ham through over-emoting, here is ham through elaborate stagecraft and straitjacketing. Leigh Hunt is reporting on the talents of Mr Pope, whom I have already had cause to mention. His comments, though cheeky, give a very good idea of what a first-class ham performance might look like, and are worth quoting at length: "Mr Pope has not one requisite to an actor but a good voice, and this he uses so unmercifully on all occasions that its value is lost, and he contrives to turn it into a defect. His face is as hard, as immovable, and as void of meaning as an oak wainscot; his eyes, which should endeavour to throw some meaning into his vociferous declamation, he generally contrives to keep almost shut; and what would make another actor merely serious is enough to put him in a passion...there is an infallible method of obtaining a clap from the galleries, and there is an art known at the theatre by the name of *clap-trapping*, which Mr Pope has shown great wisdom in studying. It consists in nothing more than gradually raising the voice as the speech draws to a conclusion, making an alarming outcry on the last four or five lines, or suddenly dropping them into a tremulous but energetic undertone, and with a vigorous jerk of the right arm rushing off the stage. All this astonishes the galleries; they are persuaded it must be something very fine, because it is so important and so unintelligible, and they clap for the sake of their own reputation." [34]

("Clap-trap" in modern speech has lost its derivation and shifted its meaning. It now denotes any verbose and windy rubbish, but in 1741 Aaron Hill invented the expression as a signal to actors how to milk applause, with no derogatory or shameful connotation attached).

Alas, we have had an opportunity to encounter the Pope kind of actor in our own day, when Peter O'Toole played Macbeth at the Old Vic in 1975 in so bizarre a style, mannered and histrionic, that the public flocked to see it and the theatre had a *succès de scandale* on its hands. This was not despite the reviews, which were uniformly horrible, but because of them. We were being informed that here was a chance to see Ham come to Life, and few could resist it. There was, I am afraid, much unkind mirth amongst the audience on the night I attended. And yet O'Toole was and is a good actor; on that occasion he didn't spot the seductive trap of overload.

Addison is said to have remarked upon watching Hamlet explode into apoplectic ire at the appearance of the Ghost ("Angels and ministers of grace defend us!") that he could not understand the cause of so much passion, as the Ghost had not offended him in any way.

O'Toole's absurdly heroic style made it seem that he was offended by every word of the text. Robert Cushman in *The Observer* wrote that "his performance suggests he is taking some kind of personal revenge on the play", and James Fenton in *The Sunday Times* thought he was contemptuous of both the rest of the company and of the audience. He wrote of the "premeditated awfulness of O'Toole's performance. There was no question of risks taken, or brave attempts which had simply failed. This was the kind of awfulness which could have been seen a mile off." Irving Wardle in *The Times* captured for posterity the manner of the actor's delivery, in much the same way that Leigh Hunt had fossilised Mr Pope. "Mr O'Toole," he wrote, "strides on in what one first takes to be the last stages of battle fatigue. His walk is an exhausted lunge, his voice thick, hoarse and full of abrupt sledge-hammer emphases. But as he begins, so he continues. His manner on the stage is not that of a man in an intricate, danger-fraught situation, but that of someone who owns the place...his verse speaking consists

above: 10. Edmund Kean in *Richard III*, by unknown artist.
(The Dionysian Actor).
below: 11. Charles Matthews, by Harlow. The Actor is seated on the
right, looking at himself in four different roles.

12. Henry Irving, the first theatrical knight, as Shylock.

13. Ellen Terry as Queen Katherine.

14. Mrs Patrick Campbell as Ophelia.

15. Ellen Terry, Herbert Beerbohm Tree and Madge Kendal in *The Merry Wives of Windsor*, by Collier.

16. Laurence Olivier in *A Flea in Her Ear*, Old Vic, 1967.

17. John Gielgud as Hamlet, New Theatre, 1934.

18. Ian McKellen as Richard III, Royal National Theatre, 1990.

of a heavy lurch from beat to beat, delivered in measured, sustained tone, and depending upon prolonged phrasing within a single breath. Arresting to begin with, if only as total departure from modern verse convention, it grows extremely monotonous and blots out the sense." Jack Tinker in the *Daily Mail* described the performance as not downright bad but heroically ludicrous, and when he confessed that it was the first time in his life a Macbeth had sent him into involuntary giggles, he was for once understating the event. When O'Toole arrived on stage after the murder of Duncan covered in gore from head to toe, blood dripping from his hands and hair, a drenched sword in each hand, and paused for an eternity of seconds before telling us, "I have done the deed," the whole theatre erupted into pitiless laughter. [35]

Peter O'Toole's fiasco made front page news, and the owner of the local Italian restaurant was delighted, because instead of having business before or after the show, it was the only time he had been full *during* the show as well. Other actors were quick to point out the dreadful curse which hung over the play, a curse so pervasive that not one of them will dare utter its title. O'Toole had apparently done so the year before at Stratford, and was now punished in consequence of his foolhardiness. Lilian Baylis had had a heart attack after the first night of *Macbeth* in 1937, and died. All of O'Toole's cast suffered mysterious illnesses and road accidents.

Laurence Olivier's *Othello* (1964) was not greeted with laughter. Rather the contrary – with awed respect. But I am glad one critic recognised it for the ham that it was. "There is a kind of acting of which only a great actor is capable," wrote Alan Brien in *The Sunday Telegraph*. "I find Sir Laurence Olivier's Othello the most prodigious and perverse example of this in a decade…he begins to double and treble his vowels, to stretch his consonants, to stagger and shake, even to vomit, near the frontiers of self-parody. His hips oscillate, his palms rotate, his voice skids and slides so that the Othello music takes on a Beatle beat."

Herbert Beerbohm Tree was a different kind of ham. He could not fall unknowingly into the trap of over-acting, he made traps for himself and leapt in gleefully. He acted according to an unvarying style, whether the part be Julius Caesar or Beethoven, and loved dressing up in resplendent uniforms, beards or vine-leaves. Underneath all this was always Tree, unlikely ever to get into the skin of any character but his own, which he found so delightfully comfortable. He was emphatically a man of the theatre, a showman, but I think he was just as surely not really an actor. We have already seen that, as Professor Higgins in the original *Pygmalion*, Tree was like a lost child when told that he would be expected to talk normally and not put on any funny hats. He could not see the character unless it were given some huge handle for him to grasp, so he tried taking snuff, using an accent, jumping on to the piano: he could only deal in the superficials of theatre practice; the depth of dramatic impersonation eluded him, if he ever wanted it. He turned the dreadful chore of learning lines, the *sine qua non* of technique one might have thought, into a joke by scribbling the difficult ones on pieces of paper which were hidden all over the stage – on the backs of chairs, under lamps, beside doors, behind curtains.

What Tree had forgotten was Hamlet's sage and simple advice to the Players 300 years before, "that you o'erstep not the modesty of nature." All ham acting does precisely that, which is what makes it immediately recognisable. This is not to say that big, bold acting must always be outside the modesty of nature – if it were, we would have no Lears. But there must always be truth within the boldness – hence the tricky line to tread. (It never surprises me that actors are nervous before going on stage; they know this might be the night they go bananas and are found out.) Look at two of the greats mentioned a little earlier – Garrick and Kean. Garrick acted the role of Virginius in a play called *Virginia* (he was the father of the title role). Virginia is claimed as a slave. Garrick/ Virginius listened to the claim being made before the tribune with his arms folded across his chest and staring at the ground. Eventually, Virginius is informed that the tribune will hear his answer to the claim. Garrick stood in the same position, moving only the muscles of his face as thoughts assailed him. He slowly raised his head, paused, turned his body round towards the questioner, again with leisurely deliberation, then fixed him with his eye. He stood there in silence, uttering not a word, while the whole theatre waited almost in anguish to see what he would do. In a low tone, and with breaking heart, he said simply, "Thou traitor!", and the audience had their release at last. There is probably nobody who could attempt that now without it seeming ludicrous, and hence it would be regarded as "ham". But with Garrick it wasn't. The tension he built was not for himself – The Actor – but for the part he was portraying, and the audience believed him. As they did Kean when, as Sir Giles Overreach, already mentioned, he was driven mad on stage by his own distempered rage and fell cataleptic, foaming at the mouth. It was said he was transcendent, and frightened every one who saw him, including others on stage; Mrs Glover had suddenly to find a chair. Reading that conclusion again, one may well see how few actors would have the courage to attempt it. The invitation to go over the top and make a fool of oneself is too rich. Kean did not make a fool of himself, because he was not, at that moment, Kean going crazy, but Overreach disintegrating before their eyes.

It is difficult to see it on the page, but there was in Edmund Kean's portrayal of Overreach enough recognisable frustration and thwarted anger for him to make even of this extreme situation a nicely balanced harmony between the possible and the real, between the flamboyant and the tame. An actor like Mr Pope could not have made it believable. It would, indeed, be too much to ask of almost anyone.

If all else fails, however, a bit of ham is preferable to a lot of boredom. There is a story that Leslie Howard played Hamlet in New York like a poetic marshmallow – muted and unmoving. Noël Coward and Joyce Carey were in the audience and, according to theatrical lore, had perforce to go backstage and see him afterwards. Carey wondered whether Coward would find anything diplomatic to say. He didn't. "Oh Leslie," he exclaimed, "you know how I hate over-acting, and you could *never* over-act. But do *please* try."

1 Jean-Paul Sartre, *Kean* (1960), Act II, Sc 1

2 Simon Callow, *Being an Actor* (1984), pp 116, 166

3 William Hazlitt, *Table-Talk* (1821-2), p 372

4 Michael Pennington, *Hamlet: A User's Guide* (1996), p 74

5 William Charles Macready, *Macready's Reminiscences and selections from his diaries and letters* (1875)

6 Philip Massinger, *A New Way to Pay Old Debts*, Act V, Sc 1

7 William Archer, *Masks or Faces: A Study in the Psychology of Acting* (1888), p 190

8 Charles Greville, *The Greville Memoirs*, ed. Strachey and Fulford, Vol I, p 377

9 Helena Faucit, Lady Martin, *Shakespeare's Female Characters* (1885), p 115

10 Ellen Terry, *The Story of My Life* (1908), p 338

11 Callow, *op. cit.*, p 165

12 James Boaden, *Memoirs of the Life of John Philip Kemble* (1825), in B Joseph, *The Tragic Actor* (1959), pp 208 216

13 G H Lewes, *On Actors and the Art of Acting* (1875), p 8

14 Michael Holroyd, *Bernard Shaw* (1988), Vol I, pp 355, 368

15 James Boaden, *Memoirs of Mrs Siddons* (1827)

16 T Cole and H K Chinoy, *Actors on Acting* (1949), pp 141, 142

17 J A Hammerton, *The Actor's Art* (1897), p 24; Archer, *op. cit.*, p 46

18 Thomas Campbell, *Life of Mrs Siddons* (1834), Vol II, p 143

19 Horace Walpole, *Letters*, ed. Cunningham (1906), Vol VIII, p 315, footnote

20 Boaden, *op. cit.*

21 *ibid.*

19 W A Darlington, *The Actor and His Audience*, p 89; Archer, *op. cit.*, p 128; Hammerton, *op. cit.*, p 23

20 *The Examiner*, 16 June, 1816

21 Thomas Campbell, *Life of Mrs Siddons* (1834), Vol I, p 285

22 Callow, *op. cit.*, p 28

23 *The Observer*, 24 May, 1992

24 Leigh Hunt, *The Essays of Leigh Hunt*, ed. Arthur Symons (1903), p 276

25 Brian Masters in *A Night at the Theatre*, ed. Ronald Harwood (1982), pp 118-119

26 William Oxberry, *Oxberry's Dramatic Biography and Histrionic Anecdotes* (1825)

27 Terry, *op. cit.*, p 130

28 John Gielgud, *Distinguished Company* (1972), pp 90-93

29 *ibid.*, pp 52-53

30 James Agate, *Ego 6* (1935-48), p 226

31 Leigh Hunt, *Critical Essays on the Performers of the London Theatres* (1807), pp 290-291

32 Nicholas Wapshott, *Peter O'Toole* (1983), pp 204-205

4

Collaborators and Comedians

If it is true that a book does not exist as an experience until it finds a reader, at least the writing of it promises to be fruitful when that reader is found and writer and reader lock in shared imaginative recreation. Moreover, the writer can bide his time. He can wait, and still pursue his art in solitude. Indeed, most of the time he will have no personal contact with his readers at all. They are invisible partners.

How much more true is it, then, that the actor's art, to exist as an experience, must depend entirely upon *visible* partners – his audience. He can practice alone if he likes, he can dress in a costume, slap on some make-up, stand in front of a mirror and speak, and I suppose that will count as acting insofar as he assumes character. But it will not matter. It will be as substantial as a summer breeze. To be truly an actor he must have an audience, he must be seen, heard, watched, absorbed, endured, by somebody, and the partnership thus created will give the performance body and life. Therefore, the importance of the audience cannot be exaggerated, extending as it does far beyond their mere presence as spectators. They contribute. They prod, they stimulate, they surprise, by their responses they aid further insights into character, by their obstinacy they may shift emphases or provoke colour. They feed the actor and in a very real sense they help shape his performance.

Henry Irving declared that audience reaction was essential to him, and that he responded to it by giving back heat for heat.

Time and again you will hear actors say that no two audiences are alike, or that it is only when they appear before an audience that the interpretation they have prepared in rehearsal finally blossoms. If I may kidnap Callow's kitchen analogy once more, the audience acts as yeast, the ingredient of growth. Actors respect and cajole them, seek to seduce them, and are occasionally humiliated by them; no wonder they sometimes stand in the wings trembling with apprehension. That right to dominate and subdue is not easily won.

Nowadays we rather expect audiences to be helpful and kind. They arrive on time, they are ready to be pleased, and for the most part they sit in silence wishing the actor to do well. An actress like Margaret Rutherford appearing in Robert Morley's *Short Story* in 1933 and achieving a personal triumph as an adorable newcomer was able to say that she "felt a wave of sympathy from the audience that seemed so solid that she felt she could almost touch it." [1] It was not always so. Had she appeared in the early eighteenth century she might not have been heard above the gossip and the din, and sympathy was not what she would have expected; she would have had to *fight.* The respect we have afforded actors and actresses since Irving would have been thought supine in an earlier age, demeaning to the proper function of an audience and lacking in that commitment to contribute to the experience. Not that they did not applaud. They applauded favourite speeches and "points" robustly and noisily throughout the performance (which Mrs Siddons claimed was useful, for it gave her voice a rest), but the kind of adulatory sanctification they accorded Irving, having first listened in rapt silent wonder to his interpretation, was entirely new. This is how Edward Gordon Craig describes an ovation: "Even in the epoch of Irving it was seldom that anybody else 'brought down the house', but Irving brought it down. A terrific sweep of applause is not 'bringing the house down'. 'Bringing the house down' is when everybody simultaneously calls out, and applauds simultaneously and electrically. A vast number of people can ponderously express approval, but that is not what I mean. You have been to the Russian Ballet perhaps on one of its great nights, or you have heard Chaliapine's reception at Covent Garden. Well, that is not what I mean either. Those are ovations, but mild ovations. The thing I mean had three times the capacity of that." [2]

One is bound to wonder if anything like it has ever happened since. Of course, Americans routinely rise to their feet for the most ordinary display of memory or distress, and so diminish the meaning of approbation. But even the 20 or 30 curtain calls with which Fonteyn and Nureyev were sometimes rewarded, lasting more than half an hour, seem pale compared with what Craig is describing. Nor did their audience often stand up, unless they were ready to leave.

In the eighteenth and nineteenth centuries, it was often difficult to persuade the audience to sit down, still less to keep quiet. They wandered in late, the box seats for the rich having been retained by servants who sat on them for up to three hours before the performance started; they gossiped and greeted, they shrieked and squabbled, they were all over the place. Thus, an actor who engaged their attention long enough to elicit applause was a very good actor indeed. There is plenty of evidence that the applause could be non-stop. Mrs Abington was applauded throughout a performance of *The Chances* every time she opened her mouth. The same happened to Edmund Kean as Shylock, when Hazlitt tells us "the applause, from the first scene to the last, was general, loud, and uninterrupted." Applause could come as much in the middle of a line or speech as at the end of it, and so used were the actors to this noisy display of approval that they were disconcerted by its absence. Macready was furious that the audience at one of his Hamlets "gave less applause to the first soliloquy than I am in the habit of receiving." A modern Hamlet would be appalled by the interruption to his concentration, whereas his predecessors felt humiliated and disappointed if the audience kept still. Today's audiences would appear mysteriously dead to them, as if mute and paralysed.

They used to be hugely demonstrative. When Mrs Pritchard appeared on stage as Lady Capulet with her own daughter as Juliet, her anxiety on her daughter's behalf was so touching that the audience burst into tears. Indeed, an entire house weeping was by no means an unusual event. [3]

A custom lasting well into the twentieth century was that of the leading lady being applauded on her entrance, before she had uttered a word or moved a muscle, to which she would respond with a gracious curtsey. The practice lingers in opera and ballet, although the welcome is perfunctory and the ballerina or singer would no longer think of stopping to acknowledge it. All this signals the new status of the actor, a man or woman adored and envied as somebody on a higher plane, hallowed with glamour and authority, distinctive and apart. They are somehow better, grander, more beautiful and more important than the rest of us, and a reverential fuss is made of them which has given rise, as we shall see, to the "star" system. Historically, however, it is an aberration. For centuries the actor was regarded as far *below* the rest of us, a creature of contamination and danger, morally reprobate and of little social worth above a beggar. Even the great Garrick, sophisticated and socially ambitious as he was and the first to make the profession of player acceptable in polite society, was held on permanent sufferance.

Walpole felt the need to warn his correspondent, who was about to dine with him, "Be a little on your guard, remember he is an *actor*." [4]

The hidden reason for distaste and distrust was the subversive, overturning power of the actor to release urges and passions within us which we feel we should suppress – the Dionysian potential we identified in Chapter One. The world was afraid of actors, hence the world despised them. There were always, however, historical and social reasons which could be substituted for the real one, and some of them now make very alarming reading. In a sermon preached just a couple of years before Shakespeare and Burbage appeared on stage, the Revd T Wilcocks affirmed, "the cause of plagues is sin, and the cause of sin are plays: therefore the cause of plagues are plays." [5] The plague which hit London in 1592 was so serious that the Privy Council determined that one remedy against it was to close the theatres, since they were breeding grounds for contagion, being frequented by whores, pimps, tramps and people with open sores. To the Lord Mayor of London they wrote, "we do hereby require you, and in Her Majesty's name straightly charge and command you, forthwith to inhibit within your jurisdiction all plays, baiting of bears, bulls, bowling, and any other like occasions to assemble any number of peoples together (preaching and divine service at churches excepted), whereby no occasions be offered to increase the infection within the city." [6] As nearly 11,000 people died of the plague within the coming year, these were sensible precautions to be adopted by the authorities, but they surprise us for the low regard in which theatres were held.

One hundred and fifty years later the situation had actually worsened, because the Puritan mentality equated going to the theatre with going to Catholic mass – both forms of idolatry! One reformer got sufficiently worked up to say that "the theatre is at present on such a footing in England, that it is impossible to enter it and not come out the worse for having been in it." He deplored the lewdness of the action, the immodesty of the actresses, the impudence of the songs, the scandal of the farces, in short everything to do with the stage, and this was four years after Garrick's tumultuous debut! Nine years earlier an indignant cleric cried, "a Player cannot be a living member of Christ, or in a true state of Grace, till he renounces his Profession." (Some might sympathise; the late Coral Browne, accosted outside Brompton Oratory after attending mass by a colleague alive with the latest gossip, ordered him to stop, with the words, "Can't you see I'm in a state of fucking grace!")

Another publication, also in Garrick's time, asserted that "play-actors are the most profligate wretches, and the vilest vermin, that hell ever vomited out; they are the filth and garbage of the earth, the scum and stain of human nature, the excrements and refuse of all mankind, the pests and plagues of human society, the debauchees of men's minds and morals." [7] (Even today, actors find it difficult to take out insurance or earn a licence to drive a car, but these are mild inconveniences by comparison.)

A measure of the lowly status enjoyed by actors was the little worth placed upon their very lives. In 1692 William Mountfort, not a run-of-the-mill actor but one of the great talents of his day and then only 32 years old, objected when two young toffs, Captain Hill and Lord Mohun, tried to abduct the famous and beautiful Mrs Bracegirdle in order to ravish her. Mountfort intervened to protect her, and so they murdered him by running him through with a sword. It was impudent of him, a mere actor, to quarrel with their pleasure. To be fair, it should be pointed out that actors were themselves prone to violence, and at least two were murderers. In 1735 Macklin killed a fellow actor called Thomas Hallam, actually in the Green Room, for having borrowed his wig without permission. Macklin was ever an irascible man who made enemies in and out of the theatre; on this occasion he first gave Hallam a mouthful of oaths, then lunged at him with his stick, which entered the poor fellow's left eye and pierced his brain. He was tried for murder, reduced to manslaughter at the insistence of character witnesses, and he was soon back on stage. Three years later he fought violently with James Quin, a dangerous thing to do, for Quin was already the murderer of two actors – Williams and Bowen. For the slaughter of Bowen he had been tried and found guilty of manslaughter on 10 July, 1718; he, too, seems to have had a light sentence. [8] There was, after all, some justification for regarding actors as people likely to fall out of control when roused.

Then, too, was the awkward fact that the theatres were situated in insalubrious neighbourhoods. Drury Lane and Covent Garden were notorious for brothels and bath-houses, and the two main theatres were stuck in the middle of them. Prostitutes lined the streets outside the theatre, hustled playgoers, hung about Stage Doors. "One would imagine that all the prostitutes in the kingdom had pitched upon this blessed neighbourhood for a place of general rendezvous," wrote one observer; "here are lewd women in sufficient numbers to people a mighty colony." Slang for a whore was "Drury Lane vestal" and for a whore's madam, "Covent Garden abbess". You would most likely contract syphilis, or "Drury Lane ague", on a visit to one of their many establishments, if you first survived the pickpockets and muggers who followed you there. Theatreland was decidedly an area to satisfy every depravity, and it was moreover blatant. On one occasion a man picked up a whore outside the theatre and forced her into the royal coach waiting outside for the Prince and Princess of Wales. Defying the remonstrances of the outraged coachman, he proceeded to have intercourse with her there and then, encouraged by a crowd of enthusiasts who threatened to break into the theatre itself. There they would have found much the same temper, for some of the boxes were known as the flesh market, and the Theatre Royal, Covent Garden was sometimes said to be tantamount to a public brothel. [9] Whether this meant that sex took place in the audience, or whether they merely made assignations, is not quite clear, but it would not be altogether surprising if some sexual activity occurred; in the twentieth century it occurs in cinemas, admittedly with less forbidding lighting.

With all this in mind, it is easier to understand why actors were often considered degenerate, and theatres dens of vice. Added to which there was the sheer exuberance of the audience, itself a sign of woeful lack of taste and dignity. You went to the theatre to let your hair down, and you made no secret to the actors that this was what you were there for.

Right from the beginning audiences welcomed the invitation to participate in the event, and their exuberance flowed from this. In Shakespeare's time the theatre was a very noisy place, with the audience bartering, gossiping, arguing, stealing, fighting and shouting amongst themselves, and when the play began it was the actor's job first to grab their attention, and second to remind them that they had to collaborate in the pretence that was about to unfold, in their imaginations and with their enthusiasm. This was to be a shared experience, in which their contribution was vital. You can hear it all in the opening lines of *Henry V*, in which Shakespeare instructs the audience to transform the building in which they stand – the theatre ("this cockpit...this wooden O") into a battlefield in France, and to help the actors by believing in them:

> ...can this cockpit hold
> The vasty fields of France? or may we cram
> Within this wooden O the very casques
> That did affright the air at Agincourt?

> O, pardon! since a crooked figure may
> Attest in little place a million;
> And let us, ciphers to this great accompt,
> On your imaginary forces work.
> Suppose within the girdle of these walls
> Are now confin'd two mighty monarchies,
> Whose high upreared and abutting fronts
> The perilous narrow ocean parts asunder:
> Piece out our imperfections with your thoughts:
> Into a thousand parts divide one man,
> And make imaginary puissance;
> Think when we talk of horses that you see them
> Printing their proud hoofs i' the receiving earth;
> For 'tis your thoughts that now must deck our kings,
> Carry them here and there, jumping o'er times,
> Turning the accomplishments of many years
> Into an hour-glass…
>   …Still be kind,
> And eke out our performance with your mind. [10]

It could not be plainer. There was no scenery as we understand it, so the audience had to *accept* that the stage represented a battlefield, or whatever, and Shakespeare is here inviting them to enjoy themselves by *seeing* it as such. He also tells them they must help the actors, who cannot do it all alone, and implicitly exhorts them to stop whatever they are doing in order to pay attention. I have always suspected that Antony's celebrated "lend me your ears" speech was addressed as much to the rowdy Elizabethan audience, who by this time were yelling their approval or dismay at Caesar's murder, as it was to the citizens of Rome. It would undoubtedly be played "out front" anyway, directly to the audience, and perhaps the audience, at that moment in the play, *were* the citizens of Rome barracking the self-important Antony – extras in their own dramatic experience.

Similarly, in Hamlet's "rogue and peasant slave" soliloquy, when he is alone on stage and speaking directly to the audience, he includes these words:

> Am I a coward?
> Who calls me villain? breaks my pate across?
> Plucks off my beard and blows it in my face?

> Tweaks me by the nose? gives me the lie i' the throat,
> As deep as to the lungs? Who does me this?
> Ha!

The Elizabethan audience is there, between each line. They jeered and howled at him, responding to each question as it was asked. There should be pauses at each interrogation mark for audience response, not the congregational hush which today greets one of the Great Speeches. Having teased and taunted Hamlet, the audience was then with him to the hilt when, finally riled by them, he rises to real anger:

> Bloody, bawdy villain!
> Remorseless, treacherous, lecherous, kindless villain!
> O! vengeance! [11]

That's more like it, they say! Now they are ready to go along with his next, more reflective, phase, when he calms himself and promises that he will catch the king his uncle by guile rather than by direct assault. They have helped him move towards this decision, they have been part of the process, having goaded him they are now willing to be persuaded by his more cautious approach to the problem at hand. Actor and audience have been two complementary halves of the performance – collaborators in fact.

When the reconstruction of Shakespeare's Globe Theatre opened on the South Bank with, appropriately, *Henry V*, it was immediately clear that the audience felt involved with the performance, invited by Mark Rylance to join him in creating it. They hissed and they cheered, they appreciated and they participated. Above all they *listened*; there is no paradox in a noisy audience being also an attentive one.

John Peter found that the attentiveness of the new Globe audience, at times rowdy, at times tense in sudden silence, was unlike anything he had ever experienced, and it made clear to him that Shakespeare had written for a living, willing, participatory crowd. "His greatest innovation, which is so vital that we entirely take it for granted," he wrote, "is the psychologically driven speech. His characters do not make speeches that sound all thought out, ready to be spoken; they express themselves as they think, dramatising the very intensity and spontaneity of the thought process." [12] Henry V's soliloquy about the loneliness of kings was delivered by Mark Rylance talking *to* the audience and confiding *in* them.

The Elizabethan audience was also bloodthirsty. They quite liked the piling on of corpses, which to a modern audience can sometimes veer close to the ludicrous unless handled with great care. Four people die within the last few minutes of *Hamlet*, and when, at a recent performance of *King Lear*, the body of Cordelia was carried on by a distraught Lear after the successive deaths of Goneril, Regan and Edmund, my sophisticated companion was heard to mutter, "Oh *No*," not out of compassion but from embarrassment at the excess of it. The original audience would have lapped it all up. Nor did they object to Gloucester having his eyes gouged out in the same play. They were a tough lot.

They wanted a good story, told with enthusiasm; good characters, clearly drawn and boldly acted; and dramatic action which demanded their input and approval. In other words, they were not louts and illiterates, but genuine playgoers, quick-witted and committed. In most respects the Elizabethan audience was superior to the Restoration audience which followed 60 years later, and it was not until after David Garrick (and due largely to him) that audiences learnt again to resume their proper role.

When Charles II was restored to the throne in 1660, one of his first acts was to reverse the damage done by Puritan darkness and re-open the theatres. He gave royal patents to William Davenant (1606-1668), who assembled a company called the Duke's men (named after James, Duke of York, the king's brother), and Thomas Killigrew (1612-1683), whose rival company was called the King's men. Both were veterans of a happier pre-Cromwellian era and Davenant, as we have seen, was Shakespeare's godson and rumoured to have been his natural son as well. His leading actor was the formidable Thomas Betterton.

Their first problem was to find a building which could serve as a theatre. Both chose Tudor tennis courts, one in Vere Street and the other in Lincoln's Inn Fields, which were long oblong spaces, about 70 feet by 30 feet, with a roof and a gallery all the way round. The division between audience and actors was marked by the net of the old tennis court, which meant that the audience of about 400 occupied half the available space, and were very close to the performance. Within three years Killigrew had built his first theatre, and by 1674 the first of the long line of Theatres Royal, Drury Lane, with a capacity of about 800. Davenant meanwhile built the Duke's Theatre in Dorset Garden. Both theatres retained a remarkable intimacy, due to the huge size of the stage and its projection into the audience. At the back was a proscenium arch, with "flats" of painted scenery sliding on and off in grooves. All of the action, however, took place on the apron stage in front of this, with doors either side for entrance and exit, which meant that the actor walked straight out into the audience and addressed them rather than other actors, who might be further away on the other side of the apron. As the theatre was lit by candle-bearing chandeliers, there was no darkened atmosphere but a feeling of hearty get-together, and the smallest gesture or facial expression was directly visible to the audience. [13]

So far, so good. We have already seen that, for the audience to contribute to the dramatic experience they must feel involved in it, and in Restoration theatres they certainly did that. The trouble was, they gradually became proprietorial and arrogant, threatening to squeeze the actor's role into subservience. Part of the fault lay in the licentiousness of the age, which exploded with excessive pleasure after years of being unnaturally corked (a little like the 1960s following the dismal grey austerities of the 1950s). People regarded the theatres as their playgrounds, a place to let off steam, show oneself to the neighbours, and flirt with the novelty of the actresses, who were introduced for the first time on the English stage. The King himself set the standard by making an actress, Nell Gwyn, his mistress (and mother of two of his children, from the eldest of whom descends the present Duke of St Albans, a chartered accountant), stealing her from Charles Sackville, Lord Buckhurst. Her first lover had been Charles Hart, leading actor of the King's Company, rival therefore to Betterton, and incidentally a great-nephew of Shakespeare's; this led wags to nickname the king as "Charles the Third".

An indication of the freedom of the age is the trial of Lord Buckhurst and Sir Charles Sedley before Lord Chief Justice Foster for acts of gross indecency in a public place. Buckhurst (later to be Earl of Dorset by inheritance and Earl of Middlesex by creation) was credited with being the first man to recognise the genius of Milton's *Paradise Lost*. Sedley's poetry and dramas were reckoned to be counted with the immortals. And what did these two eminent gentlemen get up to? Oxford Kate's was a well-known and popular tavern in Bow Street, Covent Garden, with a balcony on the first floor overlooking the street. Buckhurst and Sedley went there one afternoon, drank themselves into a stupor, and then in broad daylight appeared on the balcony, stripped naked, and acted out every possible sexual position that could be imagined including buggery, which was then becoming a popular alternative copied from the Italians. They drew an appreciative crowd of hundreds. Significantly, Pepys relates the scene without a blush, as if it were perfectly innocent to be high-spirited in this manner.

Such attitudes spilled into the theatre. Buckhurst had "bought" Nell Gwyn, it being assumed that actresses were purchasable and actors mere puppets. The grand and the rich gradually encroached on their space, as boxes were built actually on the sides of the stage, and gentlemen would take their seats on to the apron stage itself. By the first years of the eighteenth century the stage had become so crowded that actors had to weave their way in and out of trespassing playgoers who blocked their exits and interrupted their speeches with insults. Sometimes the actor had to jump into a box to get off the stage, which was full of ladies with pages holding their trains, children playing hopscotch or the like, and gentlemen eating. The Green Room – the actors' retiring room just next to the stage – was also packed with people.

Individuals in the audience did not hesitate to interrupt a performance if they felt like it, to quarrel with the actor or give him "notes" (advice), and the action would stop until they were satisfied. Once Garrick and Peg Woffington were enacting Lear and Cordelia, the old king's head lying in Cordelia's lap, when a man rushed on to the stage and threw his arms around Peg Woffington's neck. Mrs Siddons as Lady Macbeth sent a call-boy out to get her a jug of ale, with which he dutifully returned, marching on the stage to hand it to her during the sleepwalking scene. [14]

On one occasion Dr Johnson vacated his seat on the stage for some reason, and when he returned found somebody else sitting on it. The man refused to budge, so Johnson hurled him and the seat into the pit below. (Johnson also told his friend "Davy" Garrick that he would no longer join him in the Green Room since the bare flesh of the actresses excited him too much.) Boswell once imitated the lowing of a cow with such success that the audience in the pit called for more – "Encore the cow! Encore the cow!" Orange-girls yelled out the prices of the oranges, some of which were bought to be flung across the auditorium or on the stage, people squashed side by side on benches in the pit, singing or shouting, whores flaunted themselves before the gallery. A visitor described the scene as one of "noise and bombardment". In 1721 a drunken nobleman lurched on the stage and slapped the face of the theatre manager, Mr Rich. A brawl ensued, and Rich's life was only saved by the intervention of James Quin, who interrupted his lines and drew his sword. As a result of this incident, soldiers were sent by royal order to both theatres in order to protect the peace and tame the audience. [15] Fighting both on and offstage was a regular occurrence.

A man in the pit interrupted a performance when Dufresne, a leading actor from Paris, was appearing, with the words "You are speaking too low," to which the player replied with spirit: "And you, sir, too loud." The audience would not stand for impertinence from an actor and the whole theatre erupted in tumult. The following night Dufresne was made to apologise for his rudeness, telling the audience how well he realised his lowly position in life; they in turn interrupted him and told him to carry on – they did not want to rub his nose in it. [16] This was no isolated incident. In 1763 serious riots broke out at Drury Lane for days on end, in protest against Garrick's removal of the practice of getting in for half-price if you turned up only for the third act, and the audience proceeded to smash up his theatre. One of the actors, John Moody, spotting a madman in the audience with a blazing torch about to set fire to the house, seized it from his hand and put it out. For this affront, the audience demanded an apology. On the following night, therefore, Moody spoke from the stage to offer his sincere regret for "having displeased them by saving their lives by putting out the fire." His cheek was deemed to have compounded his offence, and the audience shrieked their demand that he get down on his knees. This he refused to do (others had done), but Garrick was obliged to make a promise that Moody should not be allowed to act in his company until he be forgiven by the house. [17]

John Philip Kemble fared better when he interrupted his performance to address a lady in a box who was talking loudly all the way through it. He declared that he would not proceed until she had finished her conversation. For once on his side, the audience hissed the unfortunate woman, and shouted at Kemble, "No apology! No apology!" The point of these stories is that the audience was in charge. It was they who set the parameters, made the decisions, were arbiters of what was or was not permissible on stage or in the auditorium. A French visitor deplored that "the gallery controlled the acting and thanked the players." [18] The power which spectators enjoyed over performers was used to gleeful effect, and they were not prepared to condone the smallest opposition to their wishes; "on any provocation [they] took an indecent delight in exacting apologies from the players." [19] It has been estimated that both the principal theatres of London had to be entirely redecorated once every ten years to repair depredation due to the violence or boisterousness of the audience.

When we talk today of "stopping the show", we usually mean that a musical act has been performed so well that the audience refuses to cease applauding until the performer promises an encore. In the eighteenth century, it would have meant that the audience refused to permit the performance to continue. They simply "stopped" it with their barracking, obliging the actors to give up and go home. When the play did manage to get through to the end, the manager would thank the audience for their attention and approval and crave their indulgence to admit a further performance the following night. *Never* would the entire cast be so presumptuous as to take a bow on stage without being asked, as they routinely do today. The origin of the "curtain call" was the audience calling out one actor to enjoy their congratulations; he would not come unless summoned, and he would not invite the rest of the cast to join him if he valued his safety that evening.

There were even occasions when the audience would be so dissatisfied with the play that they would muscle the actors off the stage and take on the roles themselves. More properly, this could be arranged in advance, when a gentleman who felt the itch to play Falstaff could do so without a word of remonstrance from the professional actors. G F Cooke's first season at Covent Garden involved his playing Iago to an Othello who was "a Medical Gentleman of very respectable connections and considerable literary talents". *The Times* said his performance was "shapeless and miserable...frequently below mediocrity". A printer from Winchester played Hamlet at Drury Lane, a barrister Macbeth at Covent Garden and Richard III at Drury Lane, and a man called Bludwick gave King Lear at Covent Garden with the usual announcement that it was "his first appearance on any stage". *The Gazetteer* doubted whether this was really true, but thought that it was "exceedingly clear that it ought to be his last."

These aspiring amateurs met regularly in "spouting clubs" to amuse and/or impress one another with their renditions of favourite plays, much as insurance brokers today become pop singers in their local pub on a Saturday night, and, when they could afford to pay the theatre for the privilege, they appeared before the public with real actors. A surprising number of great men began in this way; Irving paid three guineas for the part of Romeo at the Royal Soho Theatre in 1856, when he was just 18. [20]

Garrick had tried to take control by banishing spectators from the stage when his fame and authority were secure enough for him to get away with it. He also reduced the length of the apron, extinguished lighting in the auditorium to be replaced with footlights, and brought over from Paris a designer (Philip de Loutherbourg) to paint more beautiful "flats" for the scenery. He was determined to re-establish a proper relationship between actor and audience, for the benefit of both and for the dignity of the theatre. For a time he succeeded, and the generation which followed him concentrated their enjoyment upon the drama before them, although the fact that they still claimed their rights was demonstrated when Kemble tried to raise the price of tickets in 1809 and was rewarded with 67 consecutive nights of rioting. He was obliged eventually to yield and retain the old price; hence the Old Price Riots known to the history books.

As the theatre passed from eighteenth to nineteenth century, so the size of the auditorium increased and became more distant from the acting area. Covent Garden could hold 3,000 people in 1792 and even more after rebuilding in 1809 following a fire. The new stage was 63 feet deep. Drury Lane also burnt down in 1812 and was replaced by a new building with a stage 96 feet deep. The scenery, too, became more elaborate following Garrick's example and experiments were made in perspective scenery, by which ten or twelve flats were painted so as to give the impression to the eye that they diminished into the far distance. A beautiful example of this may still be seen in Palladio's perfectly preserved Teatro Olimpico in Vicenza, and the problems it presented may still be appreciated if you walk on to the stage, for the actors, appearing from between the flats, would always seem too big except in front of the first one.

The accent on scenery served to focus attention on the stage and deflect it, to some extent, from the words. As John Styan neatly put it, "by the end of the century the pictorial stage had usurped the literary theatre, and Shakespeare had begun his long struggle with the painter's art." [21] Today's actors might say that Shakespeare eventually won that particular battle as productions reverted more and more to the stark and simple, but that he has had to engage upon a new struggle with the director's ego.

We have already seen that the greater distance between actor and spectator had an inevitable influence upon technique, voice projection and expansiveness of gesture to define the smallest things. It also had an effect upon the audience. They applauded often enough, and not just at the end, but they required more to satisfy them. Whereas their Elizabethan counterparts had been rapt by the drama which unfolded right in front of them, and their Restoration and early Georgian counterparts had invaded and despoiled it, the late Georgians in their vast theatres demanded to be pleased and treated the actors as their servants, employed to provide the wares for which they had paid good money. This despite the awe they felt in the presence of a mighty talent like Mrs Siddons; she was still not quite a lady. Consequently, managers had to devise more and more bizarre confections to bring the customers in, with juxtapositions of drama and rubbish which today would seem insulting. The kaleidoscopic nature of the entertainment had already begun in Garrick's time, but by the end of the eighteenth century it was positively bizarre.

A typical eighteenth century performance would last three to four hours and consist of an overture, a big play, an interlude with music or dancing, and a shorter play or "afterpiece" (cinema audiences in the mid-twentieth century enjoyed similar distribution with a musical introduction, a "B" movie, a newsreel, and an "A" movie). The interludes and afterpieces might be farcical or acrobatic, never solemn because the main play was very probably a tragedy, the assumption being that tragedies were for the well-off and educated, whereas farces suited the relatively poor and illiterate. David Garrick fought hard to rescue Shakespeare from this tatty mixture of entertainments, but never entirely succeeded. Indeed, his most successful production was *The Jubilee*, mounted in 1764 to mark the bicentenary of Shakespeare's birth and to make use of some of the costumes which had been lavishly stitched for the Stratford-upon-Avon celebrations of which he had been in charge. But there was in this production little of the scholarly or reverential, and much that smacked of a commercial advertisement. Nineteen pageants followed one another in spectacular style, displaying the marvellous costumes to tremendous effect. Actors and actresses performed snippets from their favourite roles, Garrick himself appearing as Benedick. There was music and special tricks, a pop song and Garrick's own "Ode to Shakespeare" to finish off with, all in a carnival atmosphere with the whole cast joining in the chorus. It was what we would today term a "Gala Performance", something out of the ordinary, with as many "stars" on parade as possible, or even one of those Albert Hall performances of Tchaikovsky's 1812 Overture with several orchestras and half an army. The stage directions indicated that in the finale, "Every character, tragic and comic, join in the chorus and go back, during which guns fire, bells ring, and the audience applaud – Bravo, Jubilee, Shakespeare forever!"

John Brewer, who sniffed all this out, quotes the diary of a prompter at the Theatre Royal, Drury Lane, which gives a vivid impression of its impact. "It was received with bursts of Applause the Procession of Shakespeare's characters etc is the most Superb that ever was Exhibited or I believe ever will be, there never was an Entertainment produc'd that gave so much pleasure to all degrees Boxes pit and Gallery." Garrick himself said that the world was "mad after it", and Brewer points out that its record run of 90 performances was without precedent. [22] Briefly put, *The Jubilee* was the hit of the season and a sell-out, but essentially a sensation without substance.

To get a real notion of what an audience demanded from a night in the theatre, one cannot do better than read in full the ecstatic promise of a playbill from the year 1793, which strains credulity:

By His Majesty's Company of Comedians,
Kilkenny Theatre Royal.

(Positively the last night, because the
Company go tomorrow to Waterford)

On Saturday, May 14, 1793

Will be performed by desire and command of several respectable people in this learned Matrapolish, for the benefit of Mr Kearnes, the manager,

The Tragedy of
HAMLET, PRINCE OF DENMARK

Originally written and composed by the celebrated Dan Hyes, of Limerick, and insarted in Shakespeare's works

Hamlet, by Mr Kearnes (being his first appearance in that character, and who, between the acts, will perform several solos on the patent bagpipes, which play two tunes at the same time). Ophelia, by Mrs Prior, who will introduce several favourite airs in character, particularly "The Lass of Richmond Hill" and "We'll be unhappy together", from the Revd Mr Dibdin's oddities. The parts of the King and Queen, by directions of the Revd Father O'Callaghan, will be omitted, as too immoral for any stage. Polonius, the comical politician, by a young gentleman, being his first appearance in public. The Ghost, the Gravedigger, and Laertes, by Mr Sampson, the great London comedian. The characters to be dressed in Roman shapes. To which will be added, an interlude, in which will be introduced several sleight-of-hand tricks, by the celebrated surveyor Hunt. The whole to conclude with the farce of

MAHOMET THE IMPOSTOR

Mahomet, by Mr Kearnes.

Tickets to be had of Mr Kearnes, at the sign of the "Goat's Beard" in Castle Street

The value of the tickets, as usual, will be taken out (if required) in candles, bacon, soap, butter, cheese, potatoes etc, – as Mr Kearnes wishes, in every particular, to accommodate the public. N.B. No smoking allowed. No person whatsoever will be admitted into the boxes without shoes or stockings. [23]

An exception, perhaps? The idea of paying in potatoes or bacon is beguiling enough, but the opportunity to hear Ophelia sing a sweet ballad and Hamlet play the bagpipes (two tunes at once!) makes one shamelessly long to be there.

At least one may be quite sure the audience had rediscovered its right to participation in the event, but at what cost? With the advent of the Victorian theatre and the ubiquity of the melodrama, it seemed as if audiences were recapturing their role as collaborators, hissing and cheering the protagonists, but this was appearance only. What they had demanded, and were served, was digestible pap, predictable, safe, unenterprising, and in no sense engaging them in a joint creation as the evening progressed. It was more akin to spoonfeeding. The Elizabethan adventure was long forgotten.

The melodrama relied upon formula acting to a formula plot. There was a standard set of characters who did not vary from one play to the next – the hero, the heroine, the villain. The hero was not very bright, but good-hearted, natural and dependable; the heroine pure and unsullied, always dressed in white, with a straw bonnet "which at times of stress slipped from her head and was held by a ribbon"; the villain was swarthy, bore a moustache, carried a cane, and dressed in black. With such people you always knew where you were. If you lost grip of the story, there were well-tried clues to help guide you back on track. "If the heroine entered in rags, it was certain that she had suffered some form of moral degradation," writes John Styan. There was always some misfortune productive of misery and despair, followed by miraculous salvation and happy-ever-afterness. The misfortune sometimes involved madness, and "no leading actor was likely to refuse the histrionic opportunity of a slow descent into starvation or *delirium tremens.*"[24] The entire cast would "freeze" at certain points of high import to the narrative, and the musical accompaniment offered further hints as to the nobility or dastardy of the character about to appear, of bliss to be enjoyed or agony endured. With their appetite for this kind of packaged theatre apparently insatiable throughout the second half of the nineteenth century, audiences' taste reached a new low. They demanded trash and were served it. Their role as stimulators of theatrical invention had evaporated.

Vestiges of Victorian melodrama lingered long after the *genre* itself had dribbled to a close. Silent films are an obvious example, where the significance of the accompanying piano music to delineate character and and clarify narrative is apparent. The ballets in the classical repertoire are another; Giselle still comes on with her hair slightly out of place to indicate that she has lost her sanity, and on a particularly jolly night one may still hear the audience growl at the entrance of the wicked fairy Carabosse in *Sleeping Beauty.* Nowhere is the tradition more robust than in Christmas pantomime, at least in those theatres where they have not yet surrendered to television stars, pop singers and sports idols. The standard characters and motorless plots are a direct legacy, and when you hear the villain curse his frustration at the hands of the hero with "Hell and damnation" or "Blood and thunder" you are hearing an echo from 150 years ago.

Nor can it be claimed that the Victorian melodrama appealed to the underclass, and that more discerning audiences avoided it. On the contrary, with the change in seating which arrived in the 1840s, it was clear that customers were prepared to pay decent prices in order to witness something the outcome of which they knew in advance. The pit had previously been rows of backless benches on which people crammed as best they could. These were replaced by rows of individual chairs, as we still have today, known as the Orchestra Stalls, and the cheaper seats which had previously been the pit moved to the top of the house and became "the gods". The number of boxes multiplied as well. Popular melodramas were more often than not sold out.

The effect of all this upon the actor's art was catastrophic. An actor was required to play only the kind of part the public expected of him, and to transfer it wholesale from one play to the next. There was the Leading Lady, the Leading Man, the Heavy, the Villain, and the Juvenile Lead (still called in the theatre today the "Juve"); actors could only hope to progress from one role to the other as they grew older. The wonder of it is that such a tradition could have nurtured a great and compelling actor like Henry Irving. What he did was to take intractable material and transform it, by the mere force of his personality and magnetic appeal, into art. The word "charisma" is often overplayed these days; it is the only word which can explain the phenomenon of Henry Irving.

The cumulative effect of audience retreat from involvement with the text of drama and its interpretation was to allow too much emphasis to be placed upon simple spouting and too little attention paid to the interplay of characters on stage. Granted, it had never been much of a tradition for actors to acknowledge one another's presence, but the habit of "blocking", that is the director's arrangement of moves upon the stage and the actors' relationship with one another, a process which takes place in rehearsal, was virtually unheard of until the twentieth century. Actors spoke out front, and that was that. It had been said, perhaps with a little exaggeration, that Gerald du Maurier, a great star of the 1900s and 1920s, was the first actor ever to look at a fellow actor on stage and address his lines directly to him.

By then, the audience had become soporific. At least they reacted *to* the Victorian melodrama, even if they did not demand much *from* it. To the drawing room comedy they reacted not at all, and were the precursors of what are now derisively called "couch potatoes" – bland, blinking watchers of the television "soap operas" (which also have their unvarying heroes, heroines, villains and bitches). Occasionally one may still encounter an audience which seems to have stepped out of a previous century. I have mentioned the reconstructed Globe in London, which already shows signs of drawing audiences into the drama and asking them to breathe it and not just gawp at it. Actors will tell you of a particular evening in Oldham, say, or Crewe, when they felt that the audience was squeezing something extra out of them, although this kind of experience grows less frequent with the demise of the repertory theatre system. And there are still occasions when an audience may be so involved as to be threatening, especially in Ireland. Simon Callow has written about appearing before hostile audiences in Dublin, where riots in the theatre are still not entirely unknown, and the stage is regarded as a "gladiatorial arena". Audiences there tend to be aggressive because they know what they are watching, they have experienced it, felt it and thought about it, and they do not see why they should sit glumly non-committal. Actors much prefer these audiences to polite ones, and it is easy to see why – the shared creation is once more at work, the collaboration, the excitement of making an event.

That collaboration is essential for great performances to occur. Ralph Richardson went so far as to maintain that the audience was fired by the actor to do the major work of imagination, which he merely suggested to them by example; it was "complete contact with the deep imaginative sub-conscious inside the mind of the beholder". [25] The collaboration manifests itself in different ways, as I hope I have shown, whether volubly as in Elizabethan times or in concentrated wonder as the audience surrendered to Irving's hypnotism. (Irving's audiences were definitely not passive, though they may have been quiet – they *willed* themselves to share the intensity of his moment.) It cannot happen when the audience sinks into lethargy or contents itself with conventional signals to evoke standard responses. Hence Victorian melodrama or modern television "soap operas" cannot contain the ingredients for proper audience input. Jacobean tragedy and Restoration comedy both can and frequently do. We have covered tragedy to some extent in dealing with technique and the intensity of the actor's personal commitment (although it is interesting to reflect that until Garrick's innovations, even the great tragedies were expected to harbour "clues" to make the audience's job easier – the hero always wearing a vast headdress of exotic feathers, a convention which would now appear ridiculous). The playing of comedy requires a different set of engagements between actor and audience, and gives rise to an immediate paradox: tragedy is easier for the actor and demands much of the audience, whereas in comedy the actor must do all the work!

There is unanimity on this point, and some irritation among actors that the world does not appreciate how difficult comedy is to execute to perfection (and in comedy nothing less will do), nor how often the great actors of past and present are comedy players. Garrick himself played immeasurably more comedy parts than tragic ones, and famously declared, "You may humbug the town for some time as a tragedian, but comedy is a serious thing." Donald Sinden takes the view that two pages of farce require more expertise than the whole of *Hamlet*, and further states that the greatest actor he ever saw in his life was Ralph Lynn, a *farceur* in the great days of the Aldwych Theatre, who only played comedy and could fill in three minutes of silence with extempore improvisation which had the audience gasping with laughter. The American actress Lynne Fontanne said that with tragedy you had merely to push yourself off and roll downhill, whereas comedy was much more tiring, demanding greater breath control and attention to detail. The American actor Edmund Gwenn on his deathbed, in reply to a vapid enquiry from a member of his family as to whether it was hard dying, said, "Yes. But not as hard as comedy!"

It is also worth recalling that Irving's closest friend and contemporary, J L Toole, was a supreme actor of comedy, with his own theatre near the Strand. All the comic actors of his day worked there, and their craft has passed on to the present generation. The theatre was always full. Yet who today, outside the acting fraternity, has heard of J L Toole?

The irony is that styles in comic playing have varied far less across the centuries than those used in the interpretation of tragedy, and ought therefore (one might think) to be the easier to absorb. The plots and intrigues have altered in hardly the smallest degree since the days of the great Roman actor and playwright Plautus. They include thwarted lovers aided and abetted by enterprising cheeky servants, self-important men made risible to the world, lecherous old men lusting after young flesh (all themes much used by Molière), and the wonderful tireless old trick of mistaken identity. Shakespeare uses this several times, notably in *As You Like It* and *The Comedy of Errors*, and the joke of the first was multiplied in a recent production in which Adrian Lester played Beatrice, and was thus a man pretending to be a woman pretending to be a boy pretending to be a girl. (Boy actors in Shakespeare's day would have achieved exactly the same degree of fun, with the audience's wicked knowing connivance, except that Lester added the additional trick of being black!) As for *The Comedy of Errors*, which turns upon repeated mistakes between a double set of identical twins, making for 12 or 24 different and potentially hilarious twisted encounters, this was lifted directly from a plot by Plautus (*The Brothers Menaechmi*), passed through Shakespeare to a Broadway musical called *The Boys from Syracuse* (1938), and was adapted for the comic stage again with Frankie Howerd in Sondheim's *A Funny Thing Happened on the Way to the Forum* (1962).

Another comparatively recent variation on the mistaken identity theme was Peter Shaffer's extraordinarily ingenious *Black Comedy* (1966) with Maggie Smith, Albert Finney and Derek Jacobi. When the audience were seated and ready for the action to begin, the curtain went up on complete darkness, yet the actors on stage, whom we could not see at all, went on speaking their lines as if all was well. This went on for about five minutes, and it began to feel embarrassing. We assumed that there was an electricity failure, and that the cast were behaving in a very sporting manner by carrying on, but that they would soon receive a whisper from the wings to indicate they should stop until the fault was repaired. But no. The lights switched on to reveal four people on a fully furnished set, but they, suddenly, behaved as if the lights had all gone off. They groped around the furniture, bumped into walls, did not realise whom they were speaking to, went through the wrong doors at the wrong time to encounter the wrong people, whom they could not see, and generally spent the rest of the play floundering in a mass of glorious mistakes. Plautus had not dreamed up the lighting, of course, but he nevertheless inspired the concept 2000 years ahead of the production.

Plautus' most enduring legacy to the comic stage was, however, the establishment of a relationship between actor and audience. He introduced light banter into the script, which enabled the actor to speak directly to spectators and seduce them into being his accomplices in the plot. Again, it is the principle of performer and audience sharing in the making of an event which is at work here, although this time the audience is invited to accept, not contribute, and the performer undertakes to build his illusions upon their trust and belief. The echoes of this tradition stretch right up to the music hall and the stand-up comedian, to Tony Hancock, Eric Morecambe, Frankie Howerd and Roy Hudd, and along the way they pass through Restoration comedy, where the tradition achieved its brightest and most inventive manifestation in the actor's "aside" to the audience.

I have already mentioned that the "aside" owed some of its popularity among playwrights to the fact of the apron stage and the proximity of actor to audience on his entrance, affording him the chance to have a word with them before launching into the business of the scene (you can get a feel of this today in boxes adjacent to the stage at a number of London Theatres). It was all very intimate, appeared spontaneous, established a bond, but was entirely part of the plot. It enabled the actor to share confidences with the audience which were (they managed to believe) denied the other actors on stage, or sometimes even to carry on three separate conversations – two with different characters in the play, and one with the audience (actresses found this easier to do by astute direction of their fans to exclude some person from the chosen confidence). Sometimes the aside is accidentally overheard, but the audience knows what it means, while the person who has eavesdropped will draw a different conclusion, so the audience feels the privileged partner. When the screen falls in Sheridan's *The School for Scandal* (1777), the audience *alone* is in possession of the whole truth behind Lady Teazle's exposure behind it, by virtue of their being made privy, in a multiplicity of asides, to the intentions of all four characters in the scene, while each of them is separately and for different reasons in the dark. In some plays the asides are so frequent that the actors end up talking to the audience more than they do to one another, which is a comic device in itself.

The point is that the aside is not entirely an invention of the English stage but an inheritance from Plautus, who had insisted upon direct contact from the comic actor, and defined the role of the audience as collaborators in spirited pretence, usually at the expense of some other poor soul on stage.

There is much, of course, in the comic tradition that is peculiarly English and owes nothing to Plautus or any other legacy. The gravediggers in *Hamlet* are earthy and unexpected, philosophical with neighbourly wisdom, irreverent and witty. They come at a point in the play when the audience needed some respite from mounting disaster. But there is evidence that subsequent audiences demanded more, and that the gravedigger scene degenerated as a result into absurd buffoonery. Right up until 1831 the First Gravedigger spent a good deal of time taking off half a dozen waistcoats, one after the other, before he got down to work. This was always considered a traditional piece of "business" which survived from Shakespeare's own time, and that consequently he must have approved (or may even have invented) it. There is no evidence one way or the other.

Though Plautus had his swaggerer (*miles gloriosus*) and vain fool, he had nothing quite so outrageously florid as the various fops who adorned the Restoration stage and have been lately seen in glittering revivals. The fop is a fine example of audience influence, for he grew out of satire and flourished upon recognition. The fop was the audience looking at itself, as there were dozens of over-dressed, extravagant, bewigged and be-rouged young men-about-town, all absurdly trying to outdo one another in glitter and finery, weighed down with silk, sweating beneath outlandish wigs and endeavouring to look stylish and at ease, dotted about the auditorium. They greeted one another and were greeted by others. Then, when the curtain went up, they saw freakish impressions of themselves, often wearing the same or similar clothes, and the audience was able at once to preen itself on its good taste and to mutter knowingly about the exaggerated taste of others. Much pointing and nudging went on as people recognised who was being satirised. Lord Foppington in Vanbrugh's *The Relapse* was created by Colley Cibber in 1696, and has been fulsomely recreated in our own day by Donald Sinden (1967). A whole scene is devoted to his dressing, transforming himself from a prancing fool in undignified pyjamas (the eighteenth century equivalent thereof) into the magnificent architecture of a self-adoring dandy, all with the help, of course, of a retinue of servants behaving as if they were party to the creation of a masterpiece. In Cibber's *Love's Last Shift*, in which he himself played the role of Sir Novelty Fashion, his wig was brought on stage in its own sedan chair. Once fitted, the head had to be held aloft to keep it in place. It was by no means easy to see where one was going or to be sure where the chair was when one gingerly sat down upon it, as the arrogance of the fop demanded the actor should hold himself as if indifferent to such matters. Sinden says the way to find the style of the part was to know how to walk and how to stand – the rest followed by inevitability.

Another wonderful creation was Sir Fopling Flutter in Etherege's *The Man of Mode* (1676), which gave me one of the funniest evenings I have spent in the theatre at the Royal Shakespeare Company's 1971 revival, when the part was played with glorious élan by John Wood. His vanity and conceit were so beyond anything one could imagine would be dared to attempt in stage portrayal, but he carried it off by believing in himself 100 per cent. When he toured the stage to be admired by each person in turn, when he entered preceded by pages dressed in gold, when he turned up at a ball disguised as Louis XIV in such a pretentious and unwieldy costume that he had to be carried ("wheeled on" as we now say), Wood was the very definition of the blind, totally innocent, vainglorious and superbly ridiculous fop. The type was not entirely an English phenomenon, for Molière had made fun of the French variety, notably with Acaste and Clitandre in *Le*

Misanthrope (1666), and Sir Fopling Flutter's wardrobe, by the way, is entirely imported from Paris; but it is fair to say the English perfected the part, and still delight in using it for satire.

Eddie Izzard and Boy George are, in their different ways, modern manifestations of the tradition of the fop. They are hardly innocent, however, for both reveal a certain degree of deliberate image-building. But until a modern playwright discovers an excuse to mock the modern-day fop and give an actor the opportunity to immortalise him as Colley Cibber immortalised the eighteenth century variety, we shall lose this element of collaboration-by-wink which is the function of the audience *vis-à-vis* the affectionate caricature.

Alan Ayckbourn has created some memorable parts for actresses which, though not the female equivalent of the Restoration fop, do achieve the same degree of friendly recognition which laughs without scorn ("as soon as a comment on character is inspired by contempt or anger," wrote Athene Seyler, "it becomes tragic and loses the light of laughter.") Penelope Keith as the harassed hostess in *The Norman Conquests* (1974), frantically folding napkins to make her middle-class dinner-table correct while everyone else is miserably indifferent to her efforts, was a lovely example of a "type" which the comic actor may snatch up and make his or her own; Penelope Keith impersonated this character so well that nobody else of her generation dares attempt it.

Ayckbourn is also adept at the witty repartee, which was a crucial element in Restoration comedy. Precise, understated verbal fireworks, more like catherine wheels than explosives, have been a staple of comic acting from Vanbrugh and Etherege through Sheridan to Pinero, Oscar Wilde, Noël Coward and Ayckbourn. Once again, the verbal felicities mirrored the society of the time so that, as John Styan nicely puts it, the audience was allowed "to hear itself speaking". [26] The same could be said of the audience of 1895 (*The Importance of Being Earnest*), the audience of 1930 (*Private Lives*), the audience of 1969 (*Relatively Speaking*), and the audiences who filled the Criterion Theatre in 1996 for *Our Night With Reg*. Comic acting depends upon the verisimilitude of colloquial speech, coupled with the subtle emphases of its inherent wit, which is why it is comparatively rare to find an actor like Garrick, who was proficient in both tragedy and comedy. It also requires a mastery of silences and a rich inventiveness, like Ralph Lynn's mentioned earlier. The comic actor must, even more than the great tragedians, use his own personality in the endeavour, make himself his art, winkle out the comedy from his inner hesitations. Contrary to appearances, which suggest the comic actor is having an easy time skipping along with sparkling words, the intensity of his commitment is just as strong as for the desperate Lear or the anxious Hamlet.

One of the most lyrical, as well as the most instructive, insights into the way an actor should approach comedy is a slim but precious book by Athene Seyler, herself a comic actress of subtle finesse, entitled *The Craft of Comedy* (1943). In the form of an exchange of letters between Seyler and a young actor called Stephen Haggard, who begs for help "for a friend" who is just beginning in the theatre, it is a veritable box of jewels even for the experienced. "Comedy is the sparkle on the water, not the depths beneath," she writes. "But note, the waters must run deep underneath...it is only when one thoroughly understands a person that one can afford to laugh at him." In distinguishing between the very different techniques required to play comedy, she makes clear the fact that the audience is less required to collaborate than in drama, that the onus is on the actor to guide. "Emotional acting of a serious part involves absorption in the character – identification with it, losing one's own self in another's [which we looked at in Chapter Three]. On the other hand, comedy seems to be the standing outside a character or situation and pointing out one's delight in certain aspects of it...in essence the same as recounting a good story over the dining-table. It must have direct contact with the person to whom it is addressed, be it one's friend over the port or one's friends in the stalls and pit." [27] What the actor does is to upset the balance, to emphasise or understate, to surprise, and appear to believe in the balance of an interpretation that he has deliberately kicked off balance; in this way he makes the audience feel they have the edge on him, whereas he has engineered that feeling by a cunning performance.

It is still possible to see how some of the great comedians appeared to their audiences, and in each case one will see that it was what they did when they *weren't* speaking which mattered as much as what they said.

Describing James Nokes, who died in 1692, his contemporary Cibber says the audience burst into laughter as soon as he walked on stage, to which he responded with so serious a glance that they laughed even louder. Immediately one may recognise the grave features of Jack Benny and the sad, doe-eyed perplexity of Alastair Sim, both actors (although Benny was considered "no more than" a stand-up comedian) who established their comedy before they uttered a word. "The solemnity of his [Nokes'] features were enough to have sent a whole bench of bishops into a titter," wrote Cibber. Much careful and rehearsed use of facial muscles shook them "to a fatigue of laughter". Just like Benny and Sim, Nokes enabled the audience to supplement with their imagination what he did *not* say, yet all the effort in planting the seeds for that imagination was in his art. "When he debated any matter to himself, he would shut up his mouth with a dumb, studious pout, and roll his full eye into such a vacant amazement…that his silent perplexity (which would sometimes hold him several minutes) gave your imagination as full content as the most absurd thing he could say upon it." He still had not said anything, but the house was in continuous roar. Nokes could illustrate, by his face and with his "body language", irritation, shame, envy, distress. "What tragedy," asks Cibber, "ever showed us such a tumult of passions rising at once in one bosom?" A description which suggests Tony Hancock and Frankie Howerd, the latter especially clever at teasing out innuendo by persuading the audience they thought of it first; in this Howerd was in direct descent from the sly double entendres of Restoration comedy and, to some extent, of the self-conscious but self-deluding fop. One is also reminded of Sinden's daringly long double-takes, for which only Jack Benny was more reckless (*apparently* reckless, though in fact in absolute control of the audience). Cibber, who had a long career as playwright and actor and might be expected to know a thing or two, gave as his considered opinion that James Nokes was an actor with a different genius, unlike anyone else he ever saw. [28] This is almost a perfect echo of Donald Sinden's remark that Ralph Lynn was the greatest actor he ever saw in his life. James Nokes and Ralph Lynn. Both comic actors. Both better than anyone else alive at the time. Both now unknown to today's public. And this despite the fact that Lynn only died in 1962 I saw him perform several times in his last years.

Try as one might, it is hard to see any contemporary stand-up comic able to match any of these, save the magical Roy Hudd, a piece of tradition all by himself. There is one other, who may be caught in Victorian music halls across London, who has inherited all the tricks and techniques as well as all the spirit and purpose of comedy playing, called Peter John. Catch him if you can. He purports to limit himself to the music hall tradition, but his art goes back much further. One fancies a glimpse of James Nokes at times. In the theatre, the actor who best represents the tradition is Michael Williams, who uses his handsome and mischievous face to brilliant effect in making a farcical situation even more intolerable, bewilderment passing to anguish passing to paralysing terror; after this, words are practically superfluous. Williams' performance in *Out of Order* (1990) was one of the comic high points of the present generation.

Maggie Smith is a comic actress who skilfully uses her hands, arms and chin as part of her vocabulary. When a thought jumps into her head, the chin jerks and flicks to the side, as if somebody had hit her. The hands point and flap as if shaken by a fierce wind, when she gropes to make a point; it is like acting by semaphore.

In an earlier chapter we looked at the German traveller Lichtenberg's account of David Garrick as Hamlet. Let us now turn to the same observer's account of Garrick's most celebrated comic performance, as Abel Drugger in *The Alchemist*, wherein we can quickly discern the same art of delay and talent for facial versatility as we have identified in Nokes, Lynn, Howerd, Sinden, and Benny. "When the astrologers spell out from the stars the name, Abel Drugger, henceforth to be great, the poor, gullible creature says with heartfelt delight: 'That is my name.' Garrick makes him keep his joy to himself, for to blurt it out before everyone would be lacking in decency. So Garrick turns aside, hugging his delight to himself for a few moments, so that he actually gets those red rings round his eyes which often accompany great joy, at least when violently suppressed, and says to himself: 'That is my name.' The effect of this judicious restraint is indescribable, for one did not see him merely as a simpleton being gulled, but as a much more ridiculous creature, with an air of secret triumph, thinking himself the slyest of rogues." [29] The comic as subtle psychologist, in other words. We see the same at work in the art of Alec Guinness, the best Abel Drugger of this century, and in a comic actor like Tom Courtenay, who in Ronald Harwood's *The Dresser* went far beyond the camply loyal theatre buff he might appear, into a character of touching pathos – a limited, futureless, easily wounded and deeply affectionate aging young man. His final scene was almost unbearably moving. Yet this was undoubtedly comic acting of a very high order.

There are many other variations of style and technique, yet they all have their roots in the fertile past of English theatre; there is nothing altogether new. A central plank is the mastery of timing, of getting the audience to respond at the right moment, or, if not, adapting one's performance to synchronise with their timing (which is the same thing in reverse and requires the same control). A great actor of the 1940s,

Laurence O'Madden, was so skilled at this that he could take the script after a performance and scribble in the margin where he intended to get the laughs at the next performance. He wanted some variation, so he determined to organise it. With exactly the same lines, but an alteration in gear, he was able to cancel (in the theatre they say "kill") the laughs he had been used to getting and substitute entirely different ones in different places. Younger actors looked upon this with jaw-dropping awe. An actor today who can do it is David Jason; his long run in *No Sex Please We're British* was much enlivened by this deftness, although it kept the rest of the cast on tenterhooks (which was just as well for a farce).

Then there is the talent to detect laughs where none is immediately apparent. I, for one, can read the script of a comedy without seeing which lines could or should be funny. A comic actor of genius will not only see those that were intended, but turn those that were not. Robert Morley said of Margaret Rutherford that she could "root out a laugh like a truffle hound".

On the other hand, John Cleese is not obviously a comic actor at all, yet he is one of the funniest men working today. The reason is that he uses his own misfortunes – a social shyness bordering on illness and sometimes said to be manic depression, plus a rubbery face and awkward gait (he is so tall that he cannot stand up straight without scaring the pigeons) – as his tools to create characters of unforgettable silliness.

In all our history there is one actor who combined all these skills – the psychological subtlety, the harnessing of personal disability, the conquest of timing, the use of silence, the facial musicality, the affectionate satire – to a degree which has made him unsurpassable. Known to every actor and virtually unknown elsewhere, his name was Charles Mathews (1776-1835).

Mathews emerged from the opposite of theatrical stock, being the son of a theological bookseller, and came burdened with a face far from handsome. But he was without vanity and blessed with an irrepressible sense of fun. He said that his nurse had told him that when he was a baby she used to burst out laughing whenever she clapped eyes on him because he looked so odd, with a crooked mouth which was off-centre, seeming to slide up towards his ear. This he would turn to professional advantage. He went to the Merchant Taylor's School in London (his father's bookshop was in the Strand) where he first indulged a talent for mimicry, taking off three brothers at the school to the wonder of everybody else. He seemed to be able to crawl into another's skin and adopt his entire past, voice, movement, manner and weaknesses. On leaving school Mathews went to see the old actor Macklin, then nearly 100, who so terrified him that he fled his company after a few minutes.

Mathews' first appearance on the stage was in 1803, and he played a number of well-known parts (including Polonius with Kemble), attracting praise and building a reputation, above all establishing a loyal public following. Throughout, it was his talent for transformation which astonished, and it was no mere caricature, but a subtle, assertive, psychologically true assumption of another self. When he played an old man, for instance, he never fell into the trap of doing what a young man would expect an older one to do – stumble, stutter, prevaricate. He played the old man as an old man would play himself. (Alec Guinness has several times demonstrated the difference.) Leigh Hunt put it like this: "Mathews never appears to wish to be old; time seems to have come to him, not he to time, and as he never, where he can avoid it, makes that show of feebleness which the vanity of age always would avoid, so he never forgets that general appearance of years, which the natural feebleness of age could not help." [30]

Again, when playing Sir Fretful Plagiary in Sheridan's *The Critic*, it was the precision of Mathews' psychological understanding which informed his interpretation. In the scene where his terrible attempts at poetry are mercilessly criticised and exposed, an ordinary actor was wont to look first hurt, then angry, and the part was in his pocket. With Mathews it was all subtlety and shifting vision. He contrived to look cheerful enough, and at the same time allow his eyes and that crooked mouth to betray what he was really feeling, so that the audience felt in complicity with him against the other characters. As Sir Fretful gradually lost his self-control, the descent was heralded by much fidgeting with the buttons of his waistcoat, undoing them and doing them up again, thereby adding an affectionate audience to a complicitous one, for Mathews highlighted the humour *and* the humanity of the character; a lesser actor would have made him foolish and pitiable.

From 1818 Charles Mathews devoted himself almost entirely to one-man shows, which he called At Homes, and which were enormously popular for the next 20 years. In the space of two or three hours Mathews would assume between a dozen and 20 different characters, each so sharply distinguished from the others that people found it difficult to believe they were all performed by one man. They involved sudden transformations in voice, language, dress and manners, and some ventriloquy as well, for he could "throw" his voice to introduce one character about to make an entrance, while he was busy getting out of the costume of a previous character, and thus run smoothly from one to the other. His muscle control was so miraculous that he appeared to change the shape of his face, enabling one to *see* which character was going to speak before he said anything. Moreover, he used these talents not for simple mimicry, but to satirise the social conventions of the day. [31] No wonder he filled the theatres.

There would be a theme to the evening, Mathews showing the audience a variety of American "types", or the characters he met in the course of a day in Paris. One entertainment, called "Stories", took place on three different levels of a lodging-house in Brighton which was teeming with people. He played all the tenants and their visitors in a dizzying display of virtuosity and quick change, leaving the audience agape. [32] Sometimes he would impersonate the leading political figures of his time, and did so with such remarkable accuracy that he was reproached by the Government for imitating Lord Ellenborough too well – a fine instance of the actor's art being subversive. When *Beyond the Fringe* was first performed in London in 1963, the late Peter Cook's devastating impersonation of Prime Minister Harold Macmillan – he portrayed him as having patrician vowels and a haughty indifference to the sufferings of bothersome pensioners – is said to have contributed to Macmillan's eventual downfall. In a similar way, John Wells relentlessly portrayed Margaret Thatcher's husband as trivial and bigoted, and by extension, Mrs Thatcher herself. This may well have helped build antipathy towards her term in office. So one may easily see why a master like Charles Mathews might upset the apple-cart.

On other occasions he would impersonate other contemporary actors, and many from the immediate past, making his entertainment a veritable lesson in the history of style and dramatic technique. The At Homes grew to such a peak of popularity that Drury Lane and Covent Garden attempted to ban them (presumably through jealousy), but Mathews bore them no ill-will for this. His art was after all infused with a kindness which rendered it beneficent, and he could no more bridle his talent for mimicry than could his contemporary Kean temper his passionate outbursts of despair. He was known to indulge this talent offstage as well as on, and two stories in particular illustrate its apparently limitless scope.

A guest in a bachelor's house stayed the night and arose early for breakfast, disturbed by the sound of a little boy having his face washed. He was unaware there was a child in the house at all, but there could be no doubting the sounds of tantrums and tears, mingled with the sounds of a woman scolding and insisting, and after that the sobs of the child being swallowed up in the thickness of the towel. He could hear the dirty face bawling again when the towel was momentarily removed, then smothered once more. Having sat down to breakfast, he told his host what he had heard and how sorry he had felt for the little boy's ordeal, whereupon in walked Charles Mathews, who had been the urchin, the woman, and the towel. [33]

Another incident is related by the diarist Thomas Raikes. Mathews had one tiresomely insistent fan from the country, a man who made it his business to go uninvited to Mathews' house whenever he was in London, to follow him everywhere and seek out his company, which Mathews, being the decent soul that he was, did not refuse as often as he should. We might now call him a stalker and have him arrested. This man tracked Mathews down to the house of the actor Pope and knocked loudly on his door. The servant announced a gentleman in the hall who demanded to see Mr Mathews and would not be deflected. Mathews looked very embarrassed and apologised to the company, saying that the man was a dreadful nuisance and he would go out and get rid of him immediately. There ensued a most furious row between the actor and the fan which the people assembled in the dining room could hear, both shouting, the one determined to enter, the other determined he should retreat. The door then opened and in walked the stranger, who sat down in Mathews' place, poured himself a glass of wine, which he said was pretty awful stuff, and proceeded to claim acquaintance with everyone present and to share the latest gossip with them. For a few moments they sat astonished. Then it dawned on them that the impostor was Mathews himself, who had imitated the argument outside to give himself time to don a disguise (and presumably had made the servant his accomplice in the joke).

When he lay dying, his own servant gave him some doctor's remedy and later discovered he had mistaken the ink bottle for the medicine bottle. "Don't worry, dear boy," said Mathews, "I'll swallow a bit of blotting paper." [34]

It is possible to discern something of Mathews in the protean mimicry and astute observation of Peter Sellers, but Sellers lacked the elements of charm and kindness which made Mathews paramount.

Unexpectedly, perhaps, one may find his spirit in the work of Dawn French and Jennifer Saunders, despite their belonging to the television age and having but rarely appeared on stage. Nevertheless, neither of these actresses has quite succeeded in losing her own face, whereas Mathews regularly lost his. There is a portrait of him by George Henry Harlow in the Garrick Club, which depicts him without disguise sitting in a chair looking upon himself in five different characters, and appearing to be himself bemused at how he was able to do it. His memory lives on in that place more than anywhere else, because his matchless collection of theatrical portraits and memorabilia formed the basis of the collection which is now the finest of its kind in the world. Over 400 of the pictures belonged to Mathews and hung in his home.

That is not why he is here, however. He finishes the chapter because he is the supreme exemplar of that unequal partnership between actor and audience which prevails in comedy, where the actor has all the effort and all the imagination to muster, and the audience waits to be coaxed into believing. Kean and Siddons, working upon the imagination of the audience and expecting their collaboration, had a much easier time. Believe it or not, Penelope Keith must struggle harder than Ian McKellen.

1 Dawn Langley Simmons, *Margaret Rutherford* (1983), p 38

2 Edward Gordon Craig, *Henry Irving* (1930), in W A Darlington, *The Actor and his Audience* (1949)

3 Thomas Davies, *Dramatic Miscellanies* (1784); V C Clinton-Baddeley, *All Right on the Night* (1954), pp 41-45, 65

4 Horace Walpole, *Letters*, ed. Cunningham (1906), 1 September, 1763

5 F P Wilson, *The Plague in Shakespeare's London* (1927), p 52

6 E K Chambers, *The Elizabethan Stage* (1923), iv, p 313

7 John Brewer, *The Pleasures of the Imagination* (1997), p 333

8 *Dictionary of National Biography*

9 Brewer, *op. cit.*, pp 348-350

10 *Henry V*, Chorus, Acts I and III

11 *Hamlet*, Act II, Sc 2

12 *The Sunday Times*, 15 June, 1997

13 J L Styan, *The English Stage* (1996), pp 238, 240

14 Clinton-Baddeley, *op. cit.*, pp 20-21

15 J A Hammerton, *The Actor's Art* (1897), p 87; Leigh Hunt, *Critical Essays on the Performers of the London Theatres* (1807), p 275; Brewer, *op. cit.*, p 326; *Dictionary of National Biography*

16 Thomas Davies, *Memoirs of the Life of David Garrick* (1805), in Darlington, p 51

17 *Dictionary of National Biography*, Vol XIII, p 778

18 Brewer, *op. cit.*, p 350

19 Clinton-Baddeley, *op. cit.*, pp 77, 144

20 *ibid.*, pp 22-25

21 Styan, *op. cit.*, pp 275, 278

22 Brewer, *op. cit.*, pp 327-331

23 *Old and New London*, Vol III, pp 28-29, in John Diprose, *Anecdotes of the Stage and Players*

24 Styan, *op. cit.*, pp 314-318

25 Bryan Forbes, *That Despicable Race* (1980), p 286

26 Styan, *op. cit.*, p 262

27 Athene Seyler and Stephen Haggard, *The Craft of Comedy* (1943), pp 8-11

28 Colley Cibber, *An Apology for the Life of Mr Colley Cibber* (1826)

29 *Lichtenberg's Visits to England*, trans. Mare and Quarrell (1938)

30 Leigh Hunt, *Critical Essays on the Performers of the London Theatres* (1807)

31 Mathews' personal scrapbook, in the library of the Garrick Club

32 *The Drama: Theatrical Pocket Magazine*, March 1822

33 Leigh Hunt, *Lord Byron and Some of His Contemporaries*, in John Timbs, *Romance of London*, Vol II, pp 435-6

34 *Old and New London*, Vol IV, p 339 and Vol V, pp 410-411

5

Keep out of me Circle

One of the most arresting paradoxes in a profession which is packed with them is this: to be successful the great actor must necessarily be possessed of an almighty ego, he must want to show the audience that they cannot do without him, that their lives are to be changed as a result of having seen him, that he is justified in isolating himself from the rest of mankind to be exposed on a stage in front of them because he is special. Further, he must not only want all this, he must need it. He is liable therefore to be egocentric, smug, unbearable, vulnerable, self-pitying, delinquent and demanding. He might be also mystifyingly eccentric, or overbearingly tyrannical. And yet, in his finest incarnation as the actor-manager, this impossible beast was ever subservient to the theatre itself and to Shakespeare in particular, and saw it as his duty to bring the finest drama to the most remote corners of the country, educating the people and returning their poetry to them. Nor was this "duty" mere theory or romance. He led a life of privation in obedience to it.

The actor-managers have disappeared since the Second World War, and they are missed. They were flamboyant despots, but they brought colour and spice to the theatre where it was most needed – in the provinces. Despite the deference paid to them, despite their astrakhan coats and silver-topped canes (Anton Walbrook in the film *The Red Shoes* caught the genre to perfection), despite their air of importance, they condemned themselves and their wives to a life of touring, living in miserable one-bedroom "digs" with breakfast and supper prepared by the landlady, packing every week, travelling around the country in draughty trains, never having a chance to go home (if home there was), making do and surviving. There was precious little of luxury in such a life, and much of hard drudge. When the notice went up in a provincial theatre on a Saturday to announce arrangements for the company to move on to the next date on Sunday, it became necessary to stipulate "no brown paper bags on train-call" in order to encourage actors to invest in a suitcase.

The actor-manager took the leading role in every play, and his wife as often as not took the female lead, and he might well have played six, seven or eight different classical roles in one week. The schedule was punishing, the emotional effort exhausting. But if it was not for the actor-manager, the audiences of little theatres dotted throughout the land would never have seen Shakespeare, would never have known the experience of a cosmic theatrical performance. He was a hero of sorts.

Ronald Harwood's play *The Dresser* relates something of such a life, the central character, known only as "Sir", an actor-manager of the old ilk, mesmeric in performance, intolerable in the flesh. To an ambitious young actress who tries to flatter him into giving her a job, he warns, "You must be prepared to sacrifice what most people call life," and in a curtain call speech to the audience (a traditional part of the evening which, again, involved the audience in what had been going on), he says, "Our most cherished ambition is to keep the best alive of our drama, to serve the greatest poet-dramatist who has ever lived, and we are animated by nothing else than to educate the nation in his works by taking his plays to every corner of our beloved island." [1] The egocentricity, the responsibility, the sentiment are all there. What the audience never saw was the fear which stalked backstage, as every other actor (perchance the actor-manager's wife and daughter included), trembled lest he speak to them, and worried lest they spoil his Big Speech with a bit of acting themselves; for his part, he made sure he kept their anxieties well-honed.

And why did he get away with it? Because in the end, the actor-manager was among the finest actors in the land, and he held his audiences in thrall.

The flowering of the actor-manager occupies most of the nineteenth century and half the twentieth, but the tradition has roots which dig back to the Elizabethan era, and the tree was a long time a-growing. Queen Elizabeth I gave permission for her favourite, the Earl of Leicester, to form a company of actors and present plays in London providing they did not collide with church services nor were shown in time of plague. The leading actor of Leicester's company was a carpenter by trade, now an actor, called James Burbage. In 1576 Burbage bought the lease on a patch of land in Shoreditch and built his theatre on it. It was called, simply, The Theatre. He died 21 years later, by which time his son Richard had become established as Shakespeare's leading man, and his other son Cuthbert was the manager of the company. Not an actor-manager, however; there is no evidence that Cuthbert Burbage performed.

In 1598 the lease in Shoreditch ran out, and the landlord demanded a higher rent. Burbage refused. He and his actors (presumably including Shakespeare) tore down the old theatre and carted the timbers on their backs across the river to Southwark, where they re-erected it on a new site. They called the newly-born theatre The Globe, and it is this that has been once more recreated at the end of the twentieth century on a site not very far away.

The two celebrated theatre managers of the Restoration, Thomas Killigrew and William Davenant, were neither of them actors, but Davenant's leading man Thomas Betterton certainly was, and when he set up his own company in 1695 he effectively became the first actor-manager of the English theatre, deciding the repertoire, casting the plays, and even having his wife, Mary Saunderson, as his leading lady. Betterton, however, was a man of sober habits and discreet manners, so it would be misleading to consider him the father of the actor-manager tradition except as a matter of chronology.

David Garrick brought efficiency and revolutionary zeal to the role of actor-manager, taking over the Theatre Royal, Drury Lane at the age of 30 and giving it the best years of his life. As we have seen in other contexts, he changed the "feel" of a theatrical evening by chucking the audience off the stage, improving lighting and scenery, and generally upgrading the status of the acting profession in society. He kept all the best parts for himself, however, and Mrs Siddons, who acted with him, said he was jealous of any praise she might enjoy. "In short, I found I must not shade the tip of his nose," she said. [2]

Thus, we may not only owe to Garrick the beginning of the actor's long haul into respectability, but also his gradual slide into egocentricity. There is no shortage of evidence, even from his friends, that he was very full of himself, and there are some suggestions of autocratic behaviour on stage. When Charles Macklin announced his retirement in 1753, it was Garrick who wrote his farewell speech for him in the hope of getting rid of a formidable rival. But Macklin was back on the boards again a couple of years later! A notorious fact is that the great Garrick was never heard to praise the efforts of any other actor.

By the middle of the eighteenth century the actor-managers had become a feature of provincial life, although most of them would now have to be disinterred from county archives, such was their obscurity. One name has survived by virtue of his progeny. Roger Kemble, an actor-manager in the Midlands, was the father of Sarah Siddons, John Philip Kemble and Charles Kemble, and grandfather of Fanny Kemble. John Philip Kemble in turn became manager of both Drury Lane and Covent Garden, and Charles Kemble was manager of Covent Garden. Macready was the actor-manager who bestrode the middle of the nineteenth century, and we have a glimpse of him in action as the boss before whom all lesser fry must quake, in the diary of Fanny Kemble. "He growls and prowls and roams and foams about the stage," she wrote, "in every direction, like the tiger in his cage, so I never know which side of me he means to be, and keeps up a perpetual snarling and grumbling so that I never feel sure that he has done and that it is my turn to speak." That's how to keep them on their toes!

In London, Samuel Phelps (1804-1878) accomplished the prodigious feat of putting on 31 of Shakespeare's plays at Sadler's Wells over a period of 20 years and, as far as I am able to discover, acting in all of them. Phelps saw himself as an educator, who could also turn Shakespeare into a popular draw. His theatre became a kind of school for actors. By the end of the century the actor-manager as a species was firmly established in all parts of the country. One of the most colourful was Frank Benson (1858-1939), who ran the theatre at Stratford-upon-Avon for 33 years and had a famously skewed sense of priorities. Cricket mattered to him profoundly, and his contracts with his actors were usually worded, "To play the Ghost in Hamlet and keep wicket" or "To play Laertes and field cover point". Benson has the distinction of being the only actor to be knighted actually in the theatre, after a performance in 1916, on a sudden whim of George V who had enjoyed his performance in *Julius Caesar* and needed to show his appreciation somehow.

Yet with all these people there were two elements lacking in the cocktail which made the extraordinary hybrid of the actor-manager. One of these was reverential awe. That came in dollops with Henry Irving.

To say that Irving's actors respected him would be an understatement. Enough has been said in these pages for the reader to know by now what a giant he was (albeit an unexpected giant – he himself said he had done pretty well for somebody who couldn't walk or talk correctly), and as an actor-manager his word was never disputed. One spoke when one was spoken to, and did as one was told. With later examples of the type, submission was assured by terror, but in Irving's case it was ordained by a certain kind of astonished love. He survived the taunts of Bernard Shaw, who said he should be tied up in a sack with the works of Shakespeare and dropped into the nearest volcano in the hope he might finally understand some of them; to his actors he was beyond praise. His leading lady was Ellen Terry, who would not have a word said against him and stoutly defended him against Shaw. She is still thought by some to have been Irving's mistress as well, although it has never be conclusively demonstrated. At least the relationship reflected the actor-manager's right to have his consort at his side, and the public's expectation that she always would be. He was enough of an egocentric also to demand that no one "upstage" him; when he was speaking, nobody else on stage was permitted to budge an inch, scarcely to breathe – attention must not be deflected for a second. And you will remember with what haughty self-assurance he deserted his wife in the middle of the road on the night of his greatest success when she asked if he was going to continue to make such a fool of himself. His studied entrance as Hamlet served to emphasise his right to pre-eminence. The play opened with a procession, to establish the wealth of the court at Elsinore and the position occupied by Claudius and Gertrude on the throne and Polonius in politics. When they had all exited, lights dimmed and fanfares stilled, Irving was revealed at the back, alone in a pale glow, pensive and perplexed. That was focus. It was only partially justified by the play.

The other ingredient still lacking was vulgarity, in which Irving was singularly deficient. The acting profession has always been clear of tongue and fond of bawdy, and part of the manager's job was seemingly to entertain with the one and supply plenty of the other. Pepys tells how Killigrew talked "very lewdly" and berated Charles II for allowing himself to be henpecked by his ferocious mistress, Barbara Villiers, Lady Castlemaine (later Duchess of Cleveland). Killigrew said the lady was so imperious that the King could not get an erection and had to content himself enjoying her with his finger. Killigrew also stated his intention of employing a whore at 20 shillings a week to live in at the theatre and be continuously available for 20 or so of his lusty young actors, whom he feared losing unless they were kept happy. [3]

So, too, has the seduction attempt upon an aspiring young actress always been part of the actor-manager's repertoire, though not in Irving's case. Nowadays it is referred to as "the casting couch". Nell Gwyn is the obvious example to spring to anyone's mind. Ellen Tree (1805-1880) was fancied by Charles Kemble, who promised her all the best parts if only she would be "propitious to his flame", and when she rejected him he kept her down and promoted inferior actresses in her stead. [4]

There is an amusing story of Herbert Beerbohm Tree entertaining the young Esmé Percy to supper in his rooms after a performance. Lady Tree is said to have walked in to find the dining-table replete with delicacies and said, "Enjoy your dinner, Miss Percy. The port is on the chimney-piece, and remember, it's still adultery." Another is that of the actor who asked another more experienced colleague if he thought Hamlet had actually been to bed with Ophelia. "I don't know about the West End, laddie," he said, "but we always did on tour."

One could go on. The theatre delights in mischief of this kind, and when the actor-manager reached his apogée in the twentieth century he was often a source of gossip himself. All the ingredients were in place for the two arch-exemplars – Herbert Beerbohm Tree and Donald Wolfit (1902-1968).

Tree has already found his way into these pages, but insufficient account has been taken thus far of his influence and popularity. As manager and leading actor at Her Majesty's Theatre in the Haymarket, Tree held his public as no other had done before or has done since, by virtue of his rhapsodic devotion to his theatre and his determination to mount the most lavish productions possible on its stage. His followers "would far rather see him being bad than most actors being good," in which hope they were often satisfied, but it did not matter, for he gave them spectacle and delight. Amazing scenery, peculiar effects of light, real animals or chariots or waterfalls on stage if required, he gave it everything. He was the devil to work with, for he changed his mind without warning and his productions were never ready until a few minutes after they had their first performance, and even then his lines were not learnt and his moves were subject to whimsical amendment. Seymour Hicks said his range as a character actor was without comparison, and Huggett has deftly written that "the difference between the acting of Irving and that of Tree was the difference between hypnotism and enchantment." [5] Nevertheless, his enchantment was dearly purchased on the patience of his cast, who were never sure whether the lavish scenery would stay up or fall upon them.

Tree was so intoxicated with the fun and business of running a theatre that he rarely seemed to concentrate upon his role as actor, which gave an immediacy to his performances beyond what he intended. He entirely forgot, for instance, that there was a scene in which Eliza throws her slippers at Higgins in *Pygmalion*, with the result that when Mrs Patrick Campbell did as the script demanded and hit him square on the jaw, he was so startled that he thought it a gesture of spite on her part and looked genuinely hurt. Were one to make a sarcastic suggestion for improvement in staging, he would jump upon it as a terrific idea, for he entirely lacked the taste to distinguish invention from absurdity. Yet he was unfailingly good-natured, and broke new ground by being the first actor-manager actively to encourage friendly relations with the press. In truth, his fame and the loyalty he evoked far outweighed his talents. On the other hand, there never was a man of the stage who so infected the world with his enthusiasm, thus did his gusto bring a whole new public into the theatre. He was also bold, staging Ibsen at a time when his rivals were wary of so difficult and solemn an author.

Tree did not escape that amusing jealousy which besets the profession occasionally, especially when as actor-manager you are in a position to gratify it. He and Mrs Patrick Campbell were once appearing in a double bill, himself the lead in the first play, she starring in the second play after the interval. She was alarmed and perplexed to find that she was playing to half-empty houses night after night, until one evening she crept down from her dressing-room during the interval to listen to Tree's curtain speech at the end of *his* play – all actor-managers invariably addressed their audiences, often in a modest-avuncular manner. "Ladies and gentlemen," he said, "thank you so very much for your splendid reception of our little play tonight. I am deeply honoured, so very touched, so happy, and may I end by wishing you a safe journey home, and God bless you all."

There is an evergreen tale about "billing" on the hoardings outside the theatre, which is ascribed to Tree. Leading actors are above the title, with supporting actors below, and a special honour is sometimes given to one of these by placing him or her last in the list, and prefixing the name with "and". It is a device reserved for guest artists or for rising celebrities. A 20-year-old actor who had worked for Tree for a year, William Armstrong, asked the great man to come with him to the front of house, where he pointed out the billing and said, "You see, my name is at the very bottom." "Yes," said Tree. "Well, sir, um," faltered the young man, "do you think it could be perhaps elevated a little, or could it read, so-and-so, so-and-so, so-and-so, AND William Armstrong?" Tree paused. "Yes,, he said. "But why 'and'? Why not 'BUT'?" [6]

It was not meant unkindly, for Herbert Beerbohm Tree perhaps best represented the beneficent effect of the actor-manager at his most powerful. Wolfit, by contrast, represented the actor-manager at his most tyrannical and explosive.

Any account of Donald Wolfit's place in theatre history must begin by acknowledging that every witness attests his King Lear to have been the greatest of the twentieth century (not excluding Paul Scofield in 1962 and Ian Holm in 1997). James Agate said it was the finest example of Shakespearean acting he had seen in his 25 years as a critic, and his opinion had value. It is some loss to me that I was just too young to have caught it, but I have heard from those present something of this performance's devastating effect upon the audience.

It opened towards the end of the Second World War (12 April, 1944) at La Scala Theatre. The first night was unpromising. There were only about 60 people in the audience, and perhaps a good third of these were critics or friends. "But Wolfit took off, and the heavens opened," one of them told me. Wolfit's biographer Ronald Harwood gives a moving account of the actor's strain and tension that evening, when he sweated out the pints of Guinness handed to him every time he came off stage into the wings. What occurred was a virtuoso performance which defied description. James Agate admitted as much when he wrote, "On Wednesday evening Mr Wolfit did nothing which one could explain...the audience surrendered to the stroke of something without quite knowing what." [7]

Word passed round on the streets of London very quickly, so that on the second night the theatre was packed, with 200 people standing, squeezing round the edge or squatting in the aisles, against all regulations; most of these were in uniform, soldiers on leave. Bear in mind too that *King Lear* is not the most accessible of plays; its language is difficult, its plot subverted by unnecessary incident, its tone dark, its purpose obscure. And yet this second night audience of untheatrical, unintellectual folk were spellbound by the combination of Shakespeare and Wolfit. In the terrible scene in which the King turns upon his daughter Goneril and brings down the curse of Heaven upon her, wishing sterility into her womb, Richard Bebb said it made his flesh creep, and Donald Sinden that "you really thought he must have influence Up There." Wolfit clearly believed he did, too. He lifted his arms high above his head, physically grabbed the curse from the skies, and then, with awful ferocity, hurled it at Goneril. "I thought, there will be a flash of smoke and Goneril will disappear," Sinden recalled. "Astonishing. I had never believed an actor could be that big." [8]

Agate further made a very instructive comparison with Olivier's *Lear*, which happily supports the very distinction made between the Apollonian style of acting – contrived and controlled – and the Dionysian – fierce, demonic, unbridled, dangerous – that was introduced at the beginning of this book. "Wolfit's *Lear* is a ruined piece of nature," he wrote. "Olivier's is a picture of ruins most cunningly presented." Olivier was usually in the grip of Dionysus, but occasionally his brick-building creation of character betrayed him and uncharacteristic caution prevailed. Wolfit was never cautious.

Donald Wolfit was not born to the stage, nor did he come to it blessed with advantages. In fact, he was gifted with nothing. Short, burly even when young, moon-faced, with no chin, a big but rough speaking voice, and a broad Yorkshire accent which he had to struggle to get rid of at the beginning of his career, Agate once described him as an "amiable gorilla" [9], and Harwood "a mischievous aesthete". What he lacked in beauty he more than made up for in fire and energy, in instinct, imagination, and sense of wonder at where he was and what he was doing. On the other hand (and in this he did resemble Tree), he had very little taste.

His make-up was always bad, often using entirely the wrong colour. His wigs were ill-fitting and shifted on his head. Even his own glorious performances he seemed determined to ruin with sentimentality, exaggerated effects and the terrible temptation of "ham". There was a demon within him which was always on the edge, threatening to ruin everything. It is significant that the Lear he gave in 1944 had deteriorated within a few months into a shambles of melodrama and pose, the brilliance of his beginning having metamorphosed at his own hands. He had only himself to blame.

As an autocrat, he denied himself the possibility of help from anyone, for nobody would dare approach him with a "note" on his performance. He ran his company like a boot camp, the rest of the cast cowering before him. It is not too much to say that, though they admired him, other actors hated working with (or for) him. "You would never think of applying to join his company unless you and your family were starving," said one. "He was truly a horror, an absolute lunatic. Without the influence of his wife to keep him in control, somebody would have murdered him."

Wolfit also epitomised that egocentricity which exuded from actor-managers like steam. Every other actor on stage was required to keep well away from him, so that his spotlight should not be shared. "When I say stay at arm's length," he said, "I mean my arm as well as yours." The spot would spread a circle of light on the floor around him, and when Wolfit yelled, "Keep out of me circle", it was with the fierceness of Lear himself. On one occasion his own daughter, who acted in his company, strayed into the light when Wolfit was not even on the stage, and he would have none of it. His arm was seen stretching out from the wings to yank her back into the obscurity wherein she belonged. When he played comedy, Wolfit would routinely edit the play to excise any laughs destined for other actors, leaving his own laughs unchallenged. There seemed no end to his professional vanity. It was the custom for a small provincial theatre who could not afford to host an entire company to invite a leading actor to appear as Guest Artist, supported by their own, local company. Wolfit was invited to appear as Othello. He sent ahead a list of his requirements, two of which were that none of the other actors should ever have appeared in that play before, and that the one cast as Iago should never even have played Shakespeare.

That such a monster should also have been an inspired genius is one of the bewildering juxtapositions in which the theatre abounds, attracting as it does maverick creatures with a higher than ordinary capacity to surprise. There is a story that one young man did finally take revenge upon Wolfit in spectacular fashion. He was appearing with the great man in *Macbeth*, and one of his lines came in the last act, when he has to tell the King, "The Queen, my lord, is dead," to which Macbeth replies "She should have died hereafter" and launches into the splendid, troubling speech "Tomorrow, and tomorrow, and tomorrow/Creeps in this petty pace from day to day/To the last syllable of recorded time." It is a great moment, culminating in the familiar words that life be a tale told by an idiot, full of sound and fury, signifying nothing, and a leading actor is bound to make the most of it. Wolfit had sacked the young man, forgetting that he had one more performance to do with him. The man's pent-up frustration and bitterness at being relentlessly ignored for so long found its outlet.

He came on, went boldly up to Macbeth, and said, "The Queen, my lord, is feeling very much better." I do so hope it is true.

Wolfit was the last of the breed. Others have since combined acting with directing or administration, notably Laurence Olivier at the National Theatre, and Michael Pennington and Ian McKellen with their Prospect Theatre Company. But the colourful combination of austerity, vulgarity, flamboyance, fear and a makeshift kind of glamour have all disappeared. The only actor who attempts something like the role today is Kenneth Branagh, who likes to star, to direct, to raise the money, to cover publicity, above all (it seems) to control the casting, for his enterprises are models of the Stage Door fan's ultimate dream – to get all one's favourite actors together in the same frame. But this is to diminish a very honourable purpose. His Renaissance Theatre Company was built around the idea of a group of young actors playing with guest stars from an older generation, and thereby learning from them the very traditions we have been trying to grasp in this book, and ultimately passing them on. Branagh wants to preserve the life of these traditions at a time when they are sadly neglected by drama schools, and his commitment is as strong, though not as egocentric, as ever Wolfit's was.

No one can doubt, at least, that he has the ego-focus which must be a prerequisite for the task. Not that egocentrics were limited by any means to the actor-managers. Robert Loraine, an actor in the grand manner in his prime after the First World War, playing Othello to Elissa Landi's Desdemona, acted with rather too much realism when he had to strangle her in the final scene. Miss Landi protested that he was too violent, whereupon he thrust a pillow over her face and said, "You mind your own business, my dear young lady, and I'll mind mine." [10]

Marie Tempest (1864-1942) was an actress of imperious manner and demeanour, whose presence made her younger colleagues tremble almost as much as Wolfit's did. Had she restricted her requirements to the supply of white gloves in her dressing room and due deference from Stage Doormen it would have mattered little, but she brought her self-obsession to the stage as well. When a supporting actress tried to upstage her in a crucial scene, Tempest instructed the carpenters to screw her chair down to the floor, and at the next performance watched with grim satisfaction as the poor woman tried to move it. The only person known to have stood up to her was Margaret Rutherford, who at the beginning of her career was singled out for praise by the critics in Robert Morley's *Short Story* (1935), in which Marie Tempest was the lead. Furious, Tempest summoned the wobbly-faced newcomer to her dressing-room. "I am not accustomed to having a play stolen from under my nose," she said, presumably expecting Rutherford to endeavour to do less well in future, out of respect for rank. "I intend to play my part as well as I can," Rutherford retorted, and flounced out. [11]

Marie Tempest made her own rules. She thought she had the right, and had, in truth, allowed being an actress to become more than a vocation or a duty or a job. Disobeying the rule against smoking backstage, she had ashtrays pinned to the back of the scenery.

One could easily multiply examples of rampant egocentricity on stage, actors coughing when others are delivering their most important lines, or walking in front of them, or rattling their armour, or adding an unscripted gurgle after a drink. The most celebrated example has rightly entered into theatrical history, and concerns the quick thinking of Edmund Kean to absorb attention at a moment when it threatened to slip from his grasp. In *Richard III* there is a line interpolated by Colley Cibber in his rewrite of the text for an eighteenth century audience, and though the rest of Cibber's replacements have been forgotten, this one line remains in what is otherwise Shakespeare's pure text. It is there because it affords the actor a moment of character-building expressed in punchy iambic pentameter. Catesby rushes on to the stage and announces, "My liege, the Duke of Buckingham is taken!", to which Richard replies, "Off with his head; so much for Buckingham." The actor playing Catesby to Kean's Richard ruined the point of the scene and shape of the verse by announcing, "My liege, the Duke of Buckingham is taken, and we've cut his head off." (Apparently he was put up to it to see what Kean would do, which was brave at least.) Kean turned on him, fixed him with that big, brassy eye, and said, "Then bury him; so much for Buckingham." He had kept the iambic pentameter intact, and moreover held the focus upon himself.

Whatever fun this may be, it is obviously unhelpful to the drama to allow egocentricity to pass unchecked. The great Russian actor, director and teacher Konstantin Stanislavsky (1863-1938), subject of countless lessons in all drama schools, sought to eradicate the danger by establishing ethical rules for actors, an idea which had never occurred to anyone before. They included maxims such as, "One must love art, and not one's self in art", "There are no small parts, there are only small actors", and one in particular which would have had more than half the great names of the past in the dog-house: "lateness, laziness, caprice, hysterics, bad character, ignorance of the role, the need to repeat anything twice are all harmful to our enterprise and must be rooted out." [12] Clearly, Stanislavsky sought to establish discipline as a norm, and who can say he was wrong? In the end, art is born of discipline; Dionysus might simmer, but Apollo must control. On the other hand, the actor's work must be proud, it must seek to dominate and magnetise, it must to some extent be self-centred. Wolfit, Irving, Tree, Kean, Garrick, Olivier, and today Ralph Fiennes and Daniel Day-Lewis all knew that the audience went ultimately to see *them*, and if they underplayed, the audience would be disappointed. There is a balance somewhere to be drawn, but nobody has yet known how to draw it. Perhaps it is not a balance so much as a fusion, a melting, a recognition that the discipline of the theatrical art must absorb the indiscipline of the maverick egocentric, and trust to mutual benefit. It is a huge gamble, but when it works, it produces magic.

There are some actors who are not just mavericks, but eccentrics, wholly individual people who evade all categorisation. What, for example, is one supposed to make of Ralph Richardson or Margaret Rutherford, each entirely beyond imitation? That they were magnetic is without doubt, but to measure the degree of technique or pretence, or even acting, within their performances on stage is by no means a simple matter. I have already said that, towards the end of his career in plays by Storey and Pinter, Ralph Richardson appeared to be unaware that he was in a play at all, and would have been startled had the lights turned on to reveal a few hundred strangers staring at him. That must be due to consummate artistry, but one did sometimes wonder whether the artistry fed the eccentricity or conquered it. Stories abound of his eccentric moments, suggesting here was a man whose mind was ever half-absent.

At Richmond Theatre on a pre-London run Richardson interrupted the performance to address the audience. "Is there a doctor in the house?" he asked. A man put up his hand. "Yes," here." "Oh, doctor," said Richardson, "isn't this a dreadful play?"

Again on a pre-London engagement he forgot his lines, and was prompted from the wings. He didn't hear, so the prompter spoke more loudly. This time he pricked up his ears and turned to the audience. "Jolly useful chap, that," he said, nodding to the side.

In the last act of *Macbeth* there is a fierce duel between the King and Macduff. Ralph Richardson as Macbeth found it terribly difficult to remember the choreographed moves for this duel, and had to devise his own way in rehearsal of getting them in the right order. It went like this: "One, two, clash your swords, three, four, round we go." When it came to actual performance on the first night, however, he forgot that this was a private *aide-mémoire* and belted out the instructions at full volume. It was a hilarious moment, and typical of the man – his world was designed for himself by himself, and inhabited by himself alone. The audience were eavesdroppers; if they heard and saw genius, and they might, then they were lucky. They might also, on the other hand, hear and see an idiosyncratic Englishman amusing himself and not caring a fig whether they were present or not. His *Macbeth*, by the way, was not a success.

Richardson's eccentricity was not a pose. He was far too straight a man to play games or want to make an impression. Strangely, "acting the fool" would to him have been utterly demeaning, and yet his career was founded upon the need to act something or other all the time. Somewhere within Richardson's elusive personality must lie one of the secrets of the acting vocation which are not answered by the demands of technique or feeling or audience collaboration that we have considered so far, for he seemed to be indifferent to all of them (although the technique was inherent and masterly, he was not necessarily aware of it). He would have thanked nobody for trying to winkle the secret out, and would have had not the faintest idea where to find it. In a television interview with Bernard Levin, who was driven to lying on the floor and waving his hands and feet in the air in an attempt to get Richardson to reveal himself, the great man got up, put on his hat and coat, and walked out while the cameras were still running and the interviewer still struggling, jumped on his powerful motorbike and roared off into the traffic.

There is a story scarcely credible (and therefore not usually credited) about his coming across a man at a railway station and greeting him with old familiarity. "My dear Robertson," he said to the stranger. "How you've changed! You look so much younger; your face is round; you've got a good colour; you've shaved off your moustache; my word, how you've changed!" The man remonstrated with him. "But my name's not Robertson," he said. The old actor looked shocked. "What? Changed your name too?" he said.

If it be true, then it might indicate that Ralph Richardson's grip on reality was at best tenuous, and that the subtle tension of his finest performances arose from this very looseness, this precarious brinkmanship. The audiences hoped to see him lurch one way or the other, towards banal sanity or over the edge into glorious oddity. They were never quite sure what to expect.

When they are sure, they no longer experience theatre, but demonstration.

One story which is certainly true and comes in various versions would seem to indicate Richardson's own perplexity at the source of his art. After one especially poor performance, he said to an actor in the wings, "If ever you come across a little bit of talent with the name Richardson on it, let me know. I'd like to have it back."

It is clear that he acted with profound instinctual antennae, and the delightful stories about him must not be allowed to obscure the magnificence of his acting at its best. Richardson's Falstaff has still never been equalled. In the painful scene where the young King turns frigidly to reject his erstwhile friend, Richardson revealed what Kenneth Tynan called "the emptiness of complete collapse" – a very subtle thing to do. Bryan Forbes described him as a whale stranded without hope of rescue. He knew and understood Falstaff, therefore he had no need to invent him.

He was always refreshingly candid, as if acting were the simplest piece of nonsense to explain and not worth getting all intellectual about, and he relished stating the obvious. It needed to be stated. "I think I could come on and say, 'I'm from the Gas Works, I've come to read the meter,' and I think that people would believe me," he said. "But it's strange that John Gielgud, whose acting I admire extravagantly (I think he is one of the greatest actors living) could not come on and say, 'I'm from the Gas Works, I've come to read the meter.' People would not believe that he came from the Gas Works. Then the other curious thing is that at the end of *The Tempest*, John has come on and said, 'I am the Duke of Milan' and you believe it. He *is* the Duke of Milan, absolutely splendid. Now, I have played in *The Tempest* and I have said, 'I am the Duke of Milan,' and no one has believed me for one moment." [13]

His variety of eccentricity could only be English, and it is possible to trace a line of actors back to the nineteenth century who also appeared to have wandered from their clubs on to a stage and not noticed the difference. They include Charles Hawtrey (1858-1923), not to be confused with the later actor of the same name who played a repeating role in the *Carry On* films, Allan Aynesworth (1865-1959) and Gerald du Maurier (1873-1934). To be fair, Ralph Richardson developed into a man of danger, whereas they never wandered beyond what was safe, but there was an inch or two of character which they all shared. There was never a whisper of Dionysian energy in the performances of any of these actors, but in their way they were supreme. They made it look as if it didn't matter very much, as if they might as well be there on stage as anywhere else, and their entrances and exits were so natural it appeared they had happened on the spur of the moment. If increasing "naturalness" was the measure of every revolution in acting values from Betterton through Garrick and Kean to Brad Pitt, then there never were more natural actors than these, the kings of the effortless drama. But of course, that is not what is really meant by "natural". These men were actors by sleight of hand, masters of the ordinary. They did not stretch themselves or try to dig terrors from their souls. They knew how to fold a handkerchief and deliver a line so that its meaning was clear. They understood the music and balance of words, not their poetry. Above all, they were totally and utterly reliable.

You can imagine Aynesworth and Hawtrey as young men if you remember that Aynesworth created the part of Algy in *The Importance of Being Earnest*, and the complimentary part of John Worthing was intended for Hawtrey (Oscar Wilde had offered it to Hawtrey, who asked for some money in advance; the theatre refused, so Wilde sold the play to George Alexander, who then played Worthing). They both had ease and conviction in what they did, for they did not step very far out of themselves; they were quintessentially English gentlemen, performing on stage as quintessentially English gentlemen, with mild irony, wit, composure, good manners, style, excellent diction and intuitive decency. They were the sort of actors who drove Bernard Shaw and William Archer mad, and gave the public uncomplicated delight. John Gielgud cunningly mocked their style when he played the butler in a Hollywood film called *Arthur* (1982), for which he won an Oscar. Wilfrid Hyde-White impersonated it in dozens of films. Its modern representatives are Geoffrey Palmer and John Standing, actors of impeccable timing and taste, whom the public believe without question, and who look as if they might as well be paid for doing this as anything else. The nonchalance is, however, deceptive. These are actors of consummate control. The fact that they seem unperturbed is because their artistry demands lack of perturbability.

When you see Geoffrey Palmer playing another 'situation comedy' on television for the sixth year, you are likely to take him for granted. It is what he would want you to do; it is what Aynesworth and Hawtrey and Gerald du Maurier strove for. "Eccentric" might seem the most inappropriate word for such actors, who make a fetish of being normal. But eccentric they are, for they make it look as if they are actors by accident, which is very clever indeed. They have turned the shine and glitter on its head, and if they shine at all, it is apologetically.

Another strand of eccentricity lies within the drunkards, actors so manly and vigorous, so philistine and ashamed, that they would (apparently) rather be in a public tavern than disport themselves upon a stage. Their talent is their burden, yet they do not wish to conceal it. They therefore proclaim it with loud embarrassment. Edmund Kean, though frequently drunk, cannot fit as an eccentric of this sort, for he knew he was without equal and could afford to luxuriate in his proud supremacy. Those who are proudly drunk are usually not sure whether they can be proudly actors; it is a profession which cruelly encourages feelings of inadequacy. G F Cooke (1756-1812) on the other hand was perfectly certain that he was good, and was often right. Yet he was almost always so intoxicated that it was a wonder he could stand on the stage, let alone act on it, and witnesses declared that he acted better when drunk than when sober. After spending several terms in prison for his passion, he died probably of alcoholic poisoning; it was said that drink had driven him insane.

A whole group of working-class actors who felt odd about their profession came to notice in the 1950s and 1960s, and some of them were topers. Peter O'Toole (since reformed), Victor Henry, Oliver Reed, Richard Burton, all variously brilliant at times and all worryingly volatile. They would never have said so, but it was almost as if they thought there was something prim about being an actor, and that they must flush the primness out of their very bodies. Alternatively, their talents needed a release which they, unaided, could not grant. Dionysus needed to be let out of his cage. They might have thought there was something inconsequential about being English *and* being an actor, whereas historically Englishness has been of the highest merit and the most use. Perhaps English reticence needs to be conquered, and acting is one of the best ways to conquer it.

Charles Macklin was a boxer and rough diamond, whose untutored and non-declamatory style of acting almost exactly coincided with Garrick's arrival. Indeed, it was his example as Shylock in *The Merchant of Venice* which spurred Garrick to test his talent, so that it was Garrick who really built upon Macklin's innovations and finally took them over. The revolutionary portrayal of Shylock in 1741 as a wicked and malevolent figure rather than the buffoon which he had till then been represented as ("This is the Jew that Shakespeare drew," wrote Pope, and Quin said, "If God writes with a legible hand, that fellow is a villain." [14]) beat Garrick's début by a few weeks, and together they selected the role of Richard III for Garrick to try upon the public, Macklin even advising him on how to perform it. [15] For a while in 1742 he set up house with Garrick and Peg Woffington, all three great stars of the "new" theatre living together, but that did not last owing to Garrick's jealousy of his competition, and Macklin's instabilities of habit. He was always getting into arguments, and did in fact, as I have related, murder another actor over a wig. At the age of 75 he played Macbeth, wearing Scottish costume for the first time, to great acclaim, but the public turned against him when he stole the part assigned to another actor on a subsequent night. When he next tried to perform Shylock, the public hissed him off the stage and the performance had to be interrupted amidst the most unconscionable din. The manager, Mr Colman, came forward. "Is it your pleasure that Mr Macklin be discharged?" he said to the audience. Loud cheers and huge cry of "Yes!" "He is discharged," said Colman. Thus was a great actor sacked by a sovereign audience.

Macklin brought an action against the leaders of the riot, which was tried on 14 May, 1775, with Macklin conducting his own case in court. Judgement by Lord Mansfield was found in his favour, and he was awarded £600 plus costs against the audience. Declining to accept the award, he asked that the defendants be required instead to buy £100-worth of theatre tickets each. Lord Mansfield spotted what a clever piece of public relations this was. "You have met with great applause today," he said, "You have never acted better."

Macklin had already once retired from the stage to open the Piazza Coffee House in Covent Garden, where Boswell liked to dine. There was a small stage in the corner for lectures or recitals, but the meal was theatre enough. The bell was rung for fully five minutes to announce dinner at four o'clock, and ten minutes later it was put on the table and the door closed so that nobody else could enter once people had started eating. Macklin himself served the first course in full dress-suit, a napkin over his left arm. Then he bowed low to the diners and retired to the sideboard, surrounded by his waiters. For months he had trained them to communicate with him and with one another in sign language, so that no word could interrupt "the feast of reason and the flow of soul". At the end of dinner, he served the wine, bowed again, and "hoped that everything had been found agreeable and to their satisfaction." Then he went out of the door and left them to it. Michael Caine owns restaurants and eats in them, but to attain Macklin's level of eccentricity he would have to serve in them as well; he is unlikely to, for he is not a wayward spirit. Macklin was slightly mad.

The coffee house failed when diners got fed up with listening to him lecture on Shakespeare from his corner pulpit, and he went bankrupt. It was at that point that he returned to the stage, where he remained on and off for another 15 years. We have seen elsewhere that his last performance, aged somewhere between 92 and 97, was pathetic because he could not remember what play he was in. After that he was a living legend, telling his favourite anecdotes to whomever would listen, always drinking, often wandering the streets, and regularly calling in at the theatre, where he was venerated. People always made room for him to reach his favourite seat, the centre of the last row next to the orchestra, and applauded him as he left to walk alone through Covent Garden to his lodgings in Tavistock Street, where he died in 1797. It is not certain whether he had been born in 1697 or 1700, but he was popularly thought to have reached 100 years. He is buried in St Paul's, Covent Garden.

If I have given Charles Macklin disproportionate space, it is because he typifies that eccentricity which occasionally spawns the actor. Dogmatic, conceited, narrow-minded he may have been, volcanic, peevish, rude, unsociable, and with language so robust that ladies blushed to hear, but he was a player of genius who had lasting influence on the theatre, an intuitive and infuriating firework of an actor.

Margaret Rutherford (1892-1972) affected to be surprised that she should be asked to play so many dotty old ladies: "The parts I had been given," she said, "had begun to show signs of the eccentricity that I later developed into my own special technique." [16] Outsiders would be forgiven for supposing that the eccentricity was innate and had only to be tapped. She looked and sounded entirely unlike anyone else one would ever have the chance to meet, and she was English, both in her art and her personality, to the core. A voice rounded and clipped, precise, pedantic, and at the same time conspiratorial, taking in breath between sentences like a vacuum cleaner as the eyes suggestively swivelled. She sounded as if she were giving elocution lessons (which indeed she had done before becoming an actress), and would be unutterably shocked by any oath. She had never been young. Her jowls were part of her studied absent-mindedness – she forgot they were there and did not know what to do with them, so they shook and shuddered without her behest. She was adorably shy and ridiculously prim, and her timing was impeccable. She may not have the most important part in any play, but when she was on stage it was impossible to look at anyone else. She enticed, captured, and befriended an audience. Small wonder that Marie Tempest was a bit put out.

Rutherford's finest roles were in comedy. They included Mrs Candour in *The School for Scandal*, Mrs Malaprop in *The Rivals*, Miss Prism in *The Importance of Being Earnest*, Lady Wishfort in *The Way of the World*, and Madame Desmortes in Anouilh's *Ring Round the Moon*. She was as adept with the bicycle as with the fan, which she proved with her best role, the medium Madame Arcati in Coward's *Blithe Spirit* (1941), which she played with 100 per cent conviction that the woman was not mad, but wise. The enthusiasm she injected into the lines, "It was wonderful cycling through the woods this evening; I was deafened with birdsong," exhilarated (there is no other word) every audience she brought under her charming attack. She appeared as Lady Wishfort in Gielgud's production at the Lyric, Hammersmith in 1953, and conquered critics and public alike. One said she gave an impression of "an old peeled wall", and another wrote, "she plays with enormous gusto in the grand manner, waving her jaw menacingly at her enemies and behaving like a splendidly padded windmill; very funny, and curiously touching." *Time* magazine said she was so British "that by comparison with her even John Bull seems the son of a miscegenetic marriage."

On the face of it, these are the notices of a superb and canny artist, using technique to parade her idiosyncrasies. Yet there was always some degree of fear behind the artistry, for Rutherford knew only too well that she was an eccentric woman, for whom acting was potentially a way of taming and controlling herself. In truth, she was terrified of going insane as her father had done, and would cry long into the night through worry over it. Through acting she harnessed and gripped what she thought was her incipient dementia, and turned it into a tool of gold.

Charles Laughton (1899-1962) was an unusual actor for different reasons. Sweaty, scruffy, with dirt under his fingernails and dandruff on his collar, Laughton was blessed (though he did not think so) with unconquerable ugliness; he once described himself as looking like a departing pachyderm. In consequence, he could not play the heroic parts (though he did attempt Lear at the end of his career, with little success), but was forced to discover the humanity in wicked or distorted characters. For a season, there was nobody to touch him in the subtlety of his creations on stage and on film; his biographer Simon Callow states that one could see the thoughts forming like clouds passing through his eyes. He was in appearance and demeanour the most unlikely actor (as Charles Macklin had been).

John Cleese, Stephen Fry, Kenneth Williams have all variously suggested that the self they call upon to act is a self unguarded and disarrayed, that might threaten to disintegrate if it were not for their profession. Acting as a means of integration or re-integration is, of course, the very source and purpose of the art – to impose truth and clarity upon the diffuse and uncertain – and so it should not surprise us if some actors talk of keeping madness at bay. Acting departs from the norm, it is out of the centre, therefore it is eccentric *per se*, and those actors who reveal their vulnerability from time to time show us the wounds and the terrors which other actors, more cunning in camouflage perhaps, manage to conceal. When John Cleese reflects upon the depression which occasionally looms before him, and Kenneth Williams upon the suicide which he yearned for year after year, they suddenly show, in vibrant, garish colour, the eccentricity or abnormality which must be the lot of all actors to some extent or other, if they are to impersonate with success. It does not take long to spot the eccentricity in Edmund Kean, for example; a little longer to find it, surely, in David Suchet; and virtually impossible to detect in John Gielgud. But it must be there in all three. When Stephen Fry disappeared from the cast of a West End play in 1996 after only five performances, and fled the country, and when Daniel Day-Lewis walked out of *Hamlet* after seeing the ghost of his father before his eyes, they did what most actors long to have the courage to do at some time in their careers – to turn their backs upon the demon which consumes them and save themselves for themselves. So often do they have to reject peace in favour of enlightenment, stability in favour of truth. They are the vessels for our anxieties; it is as well that some measure of eccentricity gives them the strength to carry that charge.

1 Ronald Harwood, *The Dresser* (1980), pp 76, 84

2 Horace Walpole, *Letters*, ed. Cunningham (1906), 25 December, 1782

3 *The Diary of Samuel Pepys*, ed. Latham and Matthews, Vol V, p 230, 24 January, 1669; Vol VIII, p 368, 30 July, 1667

4 Charles Greville, *The Greville Memoirs*, ed. Strachey and Fulford, (1938), Vol II, p 182

5 Richard Huggett, *The Truth About* Pygmalion, p 60

6 *The Everyman Book of Theatrical Anecdotes*, ed. Donald Sinden (1987), p 141

7 Ronald Harwood, *Sir Donald Wolfit* (1971), pp 163-169

8 Bryan Forbes, *That Despicable Race* (1980), p 269

9 James Agate, *Ego 5* (1935-48), p 80

10 John Gielgud, *Distinguished Company* (1972), p 139

11 Dawn Langley Simmons, *Margaret Rutherford* (1983), p 37

12 Ronald Harwood, *All the World's a Stage* (1984), p 241

13 Forbes, *op. cit.*, p 246

14 John Gross, *Shylock: 400 Years in the life of a Legend* (1992), p 98

15 William Appleton, *Charles Macklin; An Actor's Life* (1960), p 57

16 Simmons, *op. cit.*, p 30

6

The Stars

In 1822 the manager of Drury Lane Theatre engaged Charles Young, an actor with an established reputation second only to Kemble, and informed the leading man there, Edmund Kean, that they would be performing together in the same plays for a month. Kean was not at all pleased. "Now this I call exceeding imprudent," he wrote. "The throne is mine. I will maintain it…go where I will I shall always bear it with me – and even if I sail to another quarter of the globe, no man in this profession can rob me of the character of the first English Actor…if Mr Young is ambitious to act with me, he must commence with *Iago*, and when the whole of *my* characters is exhausted we may then turn our thoughts." [1]

Edmund Kean is not the kind of actor from whom we would expect signs of grandeur or status-hugging. Humble beginnings, long years of struggle, dedication to the part, offstage geniality, a man of the pub or the bar rather than the posh dinner-table, one might look for his echo in Albert Finney, Michael Gambon or Stephen Rea – not among the pomposities of self-celebrating stars. But here he is talking the language of sovereignty – he actually claims a throne – and warning that he will cede his kingdom to nobody. His letter makes it clear that he will counter any threat to topple him from his pre-eminent position. There is not an ounce of magnanimity in it, not even of curiosity. It is the letter of a monster; it is the letter of a "star". (Young did play Iago.) He was even jealous of his son Charles. "Mr Kean was always averse to his son's entering the theatrical profession," states a letter now at Chatsworth, "and with the littleness of mind too often connected with greatness of talent, he always said he was determined there never should be *two* great of the name of Kean." Accordingly, he treated his son Charles with cruel severity. "He hated him also for his very virtues, for he must have felt that his son's honourable and irreproachable conduct was a silent reproach and satire on his own depraved and vicious existence." In his will, Edmund Kean left everything to his mother and secretary (Mrs Carey and Mr Ley), omitting all mention of Charles Kean, who had nursed him selflessly in the last weeks following his collapse on stage. [2]

Kean was not the first star, but he does represent the excesses to which a system of outrageous fame in the theatre might lead. Other actors were famous before him. Betterton and his wife were universally admired and liked, and they certainly drew people to the play. Garrick was treated with honour, and when Jean-Jacques Rousseau came to London and saw him perform, crowds gathered to catch a glimpse of him. [3] People queued outside the theatre all night to be sure of tickets to see Sarah Siddons, much as they might today for a show by Michael Jackson. But Kean was the first to let it all go to his head. Garrick had been guilty of a certain vanity, which his friend Dr Johnson forgave him as all London was singing his praises, but that is of a different order. The colossal self-importance of Kean was the result of a collision in his day of two influences: in the first place, the English had always gone to the theatre as much to see actors as the plays, as they still do, and thereby encouraged a sense of competitiveness amongst players, like chasers after a trophy which only one of them can win. When London boasted two principal theatres, it was not unusual for both of them to put on the same play on the same night, so that their leading actors could be seen as it were in gladiatorial contest. This is reflected in our day by the annual BAFTA or Laurence Olivier awards, whereby Emma Thompson, say, is deemed to be "better" than Maggie Smith, even when the comparison has no substance and the parts no similarity, or the Oscars in Hollywood, where stardom has frequently overtaken acting as the point of the endeavour.

The second influence which led to the star system was economic or commercial. As theatre managers fought to fill their house ("put bums on seats" is the modern phrasing) against competition not only from other theatres but against changes in social mores (the advancement of dinner time into the evening, for example), they would import a "star" actor for a fixed period as special attraction, like a special purchase at the supermarket, who would perform with people he had not met and without rehearsal of any kind. As we saw in the last chapter, this habit survived until very recently with the run of actor-managers who finally bowed out with Donald Wolfit. Some recent instances of "star" performances were Dustin Hoffman in *The Merchant of Venice*, Charlton Heston in *The Caine Mutiny*, and Jessica Lange in *A Streetcar Named*

Desire (but they all rehearsed!). Gradually, in the nineteenth century, the star became the resident magnet instead of the guest dropped in for extra gravitational pull, so that Henry Irving could be the star of his own theatre for 20 years and Laurence Olivier of his for another 20. Tommy Steele, the excellence of whose acting has too often been dazzled into obscurity by the effervescence of his personality, is a star who controls every aspect of a production in which he appears – from casting to scenery to advertising.

Thus from Kean onwards the Great Actor became a Huge Celebrity as well, treated with awe not only because he or she placed the audience in touch with mysterious forces, revealed the essence of theatrical experience, was the channel for knowledge and feelings ascertainable in no other way, all of which is in the proper tradition of the actor's role in society, but also and even primarily because he or she was famous. There had been some of this even before Kean, not in Shakespeare's day perhaps but certainly in the Restoration theatre, when gossip about which actress was being bedded by which aristocrat, who was seen where with whom and what costumes were the rage of this or that year supplanted in some minds any concern with the merit of the performances on offer. By the late eighteenth-century the only consideration was to have opinions on the theatre which were in fashion (as they then said, which were the *ton*). It was after Kean that fame became for some an end in itself. One might say he began a process which would lead inexorably to John Wayne, Mae West and others.

When an actor becomes a star, publicity takes the place of subjective reflection as his nourishment. In the nineteenth century many were the critics who already saw the dangers which loomed ahead. "An actor," wrote Hazlitt, "after having performed his part well, instead of courting farther distinction, should affect obscurity…conscious of admiration that he can support nowhere but in his proper sphere, and jealous of his own and others' good opinion of him, in proportion as he is a darling in the public eye." Above all, he should tell us nothing whatever about his private self: "Spare me this insight into secrets I am not bound to know." [4] Charles Lamb was in agreement, and lamented the habit of being more interested in Mrs Siddons than in Lady Macbeth. What on earth would these gentlemen make of today's obsessions with the colour of an actor's socks and the fibre content of his breakfast diet, the holidays, his children, his curtains, and the weekly revelations of *Hello* magazine? They would despair, were it not for the precious few who steer clear of the circus and hold on to their art as being the only aspect of their existence worthy of scrutiny. It is a wonderful paradox that Alec Guinness was one of the most famous actors in the world, adored by millions of youngsters as well as admired by seasoned theatregoers, and yet few would have been able to recognise him in the street or been able to tell you anything whatever about him. According to Hazlitt, that is as it should be, and it would be difficult to argue the contrary. Despite immediate appearances, Guinness was never a star. He was always an actor. I fancy Michael Gambon will never be a star either; Jack Nicholson will never be anything else.

Of course, it is possible to be both actor and star. In previous chapters we have examined what might be the constituent elements which go to make a great actor, and how these ingredients might be tempered or flavoured by experience and intuition. In every respect but one, quite different qualities are required to make a star. The one quality which both great actors and stars cannot do without is that indefinable, enigmatic ability to demand attention and hold it. I said earlier it was the actor's capacity to hypnotise an audience, to hold spectators in thrall, to dominate and subdue, to conquer and hold captive. The star must do this as well, and he can only do it by the exercise of his unique personality upon a whole group of people accidentally assembled and clotted, by him, into one responding heart. "Personality," wrote W A Darlington, "is the faculty of attracting public attention; and of all faculties it is the least predictable and the least explicable." [5] If you lack it, you may be a competent (but not a great) actor; you will have not the smallest hope of being a star.

It is also true that a film star can be a very impressive actor indeed, mastering an entirely different set of techniques. But the transition from stage to screen requires such a mighty adjustment that few have managed it with total success.

The other requisite qualities for stardom are many and various, and have little or nothing to do with acting. They may include unusual beauty of face or body; the knack of improvisation; bad temper and jealous rages; a thirst for fame, even for notoriety; quick wit and amusing conversation; a gift for foul language rapturously indulged; the ability to recognise good fortune and embrace it (sometimes wrongly called "luck"); and ultimately the grace of being oneself and turning one's own habits and manners into the tools of being convincing on stage.

19. Simon Russell Beale as Iago, Royal National Theatre, 1997.

20. Antony Sher as Richard III, Royal Shakespeare Theatre, 1984.

21. Ralph Fiennes as Troilus, Royal Shakespeare Theatre, 1990.

22. David Suchet as Shylock, Royal Shakespeare Theatre, 1981.

23. Derek Jacobi as Prospero, Royal Shakespeare Theatre, 1982.

24. Michael Sheen as Jimmy Porter in *Look Back in Anger*, Royal National Theatre, 1999.

25. Judi Dench and Michael Williams.

26. Peggy Ashcroft as Winnie in *Happy Days*, Old Vic, 1975.

Let us take each of these elements in turn and see how they might apply, then collect some obviously big stars, from past and present, and see which of these qualities might explain their stardom.

Female beauty is a strain which passes directly from the first days that women were allowed to appear on stage, after the Restoration of 1660, to the present day. There is little to indicate how good an actress was Nell Gwyn, although Pepys seems to have found her fetchingly funny, but there is plenty of evidence which attests to her luscious beauty. Not only do we have portraits by Lely and Verelst which leave no room to doubt the full softness of her breasts; we also have dozens of instances of her having driven men wild with lust, from King Charles himself to her fellow actor Charles Hart. History has forgotten her acting to such an extent that she is identified to schoolchildren as an orange-girl, selling oranges to the audience during the interval, which was what she did before she graduated to the stage and to the royal bedchamber. History can never forget, however, that Nell was the great star of the mid-1660s. Madame de Sévigné described her as "young, indiscreet, confident, wild, and of an agreeable humour", and queening it over Louise de Kérouaille, the Duchess of Portsmouth, whose position as official royal mistress (*maîtresse en titre*) she undermined with conspicuous delight. Nell was also one of the first to play "breeches parts" on stage. These were specially written to take advantage of the novelty of having women take female parts, by making them take male parts as well and dress in male attire, quite blatantly in order to show the shape of their legs and excite the men in the audience. Pepys was quite candid about his response: "So great a performance of a comical part was never, I believe, in the world before as Nell doth this, both as a mad girle and then, most and best of all, when she comes in as a young gallant; and have the notions and carriage of a spark the most that ever I saw any man have." [6]

Amongst the next generation of actresses Anne Bracegirdle (1663-1748) was accounted the most beautiful. Unlike Nell, however, she was also the most virtuous. When Colley Cibber wrote that "scarce an audience saw her that were not less than half of them lovers," we are not meant to understand that she was mistress to half the town, but that half the town adored her. Every man wanted to protect her, or at the very least to offer her protection, yet she remained agreeably and beguilingly aloof, smiling with a perfect set of teeth, transfixing with sparkling dark eyes, seducing her audiences at a distance. Not only that, but she was in addition one of the finest actresses of her time, especially in the plays of Congreve and Vanbrugh. She was Angelica in the original cast of *Love for Love* at Lincoln's Inn Fields in 1695, and so much did Congreve appear to capture and display her charm in those parts he wrote specifically for her that it was thought by contemporaries that they must be married.

Mrs Bracegirdle (the "Mrs" was theatrical convention) was more or less brought up in the theatre. Born in the Midlands, possibly Northampton, she was fostered by Thomas Betterton and his wife Mary Saunderson – the original happy theatrical couple who were much admired for their fidelity towards each other and their kindness to others – and played her first part on stage at the age of five. She conquered most of the roles available to her by the time she was 20 and stayed at her peak for more than a decade, until that wretched competitiveness which spoils so much of theatrical history intervened to derail her. Her rival in 1706 was the up-and-coming Mrs Oldfield, whom half of London adjudged to have eclipsed Mrs Bracegridle, while the other half hurried to her defence. Consequently, they each played the same part on two consecutive nights to resolve the issue, and Mrs Oldfield was proclaimed the winner. Mrs Bracegirdle retired from the stage that very night. She came out of retirement only once, to appear in the gala performance of *Love for Love* at Betterton's benefit in 1709, and died 40 years later, having survived well into the age of Garrick.

She has since suffered from detractors who could not abide that she be so beautiful and so chaste, and therefore denied she was one or the other; we find the same phenomenon today when confronted by actresses whose unapproachable beauty stands as an enticement. It was said she was cold and vain, that she enjoyed flirting with men and watching them suffer "in the just confidence that no flame which she might kindle in them would thaw her own ice." When her fellow-actor William Mountfort stepped in to defend her against the rogues Captain Hill and Lord Mohun, who wanted to ravish her, he was killed by Hill's sword. It is difficult to believe that this was her own fault.

Anne Bracegirdle was so popular with the people, most of whom had never seen her perform, that she would be applauded in the street and a path made through the crowds for her. It was her kindness which accounted for this acclaim, as she gave much of her money to relieve the unemployed; it was said that had anyone dared deride her in public, he would have been set upon and torn limb from limb.

Is it fanciful to see in this combination of talent, comedy timing, sense of fun, kindness, goodness, vulnerability, lostness, beauty and aloofness, the rare intangible charms of, say, Marilyn Monroe?

Mrs Bracegirdle was an old woman by the time Peg Woffington (1714-1760) came upon the scene, and she may have allowed herself a rueful smile at that lady's reputation. For she, too, was famous for her beauty, and of her, too, it was said that half the audience was in love. She also had early and unorthodox training as part of a one-woman circus act in Dublin, wherein the performer walked across the stage on a tightrope with a basket suspended from each foot, and in each basket was a baby; Peg was one of these babies. Similarities with Mrs Bracegirdle went no further, for Peg was not aloof. She specialised for a time in breeches parts, being particularly famous for her portrayal of Sir Harry Wildair in Farquhar's *The Constant Couple*, which was her début role in London and one she made so much her own that no male actor was cast in it during her lifetime. "She carried the town captive." [7] In a delicious theatrical story which has survived two and a half centuries and appears to have resisted any attempt at embellishment, Peg Woffington boasted that half the audience had taken her for a man, to which James Quin (a famous wit as well as actor) replied that the other half had good reason to know that she was a woman. [8] As we have already noted, she lived for a brief while in a *ménage à trois* with Garrick and the irascible Charles Macklin, when she was Garrick's unconcealed mistress (a few years before his very respectable and enduring marriage), and her portrait is still the one which most Garrick Club members seem strangely to know better than the others.

She suffered the consequences of the competitive spirit more dramatically than most. Not only did Mrs Pritchard and Mrs Clive consider themselves her rivals, and had their own supporters to bruit their claims, but Mrs Bellamy positively hated her; during one performance in which they appeared together Mrs Bellamy flung herself upon Peg with dagger drawn and stabbed her, driving her off the stage.

She had her temper, and it was the perception of this which eventually dissuaded Garrick from marriage, although he had apparently already bought a ring. Yet she was good-hearted, and it was her gift which endowed the almshouses at Teddington. An irrelevant footnote is added by Mrs Woffington's kindness to the unknown and wretchedly poor Gunning sisters, Elizabeth and Maria. Like her, they were Irish, and had once been driven to handing their furniture out of the window to escape the bailiffs. But they were astonishingly beautiful. Soon after they came to London they had made such a stir that people used to line the streets in the hope of seeing them, and Walpole several times in his letters explodes with ecstasy in contemplation of their beauty. The lovely clothes they wore to make their conquests were all borrowed from Peg Woffington, who had offered them. Thus she has a tiny bearing on subsequent aristocratic history, for Maria Gunning became Countess of Coventry, and Elizabeth Gunning was Duchess of Hamilton first, Duchess of Argyll later, and could have been Duchess of Bridgewater too. All four of her sons were to become dukes. The Duke of Hamilton was so eager for her, and so frustrated by her refusal to give herself before marriage, that he got a clergyman up after midnight and married her within the hour, using a curtain-ring. Presumably they were in bed by two o'clock. [9]

Peg Woffington's last role was Rosalind in *As You Like It*. In 1757 she was speaking the epilogue when she was suddenly stricken with paralysis and had to be carried off stage. She never appeared again, and died three years later.

In the next century it was Mrs Jordan who tantalised with her beauty and vivacity on stage, while being quietly demure offstage. She was a fine comedienne as well, and her audiences well knew (though nobody said) that she was the mother of all the Duke of Cumberland's children, which made her slightly royal and wholly unattainable. A measure of her effect might be gained from the effusive stammerings of the normally straightlaced Leigh Hunt, who for once dropped his guard and his critical stare to give vent to his enthusiasm. "To see her," he wrote, "shed blubbering tears for some disappointment, and eat all the while a great thick slice of bread and butter, weeping, and moaning, and munching, and eyeing at every bite the part she meant to bite next...the way in which she would take a friend by the cheek and kiss her, or make up a quarrel with a lover, or coax a guardian into good-humour ...the reader will pardon me, but tears of pleasure and regret come into my eyes at the recollection, as if she personified whatsoever was happy at that period of life, and which has gone like herself. The very sound of the little familiar word *bud* from her lips [the abbreviation for husband], as she packed it closer, as it were, in the utterance, and pouted it up with fondness in the man's face, taking him at the same time by the chin, was a whole concentrated world of the power of loving." [10]

When a seasoned critic writes like that, you can be sure he is writing about a star and not only about an actress. Stars tend to elicit fond language, for they appeal to something within us which is beyond the power of regulated language to express. They touch us with glamour, excite us with unknowable emotion, give us life and youth and vigour and abandon, and reduce us to child-talk. All this is tangential to their being actors as well – it is an additional layer of skin. And it is, alas, possible to be a star without being a noticeably good actor at all, especially if the ingredient which lifts you to stardom is that of ineffable, transcendent beauty. We come back to Marilyn Monroe. She never appeared on stage. Some who acted with her in films protest that she was unutterably awful, like a stooge who had to have her arms, eyes, lips put in place by somebody else. On the other hand, critics have melted into marshmallow before her and acclaimed her the great comic actress of her generation. She could not be ignored, and still cannot. She was unquestionably a star.

I met her once, when she came to London to film *The Prince and the Showgirl* with Laurence Olivier. My father, who worked in the laundry department at the Savoy Hotel, smuggled me in against all the rules and his own sane judgement, and I lay in wait to be drenched by her. I was not to be disappointed. Her hips and bust may have been too big, her gaze a trifle too vacant, but there was about her a sense of bafflement at her own fame, at her place in the world, at the mutterings and flatterings which surrounded her, which made one want, above all else in the world, to rescue her. She spoke to me. It was nothing much. A pouting, big-eyed request for directions to the nearest drugstore. I told her it was called a chemist's in England, and she giggled, as if that was the way to respond when you did not know what somebody was talking about. I think I offered to escort her, because she obviously wanted to step outside and in those days it would have been possible without being gobbled up by photographers. But her "minder" must have forbidden it. I dare say he was right; I was only 14.

I allow this personal digression because there was no doubt in my mind, then or since, that I was in the presence of a star. It *feels* different from talking to an actress. The heart beats faster, the pores open wider, the hand trembles; Leigh Hunt, I think I understood you then. And to those who insist that Monroe was a mere manufactured icon who has no place in a book about acting, I can only say that of all the comedy performances I have seen on screen in over 50 years, the one that

I never tire of watching again and again is Monroe in *Some Like it Hot*. For good measure one may add *The Seven-Year Itch*, and for a touch of soul and sadness *The Misfits*. I am bound to admit, however, that she could probably never have sustained a part on stage.

Although she was a contemporary, Monroe seems now to be so long ago as to be almost historical. Actresses since her time, including film actresses, have flinched at openly harnessing beauty as their route to stardom, even when they have been beautiful. It is perhaps a more serious age we live in. Actresses would rather "star", if "star" they must, for inherent ability, not for evanescent gloss. Hence Kate Beckinsale, an actress of the new generation blessed with translucent beauty, seeks hard to find roles which disregard that beauty. She is already a fine actress. With experience, she might one day be a great actress (Mrs Siddons, remember, started off without making much noise at all). And with care, she will not be a star if she can help it.

If beauty cannot help you to stardom, then tantrums might. The history of the stage is cluttered with the names of women variously known to their contemporaries as "terrors", "prima donnas" or by less polite titles, who have felt themselves bound to behave with the grandeur and pomposity which befitted their exalted station. The species did not evolve until the nineteenth century, naturally, because in earlier times no actress would have dared give herself such airs, and it has spawned some truly awesome grotesques in the twentieth, when publicity is geared to encourage them. The first actress to be created Dame of the British Empire was Genevieve Ward (1838-1922), who forthwith objected to sharing her dressing room with any untitled player. Greta Garbo, said to be neurotically jealous of her privacy, was perhaps in fact too big for her boots. She was thought not to have a cheque book because she would not sign her name, and her autograph is the rarest among film stars; it has always been assumed that she signed nothing for the last 50 years of her life. Not so; in Noël Coward's visitors' book there is a bold and confident signature, in thick black ink, written obviously with her own distinguishing pen because it is more conspicuous than any other signature written that day, and emphatically not the mark of a neurotic, shy, timid, frightened, hesitant woman. It is the signature of a woman determined to hug her stardom.

Some actresses have grown noticeably in grandeur in direct proportion to their decline in critical appreciation, as if stardom were at least a consolation prize not to be relinquished without a fight. One who only seemed to be grand, partly because in old age she played roles which demanded grandeur, was Edith Evans, in reality a sweet and unassuming lady who valued her technique more than her name. (There is a story that she excused herself from a dress rehearsal on the grounds that she was ill and had been suffering from diarrhoea, but quickly recovered when told that another actress had learnt the part and was willing to take it over; "Lead me to the lavatory," she intoned.)

Perhaps the one actress who consciously fashioned a style of imperiousness, and almost made it her purpose for living, was Marie Tempest (1864-1942), whom we already met once summoning the young Margaret Rutherford into her presence to chastise her for acting too well and to warn her not to forget her place in the hierarchy. She dressed like royalty, with long white gloves, a cloak, a veil, and what Noël Coward called one of her "crisp little hats", although John Gielgud remarked that one of them looked like an entire pheasant. Once dressed for her role, she never sat down in her dressing room, but stood on a white drugget to maintain the freshness of her costume; walking from dressing room to stage, she covered her shoulders with a white cloak. She expected deference as her right. She would not have flinched had one bowed and curtseyed at her approach. She gave orders, required favours, commanded people to attend her and listen to her advice upon life and the acting profession. The paradox was that Marie Tempest never appeared in any great role or even in any great play; her repertoire was froth and frivolity, and her august manner seemed to make up for the vacuousness of her parts. It was as if, secretly, she knew that she had to be a star to make up for not being an actress at all. Those who saw her create the role of Judith Bliss in Coward's *Hay Fever* (1925), however, maintain that she there demonstrated what a consummate and clever artist she really was. The rest of the time she was busy building an image; she would have had some very useful tips for today's armies of PR men and publicity manipulators – she did it all herself. [11]

One of her tricks was to engineer her own applause by clapping her hands in the wings immediately after coming offstage, at which the audience, thinking the noise had come from somewhere within their ranks, would follow enthusiastically. At the curtain call, she would first share with her fellow actors, then as the applause died down, her maid would throw her pet dog, a little white Sealyham, on to the stage. Marie affected to be embarrassed and tried to shoo him off, making all signs of confusion and wonderment at how on earth he had found his way, then picked the poor quivering thing up and hugged it. The audience accorded her two more curtain calls all to herself. [12]

Donald Wolfit used another method. When the curtain was down, he would stride along behind it and thump it vigorously. "Let 'em know you're coming," he said.

Stardom brings its own perils, if only because it has to be kept up and nurtured. Few sights are more pitiful than the eclipse of a star sadly seeking still to glitter in the gloom – there have been film stars eventually driven to serving behind the counter in Woolworth's and stage actresses being grand in Glasgow rather than accept a small role in the West End. The pressures are intense and constant. We have seen how competitiveness amongst actors, egged on by unscrupulous audiences, led to rival camps being formed to support Mrs Woffington against Mrs Bellamy, or Quin against Garrick, or most notoriously of all, Kean against Junius Brutus Booth in 1817. Kean accepted the challenge to play Iago to Booth's Othello, and so wiped the stage with him that Kean's stardom was assured and Booth's crushed at birth. Booth fled to America, where he pursued his craft unhindered; one of his sons, Edwin Booth, grew into the greatest of all American Hamlets, while another assassinated President Lincoln at the theatre. The rivalry between admirers of Macready and those of the American Edwin Forrest (1806-1872) actually led to riots outside the theatre in New York, in which 22 people were killed and a further 36 injured.

In the twentieth century we have been more decorous; rivalries between Olivier and Gielgud or Sybil Thorndike and Edith Evans were conducted in a friendly manner and with mutual respect, and it would be unthinkable for Maggie Smith, Diana Rigg and Judi Dench to squabble over precedence or status. For the merits to be derived from stardom are not equal to the miseries it can bring, leading to despair and, in a few cases, suicide. Take the case of Adolphe Nourritt, a singer rather than an actor, but a stage performer nonetheless and subject to the same pressures. For 16 years he was chief tenor at the Paris Opera. There arose a new sensation, a young man called Duprez, who threatened his supremacy. One day Nourritt was told that Duprez was out front, in the audience, and the shock paralysed him to such an extent that he lost his voice. He never again appeared in Paris, or in France. He left for Italy, where he had some success, but his confidence in his own stardom had been shattered, and he became more and more dejected. He imagined that the applause which followed his performances was ironical, that the audience were in truth mocking his descent from the pinnacle, having fun at his expense. In Naples at five o'clock in the morning on 8 March, 1839, Adolphe Nourritt hurled himself from the top floor of a building to death in the street below. [13]

It was also stardom, not acting ability, which was responsible for Edward Kynaston's thrashing at the hands of Sir Charles Sedley's thugs. Sedley (1639-1701) was both the most celebrated playwright of his day, and the most notorious libertine. His plays have long since been forgotten, and only a dim echo of his philandering survives. Kynaston was strolling in St James's Park in the clothes he had worn on stage when he was widely suspected of having attempted a sardonic impersonation of Sedley – such a theatrical trick was not at all unusual in the seventeenth century. Sedley gave orders to his men to turn the joke on Kynaston by pretending to believe he *was* Sedley and set upon him for insults they had received at Sedley's hands. Kynaston did not recover from the beating for over a week. [14]

"Ned" Kynaston (1640-1706) had been a star all his life. As the last man of note to play female parts, he had also been the most remarkable to look at, so that one may say, despite his sex, that it was beauty which brought him stardom just as it had for Nell Gwyn and Marilyn Monroe. He played male roles as well, and was said to be both the handsomest man on stage, and the prettiest woman. Charles II was irritated one evening by a late start to the performance, until it was pointed out to him that the Queen was being shaved. Ladies of fashion took turns to invite young Kynaston to be their passenger in drives around Hyde Park, wearing theatrical costume, and he was quite a draw, much as, say, Elizabeth Hurley might be today. What saved Kynaston from mere stardom was his talent; he survived his youthful promise and grew into a mature actor of compelling voice and authority.

Stars are much assisted by publicity. We saw at the beginning that they impose their personalities, like irresistible magnets pulling admiration to their bosom, and whether they do so during performance or in private afterwards, they need to have stories told about them for stardom to be bestowed. There are relatively few people in an audience, even fewer at a dinner party; stardom does not relish small numbers. An actor or actress might encourage people to think them witty, or relaxed, or hopelessly prone to malapropisms, and trust the reputation will spread. Gielgud, who was far too great an actor to need stardom, nevertheless got it partly because of the famous bricks he dropped every time he opened his mouth, confusing people, places and events, embarrassing himself and everyone around him; nobody minded, for it was obviously artless and not a stab for attention. Mrs Patrick Campbell (to whom we shall shortly return) retained her fame for witticisms long after she retired from the stage (the one which has spread farthest is her remark that she did not mind what homosexuals did to one another as long as they did not do it in the street and frighten the horses), and stardom clung to her because of them. So did it to Tallulah Bankhead (whose very name sounded like a piece of wit), to Coral Browne, to Lilian Braithwaite, the original Florence Lancaster in Coward's revolutionary *The Vortex* (1924); and so does it now to Maggie Smith, which in her case is a pity, for she is too fine an actress to allow her sense of humour to replace her talents in the public mind, as her famously odd, nasal, variable, sardonic and saucy voice already has.

Maggie Smith has achieved stardom for quite a separate reason, at least within theatrical circles, and that is her extraordinary ability to pick up a part and know it immediately. It is a knack which some actors, even the greatest, never acquire, while others depend upon it. At the first night of Richard Brinsley Sheridan's last play *Pizarro* in 1799, we are told that the stars, Charles Kemble and Sarah Siddons, were on stage performing Act IV while Sheridan was upstairs in the prompter's room furiously writing Act V. It was not until the interval, therefore, that they knew what they had to say, but their confidence and experience made up for small inaccuracies in delivery. One does not suggest this is a matter of photographic memory – rather is it extemporising on the bedrock of intimate knowledge. They all knew the sort of lines Sheridan was *likely* to write, and so needed the barest hint of what they in fact were. In the same way, all Alan Ayckbourn's regular company of actors in Scarborough know what is *likely* to come next, because they are so well acquainted with his tone, pace and style. Maggie Smith has the quality innately. I suppose it amounts to experienced ad-libbing, the sort of talent which enabled actors to survive a Morecambe and Wise show on television.

Yet another route to stardom is, dismally but very amusingly, through foul language. The last four centuries have not been without a generation which has its oath-spluttering actors, from Quin to Tree, Kean to Wolfit, and it appears almost obligatory for a male star to compete with merchant seamen or East End barrow-boys in the obscenity of their epithets. In the mouth of an actor, however, the oath is more of a challenge than a badge; barrow-boys might swear because the words have infiltrated their daily talk to such an extent that they lose all their strength and power to shock, but the actor will give the word its full glorious punch, relish its alliterative potential, choose its position in the phrase with a care to surprise. The cursing, blasphemous actor reminds you that words are his tools, his servants and his friends; by luck or design, he will likely have somebody to record his use of the word for posterity. Thus do anecdotes prosper.

There are dozens upon dozens of them, all amusing, nearly all true, and all subtly measuring the status of the star to whom they belong. Somehow, if you cannot give the oath its full blast, you are lacking in the bigness which makes a star. An oath cannot be half-hearted or under-rehearsed. One story will have to stand in for all the rest. It concerns Fred Terry, brother to Marion Terry and Ellen Terry, great-uncle to John Gielgud, and the original Sir Percy Blakeney in *The Scarlet Pimpernel*. Wolfit acknowledged that he learnt much from Fred Terry. An actor in the grand manner, he could press an audience to utter silence by lowering his voice an octave, was sentimental, in love with the theatre, impressive and endearing. Fred was a great clubman. On one occasion at the Green Room Club, it was reported to Fred that a young actor was using particularly sulphurous language and should be reprimanded. Fred sent for him and issued the desired reproof. The young man was a little surprised to be spoken to severely. "I seem to remember, Sir," he said, "that I have sometimes heard you use fairly strong language in the club yourself." At this Fred exploded. "God all-bloody-mighty," he said, "I'm the fucking President." [15]

An actor might become a star because he brings something new and exciting to the theatre, which need not be related to his talent at all. This it happened in 1804 when William Betty (1791-1874) burst upon the scene and monopolised attention in the capital for months. The son of an Irish linen bleacher, he was variously known as Master Betty, Young Roscius, or simply The Boy, and he played Hamlet and Romeo to packed houses at both Drury Lane and Covent Garden, earning receipts for the management in excess of £40,000. The most remarkable thing about him was that he was only 13 years old. People changed the hour of dinner so that Master Betty should not be missed, and on one occasion Pitt moved that the House of Commons should adjourn in order that MPs could attend a performance of The Boy as Hamlet.

Offstage Master Betty was like any other 13-year-old, boisterous, mischievous, fairly mindless. Though he might not be pretentious, his admirers certainly were, and he was mobbed wherever he went. His hotel was besieged by crowds. On one occasion when he was staying at a country inn in Warwickshire, the leading hostess of the county went to the manager and begged to be given a sight of the wonderful child. She pleaded and cajoled, said she would do "anything". The manager told her the only way was to spot him dining with his parents, and so the grand county lady dressed up as a waitress and served him at table. [16]

The letters of Lady Elizabeth Foster convey the sense of enthusiasm which greeted this phenomenon. To her son Augustus she wrote often on the subject. "Nothing hardly is seen or talked about but this young Roscius," she said, telling him that Sheridan had introduced the child to the Prince of Wales at Carlton House, where he had acquitted himself with the confidence of an adult. "His is the inspiration of genius, with the correctness of taste belonging generally to experience and study alone, feeling far beyond his years, and a knowledge of the stage equal to any performer, and far more graceful; in short, he has changed the life of London; people dine at four, and go to the Play, and think of nothing but the Play...the Hawkesburys stay in town for this boy's acting all next week...as to the applause, the Pit, which is filled with men, not content with applauding, over and over again cry out Bravo! Bravo! I don't suppose such applause could ever be exceeded."

Lady Elizabeth (who was, by the way, mistress to the Fifth Duke of Devonshire and best friends with the Duchess – she would succeed her as Duchess of Devonshire herself one day) related how moved and "worked up" Master Betty had been when rehearsing Hamlet; he had fainted in the arms of the prompter at the speech, "On him! On him! Look how pale he glares!" This showed how extraordinary he was, she thought. Caroline Wortley agreed, saying it was the finest piece of acting she could ever conceive. The laconic Duke was induced to attend, and he too thought it was "deuced good". [17]

Not everybody was of like opinion, however. Lord Aberdeen thought he was the greatest imposter since the days of Mohammed, and others said he was a clever mimic who could respond to direction. It was pointed out that he studied Hamlet for only three days before presuming to act the part, whereas the great Betterton had said that after 50 years of study and playing he had not even fathomed the profoundest depths of its philosophy. [18] Perhaps Mrs Siddons hit the nail on the head. Refusing to act with him, she said he was "a clever, pretty boy, but nothing more". His novelty was his pubescent blush. It was significant that the not otherwise naive Elizabeth Foster noticed how the Pit was packed with men, but did not wonder why.

William Betty did not endure beyond the one season. When his voice broke he became banal, his limitations evident. His attempt to play Richard III was hissed off the stage. He went to Cambridge, and afterwards attempted to resume his theatrical career, but he was not even mediocre. He retired at 19, his father squandered his money, and he was ignored for the rest of his unremarkable life. When he died at the age of 83 nobody had the smallest idea of what he had been in his youth. There are splendid portraits to remind us, including one very large one at the Garrick Club. What they tell us is that it has been possible to become an absolutely overwhelming star (Master Betty overshadowed Siddons and Kemble for a while), without really being an actor at all. This is still true, of course. On stage it would be hard to find anything today which approached the phenomenon of Master Betty, although there are the occasional oddities which enjoy brief attention by virtue of their unlikely flavour: Elizabeth Taylor in *Little Foxes* in 1982 for instance, or the pop singer and television performer Jason Donovan as the young psychopath Danny in Emlyn Williams' *Night Must Fall* in 1996.

There is yet another category which is rather more elusive of explanation. These are the stars who do not try to be actors, yet succeed magnificently in acting themselves in each part they take on, with triumphant and perfectly satisfying success. In a sense, they show the value of personality, with which we started this discussion, better than any other, for personality is all they have, and personality is what they have striven so well to promote in place of acting. The prime example is Gerald du Maurier (1871-1934), whom we met in the last chapter as an eccentric for the paradoxical quality of being so normal. He deserves another look.

Son of the novelist George du Maurier and father of the even better-known novelist Daphne du Maurier, Gerald perfected the stage technique of making his entrance look natural, as if the audience were not there and he was in his own home. He strolled on, walked about, smoked his pipe, held conversations with other people on stage, and strolled off again. This could not have been achieved in the classics of the dramatic repertoire, so Gerald du Maurier limited himself to lightweight comedies, in which he excelled, not because nobody was better, but because nobody else was Gerald du Maurier. He was the part in every play, the relaxed demeanour, the easy repartee, the graceful English gentleman in epitome. He took over the genre and made it his own garden, so that everyone else in light comedy was measured against him. It was not so much a question of acting, as of *being* convincingly, or *behaving* in a familiar way. Modern film stars have had to cultivate this knack, because nobody *expects* them to be actors; the prime example is John Wayne, who was as perfect an American gum-chewing haystack philosopher as du Maurier was the stylish English gentleman. This is not to say those who are primarily actors on screen cannot become stars – one only has to think of Meryl Streep, Gena Rowlands, James Dean, Julie Harris, Diane Keaton, and Elizabeth Taylor.

And what is one to make of Gertrude Lawrence (1898-1952), who fits none of these categories, defies them all, dances and skips her way around them, and yet was a greater star than any of those so far mentioned? She was certainly the most lavishly lovable and intoxicating person I ever saw on stage, even though I only caught her at the end of her career in Rodgers and Hammerstein's *The King and I*. It is easier to define Gertrude Lawrence by her negatives. She was not beautiful, with a plain face on which her nose appended awkwardly and her mouth was too small and too tight. She was not a great actress; she started as a dancer, graduated to revue, and excelled in the flimsiest of comedies – tragedy or anything profound and demanding she never once attempted. Her most famous creation was Amanda in Noël Coward's *Private Lives* (1930), in which she perfected the du Maurier trick of playing herself, a task made even easier by the fact that Coward had written it for her. But it was then that the essence of her "stardom" was uncovered by the critic James Agate, who noticed that the plain and ordinary face was a vehicle for infinite variation: "the words may be uttered in the same tone, but there is that in the face which tells you whether we are listening to trumpet truth, the full-blown lie, or the artfulness of feminine compromise. This artist is superb throughout, physically as well as mentally; there is humour in the ripple of her shoulders, fun in her head's poise, and even her elbows are witty." [19]

I think we may say that Gertrude Lawrence made Agate feel very happy that night. That is another of the unteachable gifts the star may bestow.

Coward always said her instinct was impeccable, and that she should be thrown on stage after the first reading, because she understood the part immediately. She was mischievous, "camp" in the theatrical sense, funny and endearing, wild and ridiculous – she once toured Devonshire with Fay Compton riding bicycles, and a Rolls-Royce followed them a long way behind in case they felt tired. It was fitting that this most surprising person should triumph finally in a musical, for she could not sing either, but she contrived to conquer even that shortcoming. In *The King and I,* her voice wobbled, the high notes eluded her, some of the others slipped past alarmingly in a different key, but she was magnificent and lovable. When she died suddenly during the run, at the very peak of her career, the shock felt on both sides of the Atlantic was so great that all the lights of all the theatres on both Broadway and in the West End of London were turned off. Not since the cab-drivers had placed black ribbons on their whips at the news of Irving's death had such tribute been paid. That could only happen to a star.

Forgetting film stars for a moment, if there is one characteristic the stars of the stage all have in common, whether they owe their pre-eminence to beauty, luck, wit, anecdotal panache, publicity, novelty, or the knack of being themselves, it is a glue-like devotion to the stage which is touching, almost childish, in its dependence. Without the spotlights, they would fuss and flounder, sink into the general soup of mankind from which they have hauled themselves and a return to which they would do anything on earth to avoid. Master Betty's long obscurity must have been ghastly for him. Sarah Bernhardt, a great actress as well as a star, told the Duchess of Teck (Queen Mary's mother), *"Altesse Royale, je mourrai en scène – c'est mon champ de bataille."* ("Your Royal Highness, I shall die on stage – it is my battlefield.")

Garrick, Kean, Irving, Terry, Siddons, their names have occurred again and again in this text to illustrate some point of theatrical history, some theory of technique, or some mystery of audience-control. There is room to look at them again and see to what extent and why they might be considered stars as well as great actors.

On the face of it, David Garrick looks unlikely material for stardom. Respectably married, with respectable friends, engaged in lofty pursuits and speaking an elegant tongue, an almost perfect hero in fact, there are neither the dismal flaws nor flaunted extravagances upon which stardom feeds. But he was beyond dispute one of the most famous Englishmen of the century, and fame of that order is not very far removed from idolatry. He was pictured in no less than 450 different paintings and engravings, and you could hardly go anywhere, even on the continent, without stumbling across two or three of them, much as postcards, movie "stills" and *Hello* magazine-type features bombard us today. Garrick was constantly ordering engravings of himself to give to friends or admirers. His handsome Thames-side villa at Hampton was also depicted in an engraving, and that, too, was snapped up. He was stopped and congratulated in the street, all of which he enjoyed most palpably. "Sir, a man who has a nation to admire him every night," said his friend Dr Johnson, "may well be expected to be somewhat elated." [20]

Nor did all this attention come to Garrick without some encouragement on his part. He had a good nose for publicity, and made sure that he was seen in the right places and spoke to the most useful people. His dinner guests at Hampton were hand-picked for influence, and his library and collection of pictures were also chosen with a view to posterity. "Garrick played the part of the cultivated gentleman scholar with as much skill as he ever acted Richard III." [21] When he commissioned Zoffany to paint the now-celebrated portraits of actors together in performance, which was an innovation, he had in mind not so much to preserve a record of the play as to display his performance in it.

Garrick was the proverbial life and soul of any gathering, full of enthusiasm, energy, charm, unstoppable chatter, and willing to do a turn for anyone. He was also controversial, insofar as he had his detractors, which is a help in any bid for stardom. Walpole was not at all keen on him, openly begrudging his fame. "All the run is now after Garrick, a wine-merchant who is turned player," he wrote with the manifest irritation of a wounded snob, "he is a very good mimic... His acting I have seen, and may say to you, I see nothing wonderful in it; but it is heresy to say so." [22] At other times Walpole referred to his "impertinence" and called him "that jackanapes", scornfully declaring that he was "determined to meddle with the scuffles of no green-room", thereby obliquely indicating that virtually everybody else was dying to meet the man. [23] Walpole likewise loathed Garrick's tampering with the Shakespearean text to make way for improvements of his own – removing the Fool from Lear, giving Romeo and Juliet a conversation by the tomb and Macbeth a final speech – an indignation even his admirers would share today, and when he took out the

Gravediggers from *Hamlet* to the satisfaction of the rule-driven French, Walpole wrote sarcastically that he hoped he would be rewarded with a place in the Académie Française. [24]

What Walpole resented was Garrick's popularity – that he was not only a marvellously new kind of actor, but an instant star as well. His appeal was immediate and direct, and a fastidious intellectual like Walpole was bound to find this trouble-free fame offensive. Walpole's spleen is our most convincing proof of Garrick's stardom. The noisy Jubilee celebrations masterminded by the actor in 1764 culminated in a fulsome oration with Garrick ostentatiously squeezing on the gloves which Shakespeare had worn on stage as he gazed at the sky and said, "We shall not look upon his like again." An idea of the occasion is given by the historian's sly compliment: "To Garrick's credit, however, it must be conceded that Shakespeare received almost as much attention as himself at the Jubilee." [25]

Are the clues which purport to show that Garrick suffered from the star's unhappy clutch upon fame once secured, reliable? Was he jealous of the success of other actors who might threaten it? Mrs Siddons said she had to be careful not to upstage him. And here is another witness: "Garrick is dying of the yellow jaundice on the success of Henderson, a young actor from Bath – *enfin donc désormais* there must never be a good player again." [26] But that is Walpole, whose prejudice is already pungent, and it takes no account of the fact that it was Garrick who first encouraged the impoverished John Henderson (1747-1785) to work hard at his unusual talent; Henderson is buried near Garrick in Westminster Abbey. The same source asserts that Garrick hated Mrs Pritchard because she was so much better than he was, and loathed Mrs Clive until she retired, whereupon he praised her to diminish the up-and-coming Mrs Abington; no evidence is adduced for any of this. It is to the famous feud with Samuel Foote (1720-1777) that we owe the tradition of Garrick's meanness with money (quite unsubstantiated and the very opposite of the truth, despite his having chastised Peg Woffington for brewing tea too strong). Foote never missed a chance to mock his fellow actor, but the evidence shows that Garrick never retaliated; in that, at least, he did not behave like a star, but like a gentleman. The clues to the contrary are feeble indeed.

One of the penalties of stardom which is not appreciated until it is too late, is isolation. It is possible that David Garrick gave so much energy to being a success that he left little or nothing to devote to being himself. "He had friends, but no friend," said Dr Johnson. "Garrick was so diffused, he had no man to whom he wished to unbosom himself." [27] Nevertheless, his very public funeral in 1779 drew extraordinary crowds and was attended by a pomp unprecedented for an actor. That's the point, really. In his death the enigma was finally resolved: he lived as a great actor, and he died as a star, from a stroke of death which "eclipsed the gaiety of nations".

Edmund Kean could hardly have been more different. Disdainful of society, unadorned and unkempt, often drunk, unlikely at five feet three inches to be a matinée idol, terrifyingly unpredictable, potentially manic, he was best seen with the distance of art – on stage and in his element. The statuesque and beautiful John Philip Kemble had far more of the star in him than this loutish genius. And yet we have seen that he prided himself on being the monarch of the stage – the First English Actor – which at least testifies to the arrogance necessary to establish stardom. He also had wonderful cheek, acting for three whole nights with his arm in a sling to support a story he had invented to account for his non-appearance the previous evening – his coach had been overturned and he had dislocated his shoulder (he had in fact been out cold in a tavern). As an eight-year-old child Kean had been sent to sea, which he hated. For two months he feigned deafness and lameness, even throughout a raging storm which all but capsized the ship and of which he affected not to hear the smallest whisper of wind, until he convinced the doctors, who thereupon released him. [28] Upon such stories rest the reputations of stars.

In a similar way to Kean, Sarah Siddons was too powerful and frightening an actress to really aspire to stardom, for a star must be loved as well as admired. Sheridan called her a "magnificent and appalling creature" and said he would sooner make love to the Archbishop of Canterbury, so that placed her out-of-bounds as a sex object. She was simply too good. On the two occasions when gossip attributed love affairs to her, she refused even to respond; a star like Tallulah Bankhead would have delighted in fostering innuendo. "Neither praise nor money, the two powerful corrupters of mankind, seem to have depraved her," was Johnson's gallant tribute. [29] There is this paradox about Mrs Siddons, that though several contemporaries attest that it was an event in anyone's life to have seen her on stage, and though people queued to have the opportunity of so doing, she was not quite cherished, as a star would be, beyond her hour on stage. She seemed forbidding, which was a pity, for those who knew her in private life speak of her sweetness of temper and quiet conversation; it was said, however, that she could not rid herself of the habit of speaking in iambic pentameters, of which several have survived. "You've brought me water, boy; I asked for beer" is one of them.

There is also the delicious story of Mrs Siddons in a draper's shop. On being presented with a piece of material by the nervous assistant, she asked "Will it wash?" in such tones that the assistant promptly fainted.

Nevertheless, stardom of an exemplary sort literally mantled Mrs Siddons at a Thanksgiving Service in St Paul's for the recovery of King George III from his supposed madness – she was draped in the nation's symbolic dress as Britannia. It was her only non-speaking role.

That Irving's stardom was assured by Queen Victoria and the cabbies of London, we have already remarked – the Queen by way of the first knighthood to be conferred on an actor, and the cab-drivers by going into mourning at his death. There was something of stardom also in his assumption of superiority, which was moreover never contested (although sharply and even bitterly mocked by Shaw); in the deference which always greeted him; in his dominion over the Lyceum Theatre. But especially it showed in his acting, and this may be the only example of a great actor who rose to stardom precisely through great acting. Usually, one is a great actor first, then a star for different, tangential or additional reasons, as we have seen with Kean, Siddons, Garrick. Irving had nothing additional. He was nothing but The Actor. He was not funny, not beautiful, not grand, not really interesting as a man. He was not intellectual (notwithstanding his resistance to Shaw with occasional letters of masterful scorn). His conversation was unenlightening, his friendships not profound. The manner of his leaving his wife was the only story told about him, and it was not a funny one. His affair with Ellen Terry, if it was an affair, was as tedious as everything else about him. But on stage he was magnificent, and it was on stage that he was a star, imposing his view of the world he was representing by sheer imaginative concentration. "Irving was not only able to impart more meaning to his words than they expressed in themselves," wrote a contemporary commentator, "but was addicted even to making them subservient to his own ideas, and making the public accept his conception in face of a text which was in flat contradiction to it." [30] What does this mean, if not that Irving was so great he was better than the words, than the English language, than the playwright, that he *improved* everything merely by his dignified presence and thought? Of all the actors of the past, Irving is the one most difficult to grasp, to see, to experience even at a distance. But whatever it was he did, it bestowed a kind of veneration upon him which glittered less than the stars, yet glowed with greater depth.

His leading lady for 25 years, Ellen Terry (1847-1928), was a star for the most unexpected of reasons, that she was so incredibly and manifestly *nice*, and this quality translated itself across the footlights to her audience. Her bubbling spontaneity (it was said that she spoke Shakespeare as if she had just been talking to him in the next room), her irresistible personal charm, her compassion and decency could not be concealed, whatever part it was she was portraying. When she played Portia she showed a feminine concern for Shylock and tried to dissuade him from his awful resolve to have his rightful pound of flesh, *for his own sake*, to make a better person of him. Thus did Ellen Terry's stardom shine through her acting, without quite deriving from it. She was a treat to work with, always thoughtful towards the rest of the cast, prone to giggling during rehearsals and making other actors "corpse" – always a refreshing relief of tension. Shaw told her she had a "beneficent" personality, and conducted a four-year epistolary affair with her. He referred to her as "silly, self-unconscious, will o' the wisp beglamored child actress as you still are", and affected to be affronted by her refusal to take on more serious and demanding roles. He wrote *Captain Brassbound's Conversion* for her, but knew she would take refuge in frivolity and ease. In a charming phrase, Max Beerbohm called her "the incarnation of our capricious English sunlight." In almost all the foregoing, it is difficult to resist the comparison with Judi Dench, who is also a star as herself, while being an actress on stage, simply because the effervescence and optimism of her personality cry across the stalls and into the gallery. They also have similar husky voices and are refreshingly modest. Ellen Terry said, "When people speak of me after my death, I hope they will say I was a useful actress." One can imagine Judi Dench saying precisely the same.

Long after her retirement, Ellen Terry was coaxed back on to the stage for a benefit performance of *The Cherry Orchard*, in which every part was taken by an established and revered "star". Ellen's memory and strength were both by then so fragile that it would have been catastrophic to cast her in a major role, so she was kept as the surprise to come on at the very end. When the cherry orchard has been sold and the family has departed, to the sound of trees being chopped there appears the ancient manservant Firs, alone on stage and looking forlorn and bewildered. It was Ellen Terry. The audience, recognising her, jumped to their feet in adulation. She paused, looked away, then turned and said the one line Chekhov affords the character, "They've all gone!" Tears were streaming down her face. In an instant, she had switched from being the star to being an actress.

Perhaps no one person embodies more of the ingredients of stardom in the theatre than Mrs Patrick Campbell (1865-1940), a woman whose name is invoked even today by people who have little idea who she was, how she performed, or what she looked like.

The name has survived the actress. It cannot be only because she was the last to be called "Mrs" on the billboards.

The very nature of her "discovery" was the stuff of which stardom is made, for she was the archetype of the Overnight Sensation. On her father's side she came from Anglican clergy, and on her mother's from the circus and minor Italian nobility – her grandfather had managed a circus and her grandmother ridden a horse in it. Her real name, which she hated, was Stella Tanner, but her real temperament, which contributed to her success, was Latin. When she married the unremarkable Patrick Campbell she took his name professionally and was never known by any other, and she also gave birth to a son and a daughter before embarking upon a stage career. Some discerning critics were already beginning to notice her soon after she started, but she did not make any significant mark with the public as a whole.

In 1893 Arthur Wing Pinero (1855-1934) sold his latest play, *The Second Mrs Tanqueray*, to the actor-manager George Alexander. It was a turning point for him and for London theatre in general, for it was what was called a "problem" play, which dealt with delicate matters of sex and love in a candid manner never before attempted. It would require an actress who could combine maturity and smouldering passion to carry it off. Alexander sent his wife Florence on a tour of London theatres to find someone to play Paula Tanqueray. She went with a friend, Graham Robertson, and after some discouraging days they came upon an unknown actress in a small part in a vapid melodrama called *The Black Domino*.

Years later Robertson recalled the occasion he first clapped eyes on Mrs Patrick Campbell: "She did not look wicked – a startling innovation. She was almost painfully thin, with great eyes and slow, haunting utterance; she was not exactly beautiful, but strangely interesting and arresting. She played weakly, walking listlessly through the part, but in one scene she had to leave the stage laughing; the laugh was wonderful, low and sweet, yet utterly mocking and heartless. Florence Alexander and I both realised that there before our eyes was the ideal Paula Tanqueray. If she would only move, speak, look, above all laugh like that, the part would play itself." [31]

Pinero then went to see the lady for himself, and she was summoned to attend St James's Theatre the next day. As it happened, she was then in crisis, obliged to bring up two children on her own and threatened with the sack from her part in *The Black Domino*. She was at her wit's end. Moreover, the parts she had been playing were altogether without any satisfaction, and she was more than happy to try something serious and demanding. She was engaged. During rehearsals it soon became clear that she was not going to be easy to manage, that she had her own instincts to which she was determined to be true. Pinero and Alexander both got cold feet for a while, and wondered whether they had seen a second-rate actress in a third-rate production and thought she was good merely because she wasn't bad. Alexander in particular was used to doing everything according to theatrical rules; he was alarmed that Mrs Pat might turn out to be wild and thrilling, like an unmastered stallion. He was right, of course. That is exactly what she was, and the contrast between their styles – he earnest and restrained, she mercurial and emotional – would give the play its tension and resonance. It was precisely the contrast identified at the beginning of this book between the Apollonian and Dionysian styles of acting; they often do not understand one another ("acting with him was rather like acting with a walking-stick," she said [32]), but react to each other like a naked electric charge.

For example, in one scene Paula Tanqueray was required to lose her temper. George Alexander directed her to storm over to the piano and brush all the photographs lined on it onto the floor. Mrs Pat refused. She reasoned that she was supposed to be a pianist, and that no self-respecting pianist would lumber his piano with pictures. (Mrs Pat could in fact play the piano well.) Secondly, she said, as a pianist Paula could never bear to do anything ugly with her hands. Pinero surrendered to her intuition and this saved the scene from precarious histrionics. In the end, she picked up one ornament and threatened "in tones of black ice" to drop it. [33]

The first night took place on 27 May, 1893. Mrs Pat tucked a picture of her young son in the top of her gown before going on. She need not have worried. By the end of the evening she had conquered the town, and her fame from the next morning until her death nearly 50 years later would hardly wane. An idea of the effect of her performance, and especially what that intangible attraction is which makes a star, is given by the rhapsodic words of the *Punch* review: "She is loving, she is vulgar; she can purr, she can spit; she is gentle, she is violent; she has good impulses, and she is a fiend incarnate; she is affectionate, she is malicious...she is a *bête fauve* that should be under lock and key. And not Sarah Bernhardt herself...could play this part better than Mrs Patrick Campbell. It is a wonderful performance, most striking, most convincing, from the utter absence in it of all apparent consciousness of the effects she is producing." [34] Moreover, in her most emotional scene she actually blew her nose, causing dinner-table conversations for weeks afterwards.

The audience was shocked and excited, applauding massively at each interval. The subject alone was unnerving to Victorians – a step-daughter having an affair with the former lover of her step-mother – and guaranteed rapt attention. Ellen Terry arrived from the Lyceum to see the last act. When the final curtain fell, the audience went wild, rushing towards the stage, waving handkerchiefs and cheering. Mrs Pat went home alone, "worn out by fatigue" [35], and unaware that no début in the previous 20 years could have matched hers. Coincidentally, George Bernard Shaw was also in the audience, and fell under her spell along with everyone else. "On the highest plane one does not act, one *is*," he wrote. "Go and see her move, stand, speak, look, kneel – go and breathe the magic atmosphere that is created by the grace of all these deeds." [36]

She had long, lustrous black hair, eyes which tortured with enquiry and pain, a deep sensual voice, a sexual allure which trapped men without their knowing they had been hunted. Shaw rightly called her "perilously bewitching". Women, too, were alive to her mesmerising power. "She was the beauty of the moonlight," wrote Rebecca West, "as Ellen Terry was the beauty of the sunlight." [37] She was at her best in roles which suggested fire and danger, though she was brave enough to attempt Ibsen at a time when the gloomy Scandinavian was a long way from being popular with audiences. Honest enough, also, to admit she was not much good with him: "I could never play her [Hedda

Gabler] because I could never get the Latin out of my blood. I have had Swedish masseuses who were ten times better Heddas."

Ralph Richardson did not agree. He saw her as Hedda and said she was "the finest actress I ever saw in my life. I've never seen anything to approach her since and she was wonderful at conveying terror... Mrs Pat as Hedda Gabler frightened the life out of one. A terrible appearance: large black eyes, huge mane of black hair – she walked across the stage, revolver in hand, with all the terror of the movement of a puma which you see when you go to the zoo, when you think, 'My goodness, I'm glad those bars are pretty thick.' A baleful glance, sinewy step, incredible cruelty. Never will I forget the effect when she took the letters, Lövborg's letters, and flung open the studio stove. She opened it with a poker, the lid fell back with a clang, and she took the letters in her hands, looked at them and said, 'My child and Lövborg's. I'll singe your baby locks.' Then threw them into the flames. It was like looking straight into hell." [38]

Before *Hedda* she had acted with Sarah Bernhardt in *Pelleas et Mélisande* in French, and one can now only guess at the shine from such a pair of luminaries on stage together; they became best friends for life. "I toured with her for five months," she said, "sat on her bed till five o'clock in the morning, and never heard her say a word to which a child could not have listened," which is a curiously touching tribute in the face of the huge mythological fame attached to the name Bernhardt. Mrs Pat also told of her last visit to Bernhardt before she died in 1923, at the close of which the great actress, as she was carried upstairs in her chair, kissed her finger and held it out towards her in final farewell. [39]

The other big moment in Mrs Pat's career was the part of Eliza Doolittle which Shaw wrote for her, about which we have already had something to say in other contexts. Shaw was in love with her, but she rightly saw that life with him would be annihilation for her. "I who have nothing but my little lamp and flame, you would blow it out with your bellows of self." [40] She called him "brain-proud". By this time she was not only the Actress and the Star, but the Temperament personified. She would extend intervals so that she could receive people in her dressing room, refuse to rehearse, flounce off and bang furiously at her piano for the whole theatre to hear, and one week before the opening of the play, suddenly disappear and leave an announcement that she was getting married to George Cornwallis-West (nicknamed Old Wives' Tale because of his tastes), who had previously been married to Lady Randolph Churchill, mother of Winston. She railed about her make-up ("I look like Caligula's grandmother"), her costume ("Red is a colour I abominate. It makes me look like a horrid little letter-box."), a novelist ("He has a worm in his brain. He lives in hell and likes it."). She was all wit and wonder, hypnotising people around her into silence; people looked and waited, proud to be in the same room with such a woman and anxious to hear what she would say next, and in *their* presence, too!

Gradually, Mrs Pat disappeared from view. She was besotted with a sequence of pekingese dogs which she carried under her arm and treated like royalty. Because of them, and because she spent long periods abroad, she turned down parts in England which would have meant imprisoning her poor little hounds in quarantine. She became a caricature of herself, wrinkled, haggard, shabby, and living in one room in an un-starred hotel (boarding house really) in New York. It was there that Agate, Cecil Beaton and Gielgud all visited her and brought back similar stories of sadness and wit. Agate said, "I think I have never been in contact with a mind so frivolous and at the same time so big. She talked a great deal about 'flight' in acting as being the first quality of a great actor. For four hours I listened to chatter about everything from Moses to Schnabel. On Moses: 'He probably said to himself – must stop or I shall be getting silly – That is why there are only ten commandments.' On Schnabel's piano-playing: 'like the winds of the air and the waves of the sea, without shape.'" [41]

"Chatter" is a good word for Mrs Pat's seamless verbal meanderings, sometimes funny, sometimes moving, always sharp and original. It is sometimes difficult to believe that the words tumbled out of her unprepared, but it seems they did. "Lillian Gish is a charming person, but she's no Ophelia. She comes on stage as if she'd been sent for to sew rings on the new curtains." "American parties are so noisy, like the French revolution." Noël Coward's characters "talk like typewriting". When she played Mrs Alving in *Ghosts* to the Oswald of a very young John Gielgud, she told him what Pinero had years before told her: "Keep still. Gaze at me. Empty your voice of meaning and speak as if you were going to be sick." [42] In their final scene together she whispered, "This play is worse than having a confinement." [43]

Gielgud introduced the playwright Emlyn Williams to Mrs Pat at his home, and Williams' account of the meeting is so vivid, so obviously characteristic of the woman, that it has to be quoted in full:

A stout old lady in a rag-bag of a black evening dress ornamented with what looked like jet. Her hair, an improbable black, was done in old-fashioned loops above a face to which, earlier in the evening, make-up had been applied, hastily and liberally. She looked like a grand old theatrical landlady on a night out, who had herself once trod the boards. "Stella dear, this is Emlyn Williams – Mrs Patrick Campbell."

"Oh, he won't recognise the name of an old has-been…"

She would anyway have been identified by a voice imitated in a hundred anecdotes: throaty and over-articulated, sounding anxious to please until you realise that the humble-pie was flavoured with arsenic. It was my first and last meeting with a sacred monster who so perfectly lived up to herself that next day I wrote it down. I waited for the darts, and they came. John said, "Emlyn has had a great success at the St James's, with Edith [Evans] and Cedric [Hardwicke]." I wondered if the mention of the foremost contemporary actress was the happiest of strokes. "*Do* tell me more, but you look a *child*, did you write it all by yourself?" She cannot have known how lethal that dart was. John looked nervous. "He's adapted it from the French." The black eyes fixed on me with horror and there was a weightlift of beringed fingers. "Oh, you poor dear, a *translation?*" She made it sound like a dirty book. "Translations remind me of those short-sighted spinsters slaving over their abominable copies in the Louvre. John, dear, do you remember our *Ghosts*, the programme should have read '*Mangled* from the Norwegian by William What-was-his-name?' Bowmen? Arrowsmith? *Archer*, that was it." She turned to me again, "Now I've got a *spiffing* idea, why not write a play out of your *very own head*, for a penniless old harridan who can still act? Goodbye, dear John, such lovely costumes, and goodbye you naughty *cribber*, goodbye." [44]

Her last years, clutching the last of her dogs, Moonbeam, to her bosom, were by every account pitiful. She was obsessed with the loss of her beauty. The ultra-fastidious Cecil Beaton wrote, "There was something ghastly about her dirty white gloves, her fallen chins and the tragic impedimenta of age. She bellowed like a sick cow, throwing her hands to the skies, 'Oh why must I look like a burst paper bag?'"

She showed Beaton some old photographs of herself at the height of her success. "These documents attested such beauty that it was almost frightening to compare them with what they have turned into," he said, almost with malicious glee. "'Look,' she moaned, 'at the beauty of that neck, at that line of cheek. And look at me now, all wind and water... Oh God, how can You be so unkind as to do this to me?'"

She explained that she was poor, but did not mind, for to be rich she would have had to break a little dog's heart. "I live in an old-fashioned hotel, a red-brick building full of old people who adore me. They look after me so kindly; they adore Moonbeam. I have two rooms with French windows and a high ceiling. And I don't have to hear other people's bath water." [45] What little money she had she spent on lavish food for the dog, while she herself grubbed around for left overs.

In the end, even a dump in New York was too expensive for her. She moved to a dingy hotel in Pau in southern France, where her identity was unknown and nobody ever visited. The wit was quietened with nobody to hear it, the vivacity quenched, the ugliness finally private. Another English lady at the hotel enquired why she had not seen her lately. She had been dead for three days when they found her. The clergymen who buried her had no idea who she was.

1   Joseph Donohue, *Theatre in the Age of Kean* (1975), p 80

2   Manuscripts of the Chatsworth Settlement Trust, B2779, 1 June 1833

3   John Diprose, *Anecdotes of the Stage and Players*, in *Old and New London*, Vol III, p 296

4   William Hazlitt, *Table-Talk* (1821-2), pp 373, 380

5   W A Darlington, *The Actor and His Audience* (1949), p 150

6   Brian Masters, *The Mistresses of Charles II* (1979), pp 102, 106

7   *Dictionary of National Biography*

8   Darlington, *op. cit.*, p 53

9   Brian Masters, *The Dukes: the origins, ennoblement and history of 26 families* (1980), pp 318, 289

10 Leigh Hunt, *Critical Essays on the Performers of the London Theatres* (1807), p 289

11 John Gielgud, *Distinguished Company* (1972), pp 108-110, 112-114

12 Ned Sherrin, *Theatrical Anecdotes*, p 160

13 J A Hammerton, *The Actor's Art* (1897), p 76

14 *The Diary of Samuel Pepys*, ed. Latham and Matthews, Vol IX, p 435, footn.

15 Gielgud, *op. cit.*, p 18

16 From the Diaries of Charles Macready, in Sherrin, *op. cit.*, p 76

17 Brian Masters, *Georgiana, Duchess of Devonshire* (1981), pp 258-259

18 Hammerton, *op. cit.*, p 13

19 James Agate, *Ego 6* (1935-48), 24 September, 1930

20 James Boswell, *Boswell's Life of Johnson*, Vol II, p 346

21 John Brewer, *The Pleasures of the Imagination* (1997), p 420

22 Horace Walpole, *Letters*, ed. Cunningham (1906), 26 May, 1742

23 Walpole, *op. cit.*, 15 April, 1768; 13 September, 1768

24 Walpole, *op. cit.*, 9 January, 1773

25 S Schoenbaum, *Shakespeare's Lives* (1970), p 155

26 Walpole, *op. cit.*, 4 August, 1777

27 Boswell, *op. cit.*, Vol II, p 304

28 Hammerton, *op. cit.*, p 103

29 Boswell, *op. cit.*, Vol II, p 482

30 A Filon, *The English Stage* (1897), in Bertram Joseph, *The Tragic Actor* (1959), p 367

31 John Dawick, *Pinero: A Theatrical Life* (1993), p 184

32 Alan Dent, *Mrs Patrick Campbell* (1961), p 179

33 Dawick, *op. cit.*, p 188

34 *Punch*, 10 June, 1893

35 Cyril Maude, *Behind the Scenes* (1927), p 87

36 Michael Holroyd, *Bernard Shaw* (1988), Vol II, p 295

37 *ibid.*, p 303

38 Bryan Forbes, *That Despicable Race* (1980), pp 185-6

39 James Agate, *Ego 3* (1935-48), p 111

40 Holroyd, *op. cit.*, p 317

41 Agate, *Ego 3*, *op. cit.*

42 Dent, *op. cit.*, p 188

43 Gielgud, *op. cit.*, p 48

44 Emlyn Williams, *Emlyn* (1973), pp 299-300

45 Cecil Beaton, *Self-Portrait with Friends* (1979), pp 60-63

7

Stolen Treasure

So much for stardom. The beast is slippery and sly, and will ultimately disappoint. Besides which, to seek stardom suggests that acting is a means to an end – fame – and that another means might have been chosen had it promised more rapid reward. For the great actors, no such choice was possible. Acting is and has always been an imperative, an exigent master of individual fate, whose demands could be resisted only at the expense of sanity. *Not* to act would be unthinkable, a negation of reality and of self-knowledge, a kind of spiritual suicide. If the language sounds dramatic, it is at least fitting to the subject. But countless actors have stutteringly admitted that it is so. Laurence Olivier is on record as having said that he would have gone mad had he not been an actor. The double tease of an actor playing an actor in Jean-Paul Sartre's play about Kean has him proclaim, "*On joue pour ne pas se connaître et parce qu'on se connaît trop...on joue parcequ'on aime la vérité et parce qu'on la déteste. On joue parce qu'on deviendrait fou si on ne jouait pas.*" [1] ("One acts in order to avoid facing oneself, and because one knows oneself only too well...one acts from love of truth, and because one detests it. One acts because one would go out of one's mind if one didn't.") And Michael Gambon has said, "I don't really like it. I *have* to do it."

Already, we may sense the ripples of this as they touch most of the people we have been celebrating. Their genius arose from their teetering on the edge of a sanity which they have been obliged to risk in order to show us the truth about character and situation. This is their destiny and their purpose. It is also their inheritance, the line of connection which unites them to the present day. I said at the beginning that it should be possible to see Mrs Siddons and Garrick and Kean on stage now, to restore them to our eyes and ears and rescue them from the inertia of history, by spotting their echoes among actors currently working. Now that we have looked at their styles and manner, seen how they used their voices and personalities, we are perhaps in a position at least to attempt it. I do not suggest, of course, that there is an actor today who performs in exactly the same way as Edmund Kean, or an actress who is the re-incarnation of Sarah Siddons, like ghastly and ghostly copies. No actor is like another; it is their individuality which entrances. On the other hand, we can now see bits of Kean and Irving and Macready in the way in which Ian McKellen performs, and different bits in the way Simon Russell Beale performs, and, as we do, we see the moving, speaking shadow of the originals. This is not to say they have copied. It is to say they have inherited influences which bear upon them from afar, that they hold that thread which still quivers with the presence of Richard Burbage. And also, that they are fired by the same imperative; they have inherited that common strain of stubbornness which denies all other ways of coping with life.

Acting remains a craft in which the British excel, and it would be easy to fill several pages with the names of actors who deserve our admiration, from the world-famous, like Anthony Hopkins, to the lesser-known but equally exciting Charles Kay, John Woodvine, John Normington. But by concentrating on just a few, we might better be able to isolate and draw out those echoes from the past which are discernible in their performances.

Ian McKellen's distinguished stage career exemplifies that urge to dominate the audience which we identified at the beginning as essential to the great actor. His presence on stage is magnetic. It is impossible to ignore him. A charge of energy passes through the theatre on his entrance. He contrives anticipation, so that you watch and wait to see what he will do next. He lives the experience of the part he is playing, and you live it with him. But above all, he is a consummate technician, seducing the audience into complicity with a superlative, invisible technical skill. From his alternating roles as Marlowe's *Edward II* and Shakespeare's *Richard II* in 1968 to the idealistic Dr Stockmann in Ibsen's *An Enemy of the People* in 1997, McKellen's technique has always been impressive, and it is in the Ibsen character that it is deployed in all its startling variety.

In the first place, he has great eloquence in what we nowadays call "body language", that which astonished audiences when they saw David Garrick for the first time and were immediately convinced he was the most "natural" actor there had ever been. Garrick assumed different mannerisms for the different roles he was playing. McKellen, at the beginning of *An Enemy of the People*, has to show the optimism and hearty happiness of Dr Stockmann, as well as his innocent enthusiasm. He does this by making his body speak with fun and hope, crossing his legs repeatedly, lifting his shoulders, running his fingers through his hair, waving his hands, pouting, in a kaleidoscope of visual indices of rampant joy. In print, it sounds faintly ridiculous (which is why actors *show*, and in some respects books like this should not be written), yet its effect is as subtle a portrait as a Rembrandt. It is, of course, achieved through many an acquired habit, many a borrowed piece of business, and perfect muscle control, but McKellen uses technique always at the service of truth and never in opposition to it. It is probably a small matter to portray enthusiasm on stage; he manages to convey naiveté as well, not obvious in the words he says, but lying in ambush behind them, which is a much more complicated undertaking. By his technique he must reach beyond the text and show the audience something about Dr Stockmann they did not realise they knew.

We saw earlier how Kean was able to show what Hazlitt called "subsiding emotion" for some time after the lines which prompted the emotion had passed. You can see this in McKellen's insuppressible indignation towards the end of the play, when all the allies of his idealism have turned against him for political expediency and private advantage. It distorts his body and inflames his eye. But what McKellen does which extends further (and "subsiding emotion" is after all not so innovative today as it was to Kean's audience), is to show "rising emotion", so that the early tremors of an eruption about to occur are felt in advance by the audience. This he does by another technical device, that of modulating his voice so that it may show present doubt of future intent. McKellen uses his voice with cunning. He modulates it into hills and valleys, alters its speed from express to hesitant, makes it tower and tremble, couch and cower. There is something of Irving in his resonant rotundity, in the way he flavours his voice, spreading it round his mouth before throwing it out to the audience, and he also makes careful (not extravagant) use of the Macready Pause. It enables him to spit disdain into the accusation against his brother that he is "spiritually [pause] common", and it invests warm wry irony into the observation that while it is difficult enough to be an enemy of the people it must be [pause, frown, purse lips, fiddle with shoelaces] *very* difficult to be a friend of the people.

The pause is not trivial. It is not artificial (though of course it comes from artifice). It is not an actorish trick, inserted for a laugh. It is an important statement on the character of Dr Stockmann, who in the deepest adversity can call upon his essential goodwill, expressed in gently bantering humour, to give him renewed strength. Thus McKellen shares something else with Macready apart from his pauses, and that is his artistic integrity. Like Macready, McKellen has a little of the academic in his approach to acting – it must be honest to the text, or it is mere showing-off. And this honour to the text drives him into a self-belief-in-character which, despite all the technical cleverness, can be mortifying to behold.

Another master of technique, possibly in a more absorbed, less fidgety way (one recalls George II's comment that Garrick was too much of a fidget, and wonders what His Majesty would have made of Ian McKellen) is Simon Russell Beale. A sequence of photographs of his performances in *The Seagull, Richard III, Othello, The Man of Mode, The Duchess of Malfi, Ghosts* and *Volpone* might occasion disbelief that they could all be the same person, much as Charles Mathews looked at his own array of characters in wonderment. But Russell Beale is a much deeper actor than Mathews ever was, and his chameleon quality serves a rich and bitter purpose. One critic said that he was "savage in his portrayal of the truth in people", and certainly there is no actor more psychologically probing than he. While McKellen's technique is objective, allowing the audience to peer into the heart of Edward II or Dr Stockmann until they feel they know him better than he knows himself, Russell Beale's is dedicated to showing the audience to themselves. Hence he is an uncomfortable actor, a man whose performances leave you worried.

On the final page of *The Seagull,* before Konstantin commits suicide offstage, the tormented young man is alone. Simon Russell Beale showed us, without a word of script, what was going on in his mind as he contemplated the unthinkable, and he drew both fear and compassion from the audience, because he did what we would have done. He went round the stage tidying up his affairs, arranging papers, tearing up his manuscripts, putting things in their proper place and his life in order, and dropping his pen, which he would no longer need, into the wastepaper basket. He even arranged his paperclips in meticulous fashion. It was heart-rending to behold, because it really did seem final, and psychologically all too plausible. Earlier in the play we had sympathised with his frustrated, strained, seethingly volcanic but suppressed enthusiasms, because he expressed them as we have done ourselves and would doubtless do again in his situation. He spoke not through clenched teeth but with acid on his tongue in meagre, ungenerous, self-pitying and painful short sentences, and a critic noticed that even his long sentences were broken up into short ones. All this was technical magic.

Russell Beale played Richard III as a bald, repulsive ogre, like a slithering toad, as somebody said. The moment when his nephew, the little Duke of York, in the lovely innocence of childhood asks the deformed Richard to give him a piggy-back, Russell Beale again acted without script, before the lines Shakespeare had given him. There was silent wicked fury in his face and body, fuelled by hatred of the young and a passion for revenge, all conveyed in a hesitation. It was quite chilling.

But it was Russell Beale's portrayal of Iago in 1997 which particularly made me shiver. Constructed from dozens of tiny observations and clues, he made the man utterly heartless, so that by the end the audience despised him. (I swear I heard somebody about to hiss, not the actor, who had evaporated, but the vicious Iago who had taken his place, as children will hiss the villain in pantomime.) In such meticulous detail of characterisation one may spot the attraction of Garrick, and, more recently, Alec Guinness. Some examples: the four words "I hate the Moor" are not themselves of gigantic importance. Iago's animus towards Othello is already obvious, and has been stated. The four monosyllables come unheralded at the end of a line and begin a new sentence which stretches into the next two lines of verse. Russell Beale gives them the strength of hammer blows at the end of a Mahler symphony. First, he pauses in a brooding silence which is not in the text (this is *not* a Macready pause, which would come in the *middle* of a phrase), his back shudders, he hurls a glass across the stage with such force you would think he were about to have a fit, and then shouts the words with equal emphasis on all four; we are in no doubt he means it, and I should not have wished to be anywhere near him at that point.

"Point" is indeed the word, for at such moments one may see another aspect of actors gone by in the performances of Simon Russell Beale, namely their attraction to "points" which underlined the moral of the story and could be engraved by popular artists. Russell Beale does not "freeze" at his points, nor does the audience burst into applause and beg him to hold it longer, but he has the residue of this tradition in his style. His hesitation at the piggy-back request in *Richard III* was another "point".

As Iago declares his love for Cassio, there is a shifty glance and malice in the eyes. On the famous line, "Look to your wife", he lowers his voice to a silken, furtive insinuating stiletto which is thoroughly nasty. He starts the "By the way" speech to Othello with a cunning nonchalance – the sort we have all been guilty of when about to tell a lie. He arranges playing cards to illustrate his thoughts and plans as they hatch in his mind, a telling piece of "business" which is typical of the Machiavellian villain, for whom the game of victory is more important than the reason for it (indeed, Iago offers no reason). There are moments when another character goes to touch him, and Russell Beale flinches in fear at the threatened closeness; this is standard behaviour from the semi-autistic or psychopathic person, for whom individuals are mere furniture and human tactility is loathsome. This is creative acting at its highest, the actor's insights adding to the text.

Most of all, perhaps, the drunken scene in which Iago works up the soldiers into a dangerous mob was truly frightening. Russell Beale was the epitome of the pub-crawl thug, vicious, cruel, mindless, and orgasmically fierce. He shouted and excited the men, fists clenched, mouth slobbering, face torn to a sneer, and he had me physically trembling. Then I glimpsed what it might have been like to be in a theatre dominated by Edmund Kean.

Like Garrick and Kean, Simon Russell Beale is a short, squat man, unquestionably unimpressive. Also like them, he has the ability to transform himself physically and spiritually on stage, by virtue of that valuable forgetfulness-of-self which we saw much earlier when talking of Mrs Siddons and Thomas Betterton. Russell Beale himself appears to be swallowed and dissolved by the character he has become. This quality, when allied to technical flourish, makes for the really creative actor, the actor who transcends his material and adds to it, or deepens it in some immediately accessible way so that the audience experiences something fresh. They never take anything for granted, but dismantle a role and reconstruct it from scratch. Henry Irving was a creative actor; so was Laurence Olivier. Another is Antony Sher.

There is one obvious way in which Sher "forgets" himself, and that is by fastidious attention to costume and make-up. As the Fool in *King Lear* (1982) he transformed himself into a grotesque cripple, as his research had taught him that jesters in mediaeval courts were frequently chosen from dwarfs or deformed people. As Shylock (1987) he became an oriental, complete with turban, long hair, full beard, and gorgeous flowing robe. In *Richard III* (1984), already historical for his being the first actor in that role to banish the memory of Olivier's unsettling performance 40 years earlier, he wore a hideous hunch on his back, made one leg looked withered, and supported his revolting body on a pair of crutches. Sher spent months gradually putting the part together until he resembled a startling black spider, lurching and swinging about the stage with sudden swift movement in search of a new victim. The modern play *Torch Song Trilogy* (1987) revealed an actor who could transmute into a blatant, hilariously loud and over-painted transvestite, while *Cyrano de Bergerac* (1997) was so convincing that the outsize nose really did appear to be his, and one wondered if Sher had been taking special pills to effect this extra growth. He is an intensely physical actor, recreating his appearance with every role. In this he most resembles Olivier and Garrick. While Russell Beale also disappears into his characters, Sher does so in a more physical manner. It is like somebody building a cathedral with meticulous attention to balance and shape, only to tear it all down and start again the next time.

That, of course, only gets as far as the externals. He also makes a penetrating study of the inner secret springs of the character's behaviour in an attempt to assume his mind as well as his body. In view of his long line of portraits of deeply unpleasant men, some even vile, one must hope that technique plays a greater part in these transformations than does identity, but the boldness of the attempt has a long pedigree. We are not the first age to understand the psychology of character, nor are our actors the first to get "into the mind" of the people they portray. Macklin and Irving both studied the personality of Shylock before "interpreting" him in their performances (in strikingly different ways, as it happens, Macklin as a wicked schemer, Irving as a noble victim), and despite the stage conventions in which they operated, they gave psychologically precise portrayals of the man into whose skin they had insinuated themselves. In this regard, when you see Antony Sher, you are watching the intelligence of Macklin mixed with the frank athleticism of Olivier.

Sher's Shylock was his own total creation. Wild, staring eyes, a heavy foreign accent, a high-pitched unnatural cackling laugh, you could almost smell his foreignness from the stalls. He was not somebody you would like to share a meal with, still less invite into your home. Decidedly to be kept at arm's length, Sher's creation was a technical marvel, an utterly strange individual whom one could not hope to understand and whose rather sticky presence made one's flesh creep. That, at least, was the initial impact. But then Sher took us further, and made us understand, from the inside, a character whom we thought we never could or would ever want to comprehend. It was a masterpiece of compassionate honesty. The scene in which he was mocked and beaten to the ground by a mob of thuggish Christian urchins, then spat upon and treated with fiendish contempt, was so moving as to be scarcely bearable. Sher showed us the anger of the man kept in check by his pride of race and of person. By the line, "The villainy you teach me I will execute, and it shall go hard but I will better the instruction.", delivered with cruel but justified sarcasm, he had the audience on his side. [2] One critic wrote that it was a "spectacular and thrilling conquest of the role", another that his performance had "formidable range, embracing savage irony, cries of rage, strange religious rituals, and moments of desolate grief". [3] It was possible to imagine the exciting adventurousness of Olivier before one, or the bold iconoclastic artistry of Kean.

Antony Sher's Richard III was so individual and so visually distinguished that it is one of those rare performances which are better served by painting it than by describing it in words. Again, it is Kean who comes to mind, as many of the paintings of him on stage may testify. The painting would not, however, have been able to capture the insidious charm which Sher brought to the role, making his dramatically implausible seduction of Lady Anne by the coffin of her late husband, whom he has murdered, for once not merely acceptable but shudderingly true; you felt the sexual attraction of deformity, and the guilty rustling of audiences as they recognised this response in themselves was palpable.

The style of acting which takes such huge risks must occasionally tumble over the precipice. It happened at least once with Olivier, and Kean was known to have failed in some roles. With Olivier it was usually when the technique smothered the psychology and one could watch how the thing was done; to repeat the cathedral analogy, it was like watching the bricks being laid one by one, only to realise that the finished building was the wrong shape. Sher has sometimes come close to what looks like parody. His depiction of the religious hypocrite Tartuffe in Molière's powerful play of that name was so transparently sinister that one could not understand how anyone, however pious, could have been taken in by him. His Malvolio in *Twelfth Night* was rather too obviously a raving lunatic. Both were examples of huge brush strokes of violent colour blocking out the subtle detail that was assuredly underneath. It did not matter, because the risk, with Sher, is always worth taking. In an appreciation in *The Guardian,* Michael Billington wrote, "you go to each new performance, as to Olivier's, expecting a detailed novelistic creation", and that in the classics he had the vital ability to "dismantle received ideas and stock responses". [4] Which is precisely what Garrick, Macklin and Kean all achieved.

So, one has an impression of Antony Sher the daredevil firework, lighting up the theatre with stark flashes of technical fertility, and if occasionally one is dazzled into bypassing the psychological detail which lurks within, it may be a price worth paying. He was always big, grand, expansive and intoxicating. Then, in 1996, he astonished us with a performance of quite a different stamp in *Stanley*, playing the role based upon the life and character of the painter Stanley Spencer. Not that the transformation was not complete as always, with Sher assuming a new shape, a new voice and a new demeanour, but it was totally subservient to the psychological truth of the part, and it spiked out the details. It was a meticulous portrait rather than a Rubens-like wall-covering; a piano sonata, not an orchestral blast. And the character himself was no longer villainous, oily or pathetic, he was sweet-natured and sensitive, a man of genuine spiritual goodness. That Sher could capture this man and give him to us seemed like a miracle.

On that night it was the ghost of David Garrick himself who trod the boards – the brilliant assumption of a new skin allied to stunning truthfulness of observation. One could easily imagine Garrick tackling the part in exactly the same way as Sher, tugging at his jumper, looking slily askance, bringing the audience close enough to look into his very heart. John Peter of *The Sunday Times* described him in *Stanley* with similar care of detail as Lichtenberg had described Garrick's performances. Sher had, he wrote, the "cocky but stolid walk of villagers, shy but aggressively pigeon-chested, standing with his legs bent slightly outwards like a donkey observing a friendly stranger". [5] The *Independent* noticed him "blinking sweatily as he runs his hands up skirts", and the "bumbling, innocent manner" in which he mucked up other people's lives. Another critic in the same newspaper described him as "a bespectacled nerd...you completely believe that here's a man who could marvel for hours at the beauty of woodlice in the loo." [6] All were agreed that the actor had vanished behind the performance, that Antony

Sher had accomplished that most precious of feats, to lose oneself and create another, to the point where the audience believed in the creation, no longer in the actor. One critic said he left the theatre feeling he had genuinely come face to face with the great painter Stanley Spencer, and had to pinch himself to be brought back to the world outside. The experience was "spell-binding", said another. "You genuinely believe you have met the artist himself."

These were the kinds of responses which regularly met Garrick's performances, and the use of the clichéd word "spell-binding" is justified; it is the only one that will do, for a great actor must indeed cast a spell if he is to dominate the audience and bring them to see truth through his eyes.

Juliet Stevenson did something similar in Lorca's play *Yerma*, when she utterly convinced you that she was a Spanish peasant-woman spiritually destroyed by the denial of sexuality and maternity, her whole person a festering wound of self-flagellating frustration. Her anguish was so overpowering that you felt embarrassed to be witnessing it. That was self-forgetfulness and casting of spells of a very rare order. One is reminded of Mrs Siddons' power of conviction.

If Juliet Stevenson's voice occasionally spluttered and spattered unintelligibly, that was because a voice in such turmoil would splutter; the emotional truth matters to her more than purity of sound. McKellen, Russell Beale, Sher likewise use their voices as avenues of communication, as tools, but not as fine instruments to be cherished for their own sakes. Their voices have clarity, and in McKellen's case poetic allure, yet they are secondary. There is, however, a tradition in acting style which holds that truth is brought home to an audience through the medium of a beautiful voice, that shouting and emoting are less effective than aural seduction. Johnston Forbes-Robertson was a fine exponent of this principle, as was John Gielgud. But the one actor working today who respects and reveres his voice, and draws us to his vision by encircling us with it, is Ralph Fiennes.

The sound of Ralph Fiennes is a thing of beauty, robust and mellifluous at one and the same time. He used it to great effect in two major, demanding roles on the London stage within eighteen months of one another, *Hamlet* in 1995, and *Ivanov* in 1997. The Hamlet speeches were delivered straight and honestly, in the knowledge that to alter their flow and balance would be to distort their meaning. This was Shakespeare speaking directly to the audience through the voice and intelligence of a majestic interpreter. The audience would have been disconcerted had the actor interfered with that connection (as many have), and one felt that Fiennes wanted the communication to be as unsullied as possible. Such cannot be achieved, of course, merely by a wish. It is yet another aspect of the precious technique which each actor must hone to suit his particular talents to best advantage. Ralph Fiennes appears to know that his voice is his essence. It is compelling, musical, glorious. The soliloquies came through as pure as speech, "with bite and superb phrasing" in the words of the *Observer* critic. The *Financial Times* called the voice "a shadowed baritone with innumerable lights and textures" and noticed the intensity of rhythms and of line. Another called it "crystalline", yet another "rich and resonant".

Any actor who suspected that his art was measured entirely by his vocal chords would have reason to feel resentful, and indeed Gielgud was often irritated by people who were paralysed by his voice and did not appreciate how he used it and what he achieved with it. It is no compliment to be told that your voice is so beautiful that one could with pleasure hear you read the telephone directory (although people often intend it to be). Like Gielgud, Fiennes has a voice which is a real blessing. But his intelligence, technique, and above all his heart, invest it with a depth of allusion which reaches straight to the audience and almost shocks them, stuns them, into sudden recognition; no lovely sound could do that unaided.

We saw in Chapter Two that the answer lay in an innate sense of music, and I then called the great "vocal" actors "singers in speech". Thomas Betterton sang the meaning of every phrase with such clarity that it required no additional explanation; Kean made a virtuoso musical instrument of his voice, with all the *crescendi* and *diminuendi*, drumrolls and woodwinds of an orchestral score. Mrs Patrick Campbell and Ellen Terry both had voices which shaped sense and entranced the audience; similarly, John Gielgud and Judi Dench. Ralph Fiennes is today's supreme inheritor of this tradition. The architectural skills he uses to place each syllable according to its weight and purpose turns verse into music, and enables the meaning of the verse to travel *through* and *with* the music, so that musical phrasing is not an embellishment, but the essential channel to reality. It can be thrilling to hear, and shocking to feel, for the audience is sometimes unprepared for the brightness of truth which suddenly hits them through the musicality of his voice – it is as if they have been ambushed. The words carry unanticipated punch and anguish. No wonder audiences sometimes feel seduced by Fiennes; it is not a matter of sexual allure, but of vocal enchantment.

Ralph Fiennes uses this technique, then, to insinuate the truth into the audience's mind and heart. Unlike Russell Beale and Sher, who if necessary will grapple with the verse and impose their own discordant music upon it to wrench out of it *their* meaning, Fiennes wants the music to do its job, and the effect can have an emotional intensity unlike any other. You are less standing outside the emotion and admiring its interpretation, than allowing it to reverberate through you. His Hamlet was so touching because he managed to make the audience feel *like* him; you can hear it in John Peter's agonised review, where he might almost be talking about himself. Having written of Fiennes' "immense speed but complete clarity", "cascading tumultuous passion" and "virtuosity [which was] eloquent and truthful", he went on to describe the performance as "a portrayal of pain that cannot be shared...the loneliness of personal suffering [and] deep spiritual maladjustment that nobody can understand, let alone explain...a shattering portrayal of loss and waste." [7] I personally found his closet scene with Gertrude painful and harrowing to watch. The emotional contact was immediate. No tricks. No mannerisms. Just words.

His Ivanov was even more remarkable, for it takes a rare ear to detect the musical weight in Chekhov's quotidian prose and a rare intelligence to uncover the dramatic dimensions of profound inertia and depression. Once again, the critics were instructed by the internal music of the performance ("a neurotic spontaneity suggesting agony hammered into words") and deceived into a semi-conscious identification ("one pities Ivanov almost as much as he pities himself"). The combination seemed to transcend the business of acting, as Fiennes was for the moment Ivanov and, through his art, we were too. "Fiennes is especially good at suggesting sheer inability to cope...self-loathing... we can speculate what may have produced such a condition – Fiennes presents us with the thing itself." "An unsparing look at the unloveliness of the hero's behaviour (sudden spurts of petulance, lapses into inward-staring listlessness) at the same time as innate and ineffable superiority of spirit." [8] He illustrated languor, restlessness, staleness, nobility, cruelty and pathetic uselessness not, as Kean would have done, and as such disparate qualities would seem to demand, by "flashes of lightning", but, as John Philip Kemble would have done, through a coherent wholeness of being, drawing a straight line of description in the character and showing him as he is. As with Kemble, there is an inner logic in character which Fiennes does not seek to overturn. Other actors may appear in a shambles compared with him. In this respect, he is also the inheritor of Kemble's noble art of sinking into the role and serving the words and logic of it. Like Kemble, he is heroic, statuesque, poetic. While Antony Sher will envelop and command the whole stage and transform his sound and appearance, Ralph Fiennes limits physical gesture and employs his appearance and voice to internalise his interpretation. In this way, he contrives to appear less to act and more to be.

One imagines Kemble, too, showing character through gesture of human dimension, close to the body, not inhuman, histrionic, grandiloquent, impressive conquering of space and sound-waves. The *Independent on Sunday* spoke of how Fiennes stuffed his knuckles down his mouth, stroked the air with his palm, and at one stage tried to exorcise himself, "churning his hands in front of his heart, as if scooping out of himself the shameful, complaining, dismal person that has him hostage". Oddly enough, Kemble was supposed not to have had a good voice, and Leigh Hunt never tired of chastising him for it, but he nevertheless sought to subsume himself into the words and their music, to bring forth psychological truth without resort to extravagant show.

The skill is more than usually visible, of course, on film, where emotions are habitually larger than life. Ralph Fiennes' portrayal of the Nazi soldier Goeth in *Schindler's List* was perfectly in accordance with the nature of such a man, though he scarcely moved a muscle and his sadism was torpid rather than energetic. Fiennes saw that the kind of Nazi who could kill a child with as much concern as he swatted a fly or cleaned his spectacles was ultimately autistic, emotionally divorced from humankind by some genetic flaw of arrested development. Serial killers are almost always similar in their affect. Hence he played the role with minimal notice of anyone or anything around him, and his casual nastiness was all the more disturbing for being recognisably real. That was in the tradition of Kemble, not of Kean; of Guinness, not of Wolfit. Someone said that his Goeth was "soaked through with understated detail".

His director in both *Hamlet* and *Ivanov*, Jonathan Kent, said of Fiennes that there is "a sort of hinterland, something concealed about him", which is the reservoir upon which the great actors must draw. Gielgud certainly had it, and one suspects Kemble had it too, which was why so many of his contemporaries appeared dissatisfied with his apparently half-hearted approach to the craft of acting. It was done with a whole heart, even if only half was visible. It is the same with Fiennes, and from it the actor derives his own self-knowledge and his own pleasure in transmuting this into art. Fiennes himself has said, "the moment of being, of existing in a part, is its own fine, pure moment." [9]

This matter of semi-concealment is very much a part of the acting tradition which we most celebrate today, and it can be argued that it is the one item in the baggage of inheritance which is currently most fashionable. Michael Gambon always gives the impression that he is using only half his power, and at the same time letting the audience know that the other half is there simmering, ready, threatening to erupt. Alan Ayckbourn said of his performance in *A View from the Bridge* (1987) that it was "quite daunting to be near", and Harold Pinter that he had enormous power allied to great depth and economy. Peter Hall has talked of his "catastrophic power" and *The Times* of his "knack of conveying great rage by omission". [10] Antony Sher says that Gambon had "great currents of feeling that he keeps quite secret", the result of which is a curious sense of anticipation when he is on stage, as one might feel when a tiger is prowling, displaying its musculature in repose but suggesting by a glance that the spring is coiled a little too tightly. Whether it snaps open now, in front of one, or later, when one is safely at a distance, is, you feel, a matter of chance. Hence the actor suggests continuity, time both before and after the event, instead of a momentary spectacle.

Is this what was meant by "natural" acting when Garrick first abandoned his wine shop to burst upon the stage at Goodman's Fields? Is this what was meant by "natural" acting when Betterton made you believe in the past and the future as well as the visible present? Is this what was meant by "natural" acting when Kean spoke, moved and behaved with as much idiosyncrasy and unpredictability as a man rather that an orator? Or when Gerald du Maurier used the stage as if it were his own drawing room? The answer must be in a cocktail of all of these, distilled by centuries of legacy and refined by virtually invisible technique into the great spiritual interpreters of today like Gambon. The inheritance is both shared and scattered. It would be difficult to point to two more dissimilar actors than Michael Gambon and Mark Rylance, yet they both have, in their separate ways, the ability to dissemble with such subtlety that the pretence merges with the reality and finally overtakes it. The best tribute I ever heard to the acting of Mark Rylance was that he had a "shocking capacity to make acting imperceptible", that in fact you could not tell when he had stopped. There is a kind of fresh poetry in this which is difficult to define; it is not the poetry of words (Fiennes) or of soul (Gambon) but a kind of dedication which is finally both admirable and moving.

This is not far from the forgetfulness-of-self which we examined in Chapter Three, where we saw Mrs Siddons disappear into Lady Macbeth and convince even those on stage with her that she was possessed. Derek Jacobi is another great actor of today who regularly vanishes inside his roles to assume the personality of the character and abandon his own. With him, as with Sher and Olivier, it is technical precision and inventiveness which maps the path – a stutter, a hobble, a physical shape and heaviness which he first devises and then slides into. Gambon, too, has to get the clothes right, the walk, the stance, before he knows who is the person who inhabits them. But the most obsessional of contemporary actors when it comes to disguise must be Daniel Day-Lewis, whose brilliance is so protean that no two characters he has played resemble each other in the slightest degree. He elevates the technical cleverness of impersonation to such a peak that he appears to need to submerge into a different, strange, forbidding world and breathe the very air that swirls within it. He can spend weeks, months, even on one occasion over a year, preparing himself for a role in order to encourage, or better yet, to render inevitable, the "becoming" another person. (Older actors tend to scoff at this manic amount of preparation, suggesting it might be simpler to try "acting", but they must all partake of the process to some extent.)

Nobody is closer to the dangers of letting slip than Daniel Day-Lewis. He demonstrates how the power of possession, the trick of Dionysus entering the blood-stream and nostrils of the actor possessed, can unleash forces of sublime insight or destructive havoc. With such an actor, one feels that he never knows which it will be, and the outcome of each submersion will surprise him as much as us. Thus, despite the extraordinary lengths to which he will go in researching the background and nature and milieu of the character he wishes to become, in the end his technical flourish leads to a disturbing abandonment of control. Gambon says he never does any research: "I just say what the author wrote and put my own thing on top of it." Day-Lewis, on the contrary, places all his trust in research because he does not want to rely on his "own thing"; he distrusts it. He might even fear it. As we have seen in Chapter Three, his absorption by Hamlet was in the end so intense that he fled in the middle of a performance, never to return. The point was this: Hamlet offers no disguise. There is nowhere to hide. The only way to play the part is to dig within oneself and find truth in the bowels of self-analysis. In *Hamlet*, Daniel Day-Lewis apparently found this dangerous. It is not his strong point. Sixty-five performances as Hamlet (he only missed the last seven) took their toll by obliging him to look within instead of finding his props without. The director Richard Eyre admitted that "it was the last part I should have asked him to play. It was like asking him to stand centre-stage and do archaeology on himself." [11] Which is precisely what an actor like Michael Gambon does.

The paradox is that with Daniel Day-Lewis you do not feel that sense of concealment, that something is being held back, as you do with Fiennes and Gambon. What you see is what you get; it is all there in the open, naked, scarred, scorched and weary. But it is not Day-Lewis – it is the person presented before you, an astonishing transmigration. In *Hamlet* he went perilously close to Day-Lewis and turned away in panic. No wonder the spectre of madness occasionally lurks in the wings of a theatre.

There is something so exceptional about Day-Lewis that one resists placing him in the tradition of English acting. It is not easy to find Kemble or Kean or Irving within him, impossible to locate the easy-going Garrick, awkward to place his technical obsession alongside Olivier's simpler technical tricks. His roots are Irish anyway, as were Macklin's, the one actor of the past he partly resembles. He tends to stand outside, and one has the impression that is where he wants to remain.

On the whole, however, no matter how much an actor wants to find his own truth in a part played by many others before him, and no matter how reluctant he is to admit that he has copied the felicitous insights of the greats, he has absorbed the precious examples of the past by a kind of gradual osmosis. He is not taught at drama school how Kean or Irving performed, but their shades spill over the page as he reads his rehearsal script and fill the corners of the stage behind the scenery. The legacy is both straight, in a line from Burbage down to Fiennes, Sher, Jacobi, Russell Beale, Rylance and so on; and diffuse, in that it has meandered through these people and never comes to rest. "The moment that any young actor or actress takes the first and, where talent is concerned, usually irrevocable step," wrote Bryan Forbes, "then consciously or unconsciously they become, with the passing of time, imbued with the *spirit* of previous generations of actors." [12]

What does this mean, if not that the past is present on the stage today? When we go to the theatre we have a triple experience: we are moved by the actors to find something within ourselves which lay hidden, to bring it into the light and look at it; we are, secondly, bound by the spell cast by the actor momentarily to forget who he or she is and to accept the revelation before our eyes of another, supposedly fictional but just as real, person; and thirdly, through the medium of that performance to see and feel something of the vibrancy and immediacy of performances long since past. It is this last point which I have striven to make throughout this book, and which I personally find so thrilling – that mingling of past and present in the actor's craft, the fact that we are watching not only what is happening now, but the distant ripples of what happened on other stages before, like the radiation which still reaches us on this planet from other planets which "died" millions of years ago. History is in front of us, feeding the performances of actors working today.

So it is wrong to lament the passing of an actor's magic with the ending of his life. It does not happen like that. The fashionable view, shared even by David Garrick himself, that the actor's contribution to the world is lost forever when he ceases to perform – is evanescent, doomed, mortal – takes no account of this silent but powerful inheritance. In a sense, the very opposite is true. It is supposed that a painter's work may be enjoyed centuries after his death because the painting is still there to be seen, and that a novelist's creation is recreated by every reader in every subsequent generation, the corollary being that the actor leaves nothing physical behind him to admire and enjoy. Well, that much is obvious, the only physical manifestations of his moment in time being the paintings by Zoffany and de Wilde or, in later generations, the photographs taken in rehearsal. Films and recordings available in our own age are just as unreliable, really, for they set the experience in glue, like a butterfly pinned to a board, and cannot carry the spices of immediacy, of danger, of unpredictability, which make each performance in the theatre a separate revelation. They cannot, in a word, involve us as part of the experience because we are not there.

And yet we are, still, every time we go to the theatre. And that is what I mean when I suggest that the actor's art is even more alive than the painter's or the writer's, because it is constantly awake, renewed, reborn, quickened, made alert, by an actor bearing the inherited insights and shafts of all his predecessors. There is much which is invisible in his suitcase; it is not props or cues that he carries, but the ghosts of every great actor who has preceded him. When you watch Simon Russell Beale on stage, you are brushed by the shades of Garrick and Kean and others; you are watching not just one actor, but the accumulated history of acting, just as those who saw Donald Sinden in one of his "foppish" parts were also seeing the almost-living presence of Cibber and Farren.

Indeed, the actor's art is even more alive than that, because Simon Russell Beale will adjust history even as he works, with the investment of his own personal archive of observations and knowledge of human behaviour, so that the actors who follow him will have an even richer legacy to present before the audience.

I must emphasise that this does not imply that one actor copies another (except when parody is intended), but that he locks into, yet again, the author's imagination and recreates a part previously created by other actors. The process is without end, and there are actors to come, long after this book is forgotten, who will continue it, building by accretion a lofty monument to the extraordinary ability of a few people among us who are capable of revealing truth through the obliteration of self in the service of impersonation.

It is, moreover, actors who work this miracle, not playwrights. The role of the playwright in facing up to the dilemmas of human life is another subject entirely, and it is obvious that the actor's art would be seriously impoverished were there to be no playwrights for him to interpret (as has woefully been demonstrated when actors have occasionally been invited to "improvise" on stage, which is like asking a pianist to play on the kitchen table). But the fact is, audiences go to see a play because they want to see the actor in the play, and are less beguiled by the play itself. It is in the miracle of interpretation that real theatre lies.

We go in the hope of watching an actor "take flight" and take us with him on the journey. It is an exhilarating experience unlike any other and it continues that long tradition of magic which has always belonged to the theatre and to the theatre alone. This magic is nothing so banal as "make-believe"; it is nourishment and thought and adventure and revelation all rolled into one, and I have been fortunate enough to be touched by it, as an audience, a dozen or so times in my life. I have been going to the theatre since the age of 13, always anticipating enrichment, and never completely understanding why I have been enriched. Part of the reason for writing this book has been in order to find out.

The contemporary actors I have mentioned in these pages have not necessarily studied the work of Mrs Siddons or Mrs Patrick Campbell, but they know them both, as performers, to a level far deeper than anything I, who have studied what they did and how they did it, could ever attain. The younger generation of actors, now just beginning their careers and destined one day to be mentioned with awe (Michael Sheen, brilliantly closing the last century with thrilling performances in Osborne's *Look Back in Anger* and Shaffer's *Amadeus*, is certain to hold the torch of David Garrick one day), would certainly not be able to tell you how they act. But they would be quick to point out that, not merely is it worth doing, but it is essential that it be done.

Now and again there crops up somebody who is prepared to grapple with the problem of definition. The best comment on acting I have ever come across is not from an academic historian or theatrical anecdotalist, but from an actress; it combines those elements of technique and instinct, as well as collaboration with author and audience, which this book has struggled to unravel, and it does so in the fewest and most articulate of words. Ellen Terry played Juliet at the Lyceum Theatre in 1882. On the flyleaf of her rehearsal copy of *Romeo and Juliet*, in her bold, thick, distinctive hand, she wrote:

> To act, you must make the thing written your own. You must steal the words, steal the thought, and *convey* the stolen treasure to others with great art.

1   Jean Paul Sartre, *Kean* (1960), Act II, Sc 3

2   *The Merchant of Venice*, Act III, Sc 1

3   *Daily Telegraph* and *Guardian*, 29 April, 1988

4   *Guardian*, 21 July, 1990

5   *The Sunday Times*, 11 January, 1996

6   *Independent*, 4 February 1996

7   *The Sunday Times*, 5 March, 1996

8   *Independent*, 21 February, 1997; *Independent on Sunday*, 23 February, 1997

9   *Independent*, 21 February, 1997; *Independent on Sunday*, 23 February, 1997

10 *The Times*, 24 February, 1996

11 *The Sunday Times*, 1 November, 1992

12 Bryan Forbes, *That Despicable Race* (1980), p 230

Index

Cibber, Colly, 36, 56, 63, 124, 125, 126, 127, 146, 161, 206
City Madam, 87
Cleese, John, 129, 155
Cleopatra, 18
Clive, Mrs, 163, 177
Coleridge, Samuel Taylor, 10, 22
Colman, Mr, 152
Comedy of Errors, The, 121
Commedia dell'Arte, 53, 71
Compton, Fay, 175
Congreve, William, 162
Constant Couple, The, 163
Cook, Peter, 131
Cooke, G F, 113, 151
Coquelin, 64
Coriolanus, 17
Cornwallis-West, George, 184
Courtenay, Tom, 128
Covent Garden (Opera House), 12, 23, 29, 102, 105, 106, 110, 113, 114, 131, 138, 152, 153, 171
Coward, Noël, 35, 56, 99, 125, 154, 166, 167, 170, 174, 175, 185
Craft of Comedy, The, 126
Craig, Edward Gordon, 102
Criterion Theatre, The, 125
Critic, The, 16, 130
Cumberland, Richard, 16, 27, 164
Curle, Edward, 33
Cushman, Robert, 96
Cyrano de Bergerac, 64, 195

Daily Mail, The, 97
Dark Lady of the Sonnets, The, 34
Darlington, W A, 58, 160
Davenant, William, 32, 109, 137
Day-Lewis, Cecil, 88
Day-Lewis, Daniel, 60, 62, 86, 88, 147, 155, 203, 204
de Kérouaille, Louise, 161
de Sévigné, Madame, 161
de Wilde, 205
Dean, James, 174
Dench, Judi, 11, 18, 30, 43, 56, 65, 77, 85, 89, 168, 180, 199
Dibdin, Revd., 116
Dickens, Charles, 40, 54
Diderot, Denis, 31, 44, 93, 94
Dillane, Stephen, 57
Dionysus, 14, 15, 16, 20, 26, 72, 73, 87, 143, 147, 151, 203
Donovan, Jason, 173
Dresser, The, 128, 136
Drury Lane (Theatre Royal) 20, 29, 66, 105, 106, 109, 112, 113, 114, 116, 131, 137, 138, 157, 171

Dryden, John, 34
du Maurier, Gerald, 35, 119, 150, 151, 173, 174, 202
Duchess of Malfi, The, 192
Dufresne, 112
Duke's men, The (Players), 109
Duke's Theatre, The, 109
Dumas, Alexandre, 72
Duprez, 168

Edward II, 190,
Edward II, 192
Ellenborough, Lord, 131
Enemy of the People, An, 190
Equus, 47
Espert, Nuria, 30
Etherege, Sir George, 124, 125
Evans, Edith, 30, 51, 55, 167, 168
Every Man in His Humour, 33
Examiner, The, 22, 57
Eyre, Richard, 204

Fair Penitent, The, 27
Fall of Tarquin, The, 60
Farquhar, George, 163
Farren, William, 35, 206
Faucit, Helen, 74, 77, 78
Fenton, James, 96
Feuillère, Edwige, 30
Ffrangcon-Davies, Gwen, 89
Fielding, Henry, 73
Fiennes, Ralph, 57, 147, 198, 199, 200, 201, 202, 203, 204
Financial Times, The, 199
Finney, Albert, 60, 122, 157
Fontanne, Lynne, 121
Fonteyn, Margot, 12, 89, 102
Forbes, Bryan, 205
Forbes-Robertson, Johnston, 19, 32, 65, 66, 198
Forrest, Edwin, 168
Fortune Theatre, The, 32
Foster, Lady Elizabeth, 172, 173
French, Dawn, 133
Fry, Stephen, 155
Funny Thing Happened on the Way to the Forum, A, 121

Gaiety, The, 25
Gambon, Michael, 31, 56, 57, 157, 160, 189, 202, 203, 204
Gamester, The, 82
Garbo, Greta, 166
Garrick Club, The, 24, 33, 53, 120, 133, 173
Garrick, David, 10, 11, 12, 13, 16, 17, 18, 22, 26, 27, 28, 29, 30, 31, 32, 35, 39, 43, 44, 45, 46, 49, 51, 52, 59, 60, 61, 62, 63, 64, 66, 72, 73, 74, 79, 82, 87,

INDEX

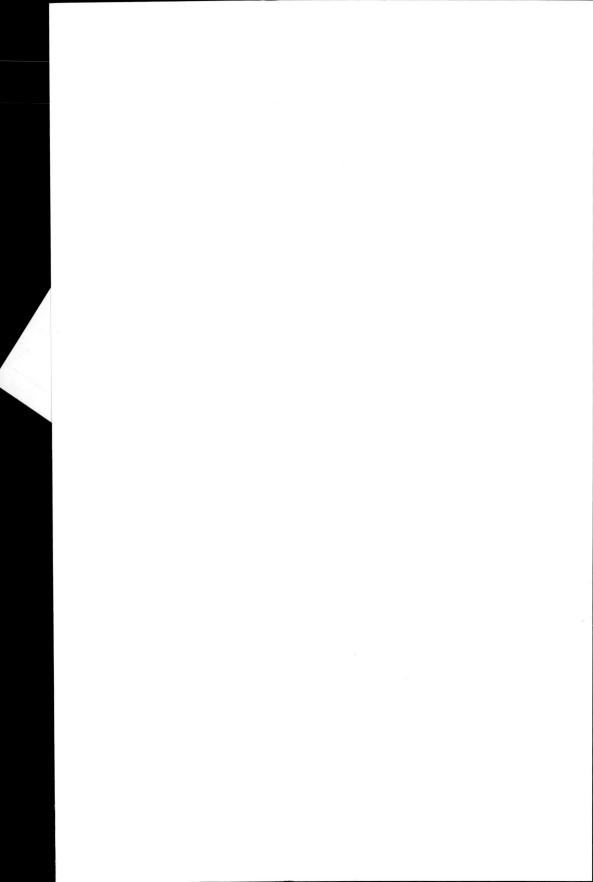

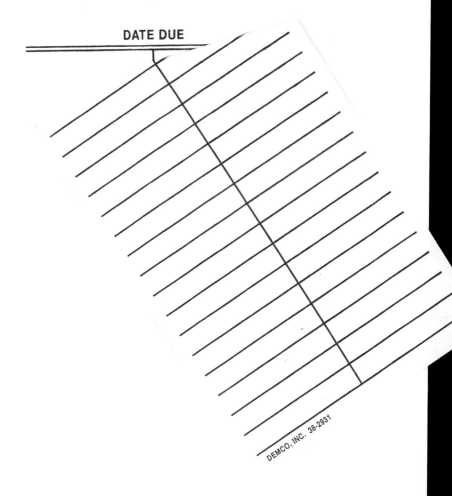

DATE DUE

DEMCO, INC. 38-2931